Britain's Two World Wars Against Germany

Britain's role and performance in the two world wars continues to generate considerable debate but the wars are rarely considered together. Leading military historian Brian Bond here challenges the popular view of the First World War as catastrophic and futile in contrast to the Second World War as a well-conducted and victorious moral crusade. He focuses on the key issues that have caused controversy and distortion, to demonstrate how these views became deeply rooted in popular culture in the years since 1945. These issues range from policy and strategy, combat experience, the attritional strategies of naval blockade and strategic bombing to British generalship and gains and losses in the aftermath of both wars. He also considers the learning process of the British Army in both world wars. He boldly concludes that in a number of important respects Britain was more successful in the First World War than in the Second.

Brian Bond is Emeritus Professor of Military History at King's College London and author of *The Unquiet Western Front* (2002) and *Survivors of a Kind: Memoirs of the Western Front* (2008).

Britain's Two World Wars Against Germany

Myth, Memory and the Distortions of Hindsight

Brian Bond

CAMBRIDGE
UNIVERSITY PRESS

CAMBRIDGE
UNIVERSITY PRESS

University Printing House, Cambridge CB2 8BS, United Kingdom

Cambridge University Press is part of the University of Cambridge.

It furthers the University's mission by disseminating knowledge in the pursuit of education, learning and research at the highest international levels of excellence.

www.cambridge.org
Information on this title: www.cambridge.org/9781107659131

First published 2014

Printed in the United Kingdom by Clays, St Ives plc

A catalogue record for this publication is available from the British Library

Library of Congress Cataloguing in Publication data
Bond, Brian.
Britain's two world wars against Germany : myth, memory and the distortions of hindsight / Brian Bond.
    pages   cm
Includes bibliographical references and index.
ISBN 978-1-107-00471-9 (hardback) – ISBN 978-1-107-65913-1 (paperback)
1. Great Britain – History, Military – 20th century.   2. World War, 1914–1918 –
Great Britain – Historiography.   3. World War, 1939–1945 – Great Britain –
Historiography.   4. Great Britain – Foreign relations – Germany.   5. Germany –
Foreign relations – Great Britain.   I. Title.
DA69.B65   2014
940.4′0941 – dc23   2014018298

ISBN 978-1-107-00471-9 Hardback
ISBN 978-1-107-65913-1 Paperback

CONTENTS

Acknowledgements   vii

Introduction   1

1   The creation of myths after 1945   8

2   British policy and strategy   25

3   British generalship in the two world wars   42

4   At the sharp end: combat experience in the two world wars   62

5   Attrition in the First World War: the naval blockade   88

6   Attrition in the Second World War: the strategic bombing of Germany   100

7   The transformation of war on the Western Front, 1914–18   125

8   The British Army's learning process in the Second World War   144

9   After the wars: Britain's gains and losses   164

Appendix   177
Select bibliography   179
Index   184

ACKNOWLEDGEMENTS

Many individuals have helped me indirectly in discussing the themes of this book as it took shape, but for practical assistance or advice I should particularly like to thank: Catherine Boylan, Jeremy Crang, Michael Dockrill, Simon Doughty, Colin Hook, Halik Kochanski, Sir Michael Howard, Andrew Lambert, Penny McLeish and Gary Sheffield.

I first outlined my main arguments in the Saki Dockrill Memorial Lecture at King's College, London in November 2011 and was much encouraged by the positive response, especially from Philip Bell and the late M. R. D. Foot.

I am extremely grateful to Sebastian Cox for vetting my draft chapter on strategic bombing and for giving me a copy of his unpublished paper on Sir Arthur Harris. John Ellis has generously permitted me to draw heavily on his book *The Sharp End of War* in my chapter on front-line combat. I am, above all, indebted to John Bourne for reading all the chapters, except that on strategic bombing, at a particularly difficult time for him, and providing me with a judicious mixture of praise and criticism. I have done my best to take full advantage of my readers' expert help but am entirely responsible for any remaining errors or omissions.

As with all my previous publications, my wife Madeleine typed nearly all the first draft of this book, but was obliged to stop when our home was flooded, first on 29 November 2012 and secondly, and even more severely, on Boxing Day. In the ensuing chaos, which lasted for five months, I was very fortunate indeed to find an excellent replacement in our friend and neighbour, Emily McLeish, who re-typed the whole work, including the revised references and the index.

Finally, my thanks are due to Michael Watson, History Publisher for Cambridge University Press, and his Assistant Editor, Kaiya Shang.

Medmenham, Bucks. October 2013

INTRODUCTION

In 'A Personal Reflection on the Two World Wars' John Bourne neatly captures the public's view of Britain's contrasting roles in the two conflicts.

> The First World War was not really about anything, or not about anything important; the Second World War was about national survival at home and the defeat of a vile tyranny abroad. The First World War was hopelessly mismanaged by incompetent generals... compared with the Second World War generals who understood technology and fought wars of manoeuver that avoided heavy casualties.[1]

Furthermore, he writes, 'the outcome of the First World War was futile... making another war inevitable; the outcome of the Second World War, sanctified by the discovery of the Nazi death camps, was not only a military but also a moral triumph'.[2]

As regards the experience of combat, the First World War, invariably associated in popular mythology with the horror of the trenches, is imagined as an unending hell on earth whereas the later conflict, being more mobile and with far fewer British casualties, is thought to have been easier, or at least more tolerable.

---

[1] Peter Liddle, John Bourne and Ian Whitehead (eds.), *The Great War, 1914–1945*, Vol. I (Harper Collins, 2000). See especially John Bourne, 'A Personal Reflection on the Two World Wars', p. 17.
[2] Ibid.

It is not the objective of this study to reverse the myth of First World War very bad – Second World War very good, but rather to argue that both of these stereotypes are flawed and, in particular, that Britain's role in both wars has been distorted in hindsight.

In the last thirty years or so a great deal of scholarly work has been published on virtually every aspect of the First World War, including controversial topics such as casualties, battle conditions, generalship (and Haig's role in particular), strategy, tactical and technological innovations and the notion of a 'learning curve'. Most, though not all of this work, has tended to place Britain's role in a more positive light. But, at the very least, recent scholarship, based on archival research and a more objective approach, has moved the debate forward from the emotional and polemical approach typified by phrases such as 'butchers and bunglers' and 'lions led by donkeys'.

Unfortunately this innovative and revisionist work has, on the whole, not filtered through to the non-specialist general public. Many school children are introduced to the First World War through a select number of war poets who, whatever their merits, do not provide a sound historical basis. The media – especially television, fiction and the theatre – incline towards a negative or farcical interpretation with entertainments such as *Oh, What a Lovely War!* and *Blackadder* still exerting a powerful influence. The Somme campaign, especially its disastrous first day, and the Third Ypres offensive – now invariably referred to as 'Passchendaele' – are given undue emphasis as representative of the whole war on the Western Front. This outmoded approach is badly in need of revision, particularly its depiction as a disastrous and futile conflict in contrast to the 'good war' of 1939–1945.

The First World War had already acquired a negative image in the 1930s, due mainly to the unprecedented scale of British losses and disappointment with the outcome both at home and in international relations. Whether the publication of a few 'disenchanted' writers truly represented national reactions to the war may be doubted but they have since, especially from the 1960s, been widely viewed as the true interpreters of the conflict and key contributors to a powerful myth. In reality, as common sense suggests and recent publications confirm, 'middlebrow' literature with a mainly positive, patriotic and reassuring message was much more widely read. Disenchantment with the First World War certainly did not prevent the nation from responding readily, albeit in a grim and stoical spirit, to the renewed challenge from Germany in the late 1930s.

Britain's achievement in helping to defeat Nazi Germany was certainly important and worthy of celebration, but it was magnified in hindsight by the full, horrific revelations of the enemy's barbarism after the liberation of the concentration and extermination camps at the very end of the war, and by the massive documentary and visual evidence provided at the Nuremberg Trials. Numerous considerations contributed to British euphoria and exaggeration of Britain's role in relation to allies in the decades after 1945, but two influences receive special attention in this study: namely the spate of extremely popular British war films produced between the end of the war and the early 1960s; and Churchill's remarkably successful promotion of his own colossal status as war leader in his massive history *The Second World War*.

The sharp contrast in the popular view of Britain's role in the two world wars is now determined largely by comparative casualty statistics. Britain and the Dominions suffered approximately one million military deaths in the First World War as against only about one-third of that number in the Second. But the essential fact that cannot be over-stressed is that Britain fought the whole of the first great industrial war of mass armies on the principal front against the outstanding military power of the day. By contrast, in what seemed a disaster at the time but on a longer view may be deemed a blessing in disguise, British forces were expelled from Western Europe in June 1940 and did not return until precisely four years later. The numerous campaigns waged in this long interval, notably in North Africa, Burma and Italy, were far from irrelevant to Britain, but they were peripheral and on a very small scale compared to the titanic struggle on the Eastern Front where the bulk of the German forces were eventually driven back and annihilated. This seems almost too obvious to mention now but it took decades to be recognised in Anglo-American historiography.

A century after the outbreak of the First World War it is harder for critics of the ensuing conflict to grasp Britain's strategic interests in the security of the Low Countries and the Channel coast, which were widely held to justify her intervention in the war, albeit on the erroneous assumptions that it would be comparatively brief and require only a limited contribution. Later concentration on terrible conditions and heavy losses lends weight to the argument that the war was too costly and not worth fighting, but this attitude was held by only a small minority at the time. Even influential 'anti-war' writers such as Robert Graves, Edmund Blunden and Richard Aldington hated the conflict as they experienced it but still believed that it had to be endured until victory was won.

Britain entered the Second World War for similar concepts of national and imperial strategic interests as had motivated her leaders in 1914. The threat posed by the Kaiser's Germany now seems, in distant hindsight, far less serious than that of Hitler, but arguably it was the other way round. Germany saw Britain and her empire as the vital obstacle to her global ambitions in the 1900s and had been planning for naval confrontation and invasion since the 1890s. By contrast Hitler had not been planning seriously for war against Britain until the late 1930s, and even hoped in 1939–1940 that she would accept German domination in Europe.

As regards battlefield conditions, the belief that the Western Front in 1914–1918 was uniquely horrific has taken such a deep hold on the public imagination that it seems almost irrational to query it. Yet those few historians who have carefully compared the two world wars (and other large-scale conflicts) concur that modern, industrialised war is always horrific for soldiers 'at the sharp end'. This study will attempt to demonstrate the dreadfulness of combat conditions prevailing in Italy and North-West Europe between 1943 and 1945 while excluding the even more hellish climatic and logistic experience of the campaign in Burma.

First, however, it is necessary to touch on some of the reasons why the Western Front in 1914–1918 acquired its reputation for unique awfulness. Romantic illusions and ignorance about the likely nature of a great European War before 1914, especially in Britain where recent experience was lacking, made the impact more shocking, witness the reaction of cinema audiences to the film of the battle of the Somme in 1916. The conflict was not 'over by Christmas' but developed into a protracted siege war in which front-line conditions were often appalling. The failure of either alliance to deliver a knockout blow or negotiate for a peace without victory made the conflict seem unending. For the Western Allies victory only began to seem possible in the summer of 1918, whereas in the later war Germany faced unavoidable defeat from early 1943.

Popular representations have given a distorted impression of the Western Front as resembling conditions on 1 July 1916 all the time. The common experience for most soldiers for much of the time was boredom and weariness, endless marching, drilling, fatigues and, above all perhaps, lack of sleep, with occasional episodes of fear and danger. A huge popular misconception is that the troops were herded into the trenches en masse and kept there for weeks without a break. The much more complex reality of front-line routines will be explained in detail.

An important and valid explanation of the First World War's negative image is that the civil population had little understanding of conditions at the front; hence the frustration and anger of many soldiers on leave, even to the extent of preferring to be back with their comrades. This justified rage at complacency and ignorance at home goes far to explain the bitterness of some of the veterans' memoirs and poetry, Siegfried Sassoon's satirical war-time verses being a good example.

The First World War left a powerful legacy that greatly influenced the British nation before and during the second conflict. Clearly, modern warfare was not romantic – if indeed it ever had been – and another struggle with Germany was likely to be a long attritional fight for survival in which every aspect of the nation's staying power would be tested to the limit, civilian morale not least important. Another war with Germany had been expected since the mid-1930s and its immediate horrors even exaggerated in the anticipation of all-out bombing of cities with the widespread use of gas. Consequently there was little euphoria or idealism evident in 1939, in contrast to the opening phase of the First World War.

Britain suffered a series of humiliating defeats between the spring of 1940 (Norway, followed by Dunkirk) and mid-1942 (Tobruk) but their impact at home was muffled by Churchill's rhetoric and, after a shaky start, skilful propaganda that even contrived to distil the 'Dunkirk spirit' from the Allied defeat and the Field Force's fortunate escape.

A vitally important contrast with the earlier conflict was that in the Second World War there was far less of a gap between home and military 'fronts'. A form of conscription was in place from the outset, civilians were heavily involved in war work and suffered from bombing, constant anxiety and fears of possible invasion, evacuation of children, homelessness, rationing and other privations. Indeed many servicemen had an easier war than their families at home. Propaganda effectively exploited these hardships by stressing that it was a 'people's war', involving even the Royal Family, and that eventual victory would bring greater benefits than after 1918. Despite continuing shortages and austerity through the 1940s and early 1950s this promise was, on the whole, realised.

The comparatively light scale of battle casualties compared with the First World War ensured that there was much less of a backlash against the generals and political leaders. Army commanders were acutely conscious of the need to minimise losses, on practical grounds of limited available manpower as well as due to greater sensitivity about morale, but they were considerably helped by the comparatively small scale of British battles. Greatly improved medical supplies, treatment of casualties in the battle zone and evacuation transport – especially by airlift – also saved thousands of wounded soldiers who would have died in the earlier war.

Even so the remarkable fact has to be confronted that casualties 'at the sharp end' were as heavy, or indeed heavier, than in the worst phases of the First World War, in proportion to the numbers engaged in the front line. Brutal, relentless attrition was the prevailing feature of the Second World War as all accounts of fighting in Italy and North-West Europe between 1943 and 1945 make abundantly clear.

In terms of national effort, military achievement and realisation of war aims, Britain was more successful in the First World War than the Second. From a very modest military base in 1914 Britain (and the Empire) created a truly remarkable nation in arms. After an undistinguished start in unexpected conditions the Army's leaders gradually learnt lessons in command and control and developed impressive tactical, technical and training innovations. By 1918 a truly modern military machine, with excellent inter-arm and inter-service co-operation, was in being. Although the French Army's role was still significant and the American forces were just beginning to make an impact, it was the British (and Dominions') land and air forces that played the major role in the culminating advance to victory in the autumn of 1918. This astonishing achievement was generally understood and appreciated at the time, giving Britain a strong diplomatic position in the post-war settlements.

After victory over Germany in 1918 Britain secured virtually all her war aims. France and Belgium were liberated and the former recovered Alsace-Lorraine. German naval and air power was destroyed and her Army limited to 100,000 regular soldiers; France's security was safeguarded by a demilitarised buffer zone in the Rhineland; and the new Western frontiers were guaranteed by the Locarno Treaty in 1925. With the award of mandates in the Middle East the British Empire was enlarged to its greatest extent. These settlements reflected Britain's military might: powerful only at sea in 1914 but with vastly expanded land and air forces also in being at the end of the war.

In sharp contrast, Britain enjoyed her 'finest hours' early in the Second World War but thereafter her relative power vis-à-vis the United States and the Soviet Union declined steadily. Consequently Britain ended on the winning side in 1945 but with her industrial and financial bases severely weakened and her hold on the Empire fatally undermined. Churchill strove valiantly but in vain to counter this comparative loss of power by the exercise of personal leadership, and by appealing for continuing co-operation on the part of his war-time allies. In the event Britain did not even achieve her initial reason for going to war: the restoration of a free, independent Poland. Even worse, it soon became clear that Britain and the United States had defeated one terrible tyranny only to see it replaced by another, with much greater staying power, in Central and Eastern Europe.

The argument in the following chapters is that the stark contrasts between the character and historical legacy of Britain's two world wars against Germany have been exaggerated and clouded by hindsight. Recent research and publications have tended to put Britain's performance and achievement in the First World War in a more positive light; but a more thorough and objective reappraisal of the nation's contribution to the defeat of Germany in the later war has scarcely begun.

So deeply rooted are the beliefs about these contrasting 'bad' and 'good' wars, particularly negative interpretations of the First World War, that they will be difficult to alter in any radical way. But the passage of time provides ground for hope, and exactly one hundred years after the outbreak of war in 1914 this exploratory study should at least stimulate debate.

1 THE CREATION OF MYTHS AFTER 1945

In Britain in 1945 victory was greeted with relief rather than euphoria. Living conditions remained harsh and an 'Age of Austerity' was dawning. It would soon become clear that although Britain had emerged on the winning side she was markedly in decline as a world power and her Empire was breaking up. Nevertheless Britain's role in the Second World War continued to be viewed in a very patriotic light in sharp contrast to the First World War, whose negative attributes were ever more grimly emphasised.

As the editors of a two-volume study entitled *The Great War, 1914–1945* remarked, 'The First World War has more often than not been regarded as a "bad" war resulting from failures in diplomacy, and a war characterised by the "futile" sacrifices of trench warfare on the Western Front; standing in stark contrast to the justifiable and necessary struggle, between 1939 and 1945, against Nazi tyranny and Japanese militarism'.[1] One of the contributors neatly summarised the contrasting myths of the two world wars: 'The First World War was not really about anything, or not about anything important; the Second World War was about national survival at home and defeat of a vile tyranny abroad'.[2] Moreover, whereas the earlier war had been hopelessly mismanaged by incompetent generals, their successors had been technically proficient and had avoided heavy casualties by conducting mobile wars of manoeuvre.[3]

---

[1] Liddle, Bourne and Whitehead (eds.), *The Great War, 1914–1945*, Vol. I.
[2] Bourne, 'A Personal Reflection on the Two World Wars', p. 17.   [3] Ibid.

Why, despite years of hardship and suffering and a series of military disasters between 1940 and 1942, cumulatively worse than any single defeat in the First World War, did positive attitudes, bordering on triumphalism, persist after 1945?

During the conflict Winston Churchill had established a colossal personal reputation as the supreme leader, who by his courage and fortitude, had pulled the nation through its greatest crises. His status might have suffered a steady decline after his, and his party's overwhelming defeat in the 1945 general election but, as after the First World War, Churchill the historian and publicist came to the rescue of Churchill the statesman.

As David Reynolds notes in his brilliant, and aptly titled analysis, *In Command Of History*, Churchill was remarkably 'quick off the mark, wrote on an epic scale and reached a global audience'. The six weighty volumes of *The Second World War*, which appeared between 1948 and 1954, were published in fifteen countries, while extracts appeared in some fifty newspapers and magazines in forty countries. Reynolds adds that numerous people who never opened the books would have become familiar with Churchill's themes and viewpoints from these serialised versions and also from reviews. The Churchill legend also received a tremendous boost by the TV serialisation of his war memoirs in *The Valiant Years* (1960–1963) with Richard Burton reading Churchill's words.[4]

In addition to the unique position he had enjoyed as a war leader who really did try to dominate events as a grand strategist and even as a battlefield tactician, Churchill possessed at least two great advantages. Although a great deal of his text was originally drafted by a team of researchers and advisers, it was Churchill's gift for purple prose and memorable phrases that stamped his authority on the history, not least in the volume titles (beginning with *The Gathering Storm* and *Their Finest Hour*), and provided a structure of chronology and themes for later historians. Secondly, thanks to a remarkable arrangement with the Cabinet Office, Churchill was able to quote from and publish a mass of war-time documents that would remain closed to other historians for several decades, thereby giving his account an unrivalled authority. Of course, Churchill's version of events did not command universal

---

[4] David Reynolds, *In Command of History: Churchill Fighting and Writing the Second World War* (Penguin Books, 2005), pp. xxi–xxvi.

accord, particularly in the United States, whose war effort had been, to say the least, understated; in Britain it is hardly an exaggeration to say that this epic history consolidated Churchill's reputation as the supreme leader who had won the war.

For millions of British citizens, whether or not they were much influenced by Churchill's history, cinema in the 1940s and 1950s (as indeed during the war years), exerted an overwhelming attraction that it is difficult for later generations to grasp. It is important to stress that in the later 1940s and 1950s cinema was still a key mass medium and it was precisely then that the British war-film output reached its peak. After 1945 war films could celebrate victory and Britain's role in winning it. The conflict was generally depicted as a good war in which Britain's national solidarity and heroic deeds were emphasised. Most war films were up-beat and exciting, some even depicting the struggle as a 'great game' – an approach also evident in popular comics like *The Eagle*. British war films, and their leading actors, remained popular throughout the 1950s. For example they constituted eight of the top sellers in 1958.[5]

On a personal level John Bourne (born in 1949 and later to become a distinguished historian at Birmingham University) grew up a keen student of the Second World War, finding it first and foremost 'glorious'. On television he watched war-time newsreels in the series *All Our Yesterdays*, and repeats of earlier war films. The cinema supplied what he could not view on television with the result that by the age of ten he could recite the litany of landmark events from the *Graf Spee*, Dunkirk and the Battle of Britain to D-Day, Arnhem, the V2s and Belsen. Thus he grew up believing that 'we' had won the war. Britain always seemed to play the key role, with foreigners having only walk-on parts in the drama. Allied efforts, except for those of the gallant Poles, were not really recognised. The Eastern Front was seen to have been bloody and important, but the Soviet Union was now the mortal enemy. Whereas the earlier war seemed to be one of mass victims, the Second World War, especially in British films, was characterised by the heroic deeds of individuals and small groups.[6]

[5] John Ramsden, 'Refocusing "The People's War": British War Films of the 1950s', in *Journal of Contemporary History* 33(1), (January, 1998), pp. 35–63.

[6] Bourne, 'A Personal Reflection', pp. 14–19.

As the late John Ramsden pointed out in an excellent article on 'Refocusing "The People's War": British War Films of the 1950s', academic critics would later underplay the very wide influence of middlebrow writers in the later 1940s and early 1950s, including Nicholas Monsarrat, Alastair MacLean, C. S. Forester, Nevil Shute and Nigel Balchin. Exciting war books, such as *The Cruel Sea*, Paul Brickhill's *The Dam Busters*, and *The Wooden Horse* were bestsellers several years before they were transformed into hugely successful films. The climax of the British war-film boom was reached in the later 1950s when about eight a year were issued, but by 1963 the number had sunk to only one or two per year. Thus, notwithstanding that the Suez crisis in 1956 had demonstrated Britain's drastic decline in influence vis-à-vis the United States, the public was still exposed to a 'large dose of films about British heroism and ingenuity'.[7]

There were clearly several overlapping reasons for the phenomenal popularity of British war films through the 1940s and 1950s and into the 1960s. After the war the British people were tired and needed a kind of ego boost with nostalgic reminders of recent greatness, especially at a time when the British economy was already falling behind that of the defeated nations of Germany and Japan. Although a few hints of social criticism and subversion could already be detected, most war films made then were essentially conservative and patriotic. Thus prison-camp and espionage films emphasised British endurance and ingenuity, while combat films concentrated on inventiveness, team spirit and willingness to make sacrifices for the greater good – as determined by those in political and military authority.

By the early 1960s the spate of tremendously popular war films had established a nostalgic and reassuring view of Britain's role in the Second World War.

In the 1960s, however, radical changes in the social and political climate would make it virtually impossible to make more war films in the previous patriotic and uncomplicated style. But parodies and satires, as in such television programmes as *Hancock's Half Hour*, *Dad's Army* and *Beyond the Fringe*, were only acceptable on the assumption that the truth had been established and was impervious to these forms of entertaining mockery.[8] The same cultural and political

---

[7] Ramsden, 'Refocusing "The People's War"'.   [8] Ibid., pp. 59–63.

changes profoundly influenced an opposite reaction to the First World War; namely a tendency towards intemperate vilification of the military leadership, conduct and outcome that was hardly less bitter than the most disenchanted poetry and memoirs of the earlier conflict in the 1920s and 1930s.

Britain's reasons for going to war with Germany are generally viewed as more principled and idealistic in the Second World War than the First World War. Whereas the First war is often seen as an old-fashioned balance of power conflict brought about by rival alliances, the Second has been portrayed as a moral crusade against the barbarous Nazi tyranny. In truth Britain's motives were very similar at the start of both conflicts: namely a reluctant acceptance of a Continental military commitment to protect the home islands, their vital lines of communication and the Empire against an aggressive, expansionist European Great Power.

Germany was singled out for strategic planning purposes as Britain's 'ultimate enemy' soon after Hitler came to power in 1933, but this by no means implied that war was inevitable.

The Nazis' ruthless destruction of democracy, violent behaviour towards all domestic opposition and strident anti-Semitic propaganda were all thoroughly reported in the British press but were not deemed to be reasons for going to war. On the contrary, British governments in the 1930s focused on German territorial and nationalist grievances in the belief that if these could be settled amicably Hitler would be appeased. As the late John Grigg wrote in a provocative article in 1990, 'Germany was challenged not because its regime was odious internally, but because it was a menace externally'.[9]

The murderous policies of the Nazis were known from the outset and in the course of 1942 the British and American governments received overwhelming evidence regarding the mass killing of Jews and other 'undesirables' in Eastern Europe. However, Allied policy and strategy were not substantially altered in the light of this intelligence, nor was it much used as a propaganda weapon to inflame public opinion.[10]

[9] John Grigg, 'Nobility and War: The Unselfish Commitment', *Encounter* (March, 1990).

[10] For early information about the Holocaust reaching the West, mainly from Polish sources, I have used E. T. Wood and S. M. Jankowski, *Karski: How One Man Tried*

Consequently, it was only in the final weeks of the war with the liberation of Bergen-Belsen in the West and revelations about the existence of the extermination camps such as Auschwitz and Treblinka in the East, that the full horror of Nazi barbarism was revealed to the wider world. Thus A. J. P. Taylor's concluding remark in his *English History 1914–1945* that for soldiers who liberated Belgium and the death camps the war ended as a noble crusade was true but needed elaboration. It was essentially after the war with an outpouring of revelations about Nazi atrocities on an unimaginable scale and the staging of the Nuremberg Trials that the British war effort came to be seen as a moral crusade against evil. While it would be unduly cynical to deny any moral element in Britain's war policy, the sober truth is that between 1939 and 1942 the overriding concern was to avoid defeat, and after that to ensure, in company with vastly more powerful allies, that Germany was absolutely defeated.

This aspect of the war merits more discussion because it illuminates the intractable political and ethical problems posed by the alliance with the Soviet Union, and why the notion of a 'crusade against the evil of Nazism' was to a considerable extent a retrospective distortion that could only flourish after 1945.

By the autumn of 1942 information about the slaughter of the Jews in Poland and the establishment of death camps at Chelmno, Belzec and Treblinka had reached the West via Switzerland, and from British intercepts of German police and SS radio traffic. Churchill was fully informed and wrote to the Archbishop of Canterbury on 29 October 1942, before a protest meeting at the Albert Hall, deploring these systematic cruelties and promising that such racial persecution would be ended when the war was won.

Dramatic personal evidence, amplifying previous reports, was provided by a remarkable individual, Jan Karski, a Polish soldier and diplomat who had been tortured by the Nazis and had witnessed the suffering of the Jews in the Warsaw ghetto and the experiments carried out at Belzec. Karski arrived in London on 25 November 1942 and secured an interview with Anthony Eden, who was initially cautious in his response. Foreign Office officials were inclined to deny that Karski's

to *Stop the Holocaust* (Wiley, 1994) and R. Breitman, *Official Secrets: What the Nazis Planned. What the British and Americans Knew* (Hill and Wang, 1999).

information about the Holocaust was convincing, and took the position that nothing could be done about Nazi persecution of the Jews. By 6 December, however, Eden had received confirmation of the plight of the Jews from the American and Soviet ambassadors, Winant and Maisky, and was convinced that a public statement was warranted. Accordingly on 17 December an Allied Declaration was published denouncing Nazi atrocities and promising that evil-doers would be punished after the war was won. Eden declared that 'Their [the Jews'] suffering, however horrible, would not be allowed to influence the military effort.' Eden was impressed by Karski, but at a second meeting depressed the Polish envoy by asking what would be the reaction if his country were pressed to cede Eastern territories to Stalin. In July 1943 Karski had a personal meeting with Roosevelt, who, unlike some senior American officials, seemed convinced that he was telling the truth but, like Britain, he would promise no action to help the Jews – or indeed to support the Polish government in London, which was making allegations of Soviet crimes and perfidy. Roosevelt's pro-Stalin policy made Karski realise that his visit to America was futile: he had backed the wrong horse. Eden echoed Roosevelt's pro-Stalin sentiments, speaking of the latter's moderation and goodwill, Russia wanted very little from Poland – only the land east of the Curzon Line.

Shortly before Karski arrived in the United States an event occurred that had ominous implications for the fate of Poland and for any prospects of the Western Allies intervening to stop the Nazi mass extermination policies in the East. In April 1943 the Germans announced the discovery of the mass graves of murdered Polish officers in Katyn Forest. The location, timing and documentary evidence from the bodies strongly indicated that this crime was perpetrated by the Soviet Union, but in the face of Stalin's denials Britain and the United States chose to accept his word against that of the Germans. It was eventually established that the Soviet Union *was* responsible. The Polish government in exile expressed outrage but Stalin retaliated by breaking off all contacts with it.[11]

Only on 7 July 1944 did Churchill learn of the full extent of the mass murder of the Jews at Auschwitz, where they were being gassed

---

[11] For Britain's reluctance, long after 1945, to acknowledge that the Poles had been right about the Katyn Massacre see Halik Kochanski, *The Eagle Unbowed* (Allen Lane, 2012) especially pp. 579–584.

at the rate of about 12,000 a day. Churchill minuted to Eden to urge the RAF to bomb the railway line from Budapest to Auschwitz to stop the transport of Hungarian Jews, but the Air Staff replied that this was impractical as it had to previous requests. As for bombing the gas chambers themselves, this would have to be a task for the United States' Air Force in daylight, but this was also refused on several occasions.

It was clear by 1943 that Britain and the United States (and more especially the Foreign Office and the State Department) were giving the higher priority to good relations with the Soviet Union, and were not willing to risk bombing operations to mitigate the annihilation of the Jews and other groups being exterminated by the Nazis. This latter decision was strengthened by the extreme reluctance of the Soviet Union to give any ground facilities in support of Allied air operations. Against mounting evidence of Soviet ingratitude towards aid delivered at great cost in lives by the Allies, cynical failure to support the Warsaw Rising and determination to secure a pro-Communist government in Poland at the end of the war, Roosevelt and Churchill could only hope that Stalin would display some moderation in order to continue the Grand Alliance after the defeat of Germany.

It is not difficult to grasp why there was no wave of bitter, disenchanted anti-war novels, memoirs or poetry after 1945. To become disenchanted one must be motivated by idealism and hope and there was little of these in the later 1930s. By 1938 it was grimly accepted that there would soon be a second more desperate struggle to stop German expansion. Older men who had seen it all before prepared stoically for another war 'in the trenches' while the younger generation already had a war in their heads; namely the war depicted after 1918 in the memoirs of a small number of middle-class survivors. So powerful were the images of 'the horror of the trenches' that many soldiers noted in the Second World War that their experiences, though dreadful, could not be anywhere near as terrible as their fathers'.[12] Another of the causes of the angry poetry and memoirs of the First World War subalterns such as Graves, Sassoon, Blunden and Aldington was also lacking: that is the justified belief that the civilians at home had no idea of the hardships and suffering they were enduring at the front. After the brief period of

---

[12] Gary Sheffield, 'The Shadow of the Somme', in Paul Addison and Angus Calder (eds.), *Time to Kill: The Soldier's Experience of War in the West 1939–1945* (Pimlico, 1997) pp. 29–39.

'phoney war' in 1939 and early 1940, the home population experienced the Battle of Britain, the Blitz, the Doodlebugs and V2s accompanied by continuous anxieties and shortages of fuel, food and other vital commodities. Indeed, given the British forces' long administrative tail compared to the First World War and several quiet backwaters where there was little action, it was not fanciful to suggest that many soldiers enjoyed a 'cushier' time than their families back home.

Lastly, though doubtless exaggerated by propaganda and in Churchill's rhetoric, there was a much greater feeling of national solidarity than in the earlier war. A very high proportion of the population was involved in war work, and although class divisions and resentments remained, there was a greater sense of pulling together through a long crisis. In particular, leadership in the Services was more democratic and open to merit, and there was greater understanding that citizens in uniform must be treated more humanely, especially in the matter of punishments.[13]

Fascist leaders, including Sir Oswald and Lady Mosley, and other prominent individuals thought to be sympathetic towards Germany, were locked up. At the other political extreme, Communists were thrown into confusion by the Nazi–Soviet Pact of August 1939, but their dilemma was not merely resolved with the Nazi attack on the Soviet Union in June 1941: 'Uncle Joe' Stalin and the Russian war effort were henceforth given heroic status in British publicity. Sir Stafford Cripps, Ambassador to Moscow 1940–1942, publicly pressed for more arms, raw materials and food to be sent to the Soviet Union. Lord Beaverbrook, until recently Minister of Production, led a public campaign for a Second Front to be opened in 1942. This gained momentum in the first half of 1942 but was played down after the loss of Tobruk and the tragic failure of the Dieppe Raid.[14]

Thus by the 1950s a positive and exaggerated view of Britain's and the Dominions' role in deciding the outcome of the Second World War had been firmly established. The war had been manifestly just, comparatively economical in lives lost, brilliantly successful in

[13] For the sensitive handling of the Home Front in the Second World War see Jeremy Crang, *The British Army and the People's War 1939–1945* (Manchester University Press, 2000).

[14] P. M. H. Bell provides an excellent account of Anglo-Soviet relations during and after the war in *John Bull and the Bear: British Public Opinion, Foreign Policy and the Soviet Union 1941–1945* (Arnold, 1990).

mechanical innovation and in Deception and Intelligence generally (though the outstanding work at Bletchley Park and the vital importance of 'Ultra' were not made public until the mid-1970s). The Armed Services were all deemed to have served the nation well, and the embarrassing run of miscalculations, defeats and disasters were as yet not much studied, let alone pilloried by an equivalent of *Blackadder*. Above all, with every passing year it became more evident that this had been a conflict vital to win and Britain and the Dominions (that is Churchill and the 'Anglo-Saxon Peoples') had won it. The concepts of 'the Dunkirk Spirit', the 'Finest Hour' and 'taking it' through the Blitz achieved mythic status and were stretched retrospectively to cover the whole conflict. Writing in the mid-1970s, the radical historian A. J. P. Taylor, no admirer of wars or military leaders, could conclude his popular illustrated history,[15] somewhat parochially, by stating that for all the killing and destruction that accompanied it, the Second World War was a good war.

He would not have passed such a positive judgement on the First World War, and nor would the great majority of opinion-formers in publishing, the press, the theatre and the media in general when the earlier conflict again became a focus of interest and controversy in the 1960s. Of course, public interest in the First World War had never been completely eclipsed thanks to the role of popular historians like Basil Liddell Hart (knighted in 1965), and the extremely slow gestation of the official histories, which was prolonged into the late 1940s. But, for reasons that are not entirely clear, once Churchill's monumental history of the Second World War had been published and numerous statesmen and service leaders had fought their corners in the 'battle of the memoirs', the media appeared to tire of Hitler's war and turned once again to new appraisals and interpretations of the earlier conflict.

From the viewpoint of scholarly objectivity, the 1960s was an inauspicious decade for the revival of Great War revisionism. Official documents were still unavailable under the then 'Fifty Year Rule'; but, more importantly, this was a period of radical political and social agitation and change, under the shadow of possible nuclear annihilation, when authority in general and military authority in particular came under fierce attack. To a considerable extent the new critical approach simply resurrected the expressions of disillusionment of the inter-war

---

[15] A. J. P. Taylor, *The Second World War: An Illustrated History* (Penguin, 1974).

decades. There is also the suggestion that the passing of the generation of those directly bereaved liberated the critics from restraints they
had previously observed. But, in the 1960s, with the fiftieth anniver-
saries of the outbreak of war in 1914 fast approaching, it is hard to
resist the simple explanation that this seemed an opportune moment
for left-wing, anti-establishment writers to 'put the boot in' rather as
Lytton Strachey in 1918 had savaged the idols of an earlier generation
in *Eminent Victorians*.

In the sequence of the publication of campaign and general
histories, Alan Moorehead got in early with his very critical account
of *Gallipoli* (1956), Leon Wolff published a doom-laden account of
Third Ypres entitled *In Flanders Fields* in 1958, and A. J. P. Taylor
an irreverent *Illustrated History of the First World War* with impish
cartoons and captions in 1963. But it was Alan Clark's *The Donkeys*
(1961) that most successfully captured the ethos of the time. Clark
wrote the book in a great hurry to meet a profitable deadline, and
it had little merit as a serious study. But he had hit on an inviting
target in the disastrous Loos offensive of September 1915. Sir John
French, the Commander-in-Chief, and Sir Douglas Haig, his senior
Army commander, were certainly open to severe criticism, but Clark's
sarcasm and innuendos were intended for a popular readership that
seemed ready to applaud the mud-slinging. Above all, his employment
of the phrase 'lions led by donkeys' not only echoed his catchy title,
but perfectly suited a generation ready to believe that the true heroes
were the previously unsung private soldiers who had been callously
sacrificed by incompetent generals. As Peter Parker has recently noted,
The Donkeys was an important document for the 1960s; Clark's version
of courageous soldiers sent heedlessly to their doom set the tone for the
whole decade. 'It fixed ever more firmly in the public mind, the mud,
blood and futility view of the war.'[16]

If these anti-First World War publications had already made an
impression in 1961, they were enormously strengthened and extended
to a much wider public by Joan Littlewood's theatrical entertainment
Oh! What a Lovely War (1963), and the considerably adapted film
version (1969). Joan Littlewood made no secret of her radical intentions; hers was a scathing, uninhibited attack on the ruling classes and

[16] Peter Parker, *The Last Veteran: Harry Patch and the Legacy of War* (Fourth Estate,
2009), pp. 179–180.

particularly the military hierarchy. As Peter Parker neatly put it, this was 'agit-prop theatre of the most effective kind'.[17] The play was attacked by senior military historians, such as Correlli Barnett and John Terraine (and subsequently the present writer) for its breath-taking liberties with First World War history: for example by omitting the final months of the war it evaded the awkward question of how these 'Donkeys' had won one of the greatest ever British victories. Nevertheless the performance flourished because it provided superb entertainment, most notably in the soldiers' songs, some of which were moving as well as irreverent.[18]

> The play's most original feature was its presentation of the war from what was assumed to be the common soldier's viewpoint: a revolutionary inversion of class authority in the 1960s though since then a much more common approach. A new generation in the 1960s was provided with the disturbing argument – later to be comically trivialised in the 1989 BBC television series *Blackadder Goes Forth* that the Great War represented a betrayal of the ordinary people by the ruling class.[19]

These strident attacks on the military leaders' incompetence and lack of concern for the soldiers' lives have achieved the status of popular myth, so much so that to many people it now seems perverse even to suggest that the majority of soldiers did not see themselves as hapless victims of a pointless war; that there were thousands of brave and popular junior officers; and that most of the senior officers were neither callous nor incompetent.

The film version of *Oh! What a Lovely War* disappointed some critics because it somewhat muffled the stage version's radical political message and the film's tone sentimentalised in order to entertain mass cinema audiences. But this limitation was more than offset by an all-star cast with John Mills presenting a caricature of Sir Douglas Haig as completely unimaginative, stubborn and inhuman in his cold acceptance of huge losses. But the film's most audacious

[17] Ibid., pp. 155–156.
[18] Brian Bond, 'Oh! What a Lovely War: History and Popular Myths in Late Twentieth-Century Britain', in William Roger Louis (ed.), *Yet More Adventures with Britannia* (I. B. Tauris, 2005), pp. 149–164.
[19] Ibid., pp. 154ff.

coup was to transfer the unending field of white crosses from the body of the text to a surreal concluding scene. In crowded cinemas the impression of sadness at the useless sacrifice of so many young men was reportedly overwhelming. These young 'lions' were seen to have thrown their lives away for nothing: the meaning that the producer, Sir Richard (later Lord) Attenborough, believed to be true and intended to stand as the film's final message. The film won numerous international awards.

In the same year that *Oh! What a Lovely War* was first produced (1963), John Terraine published his biography *Haig: The Educated Soldier*. Though not entirely blind to his hero's limitations, Terraine remained a staunch and obstinate defender of the Commander-in-Chief and, more widely, of Britain's successful war effort in numerous publications for the rest of his life. With few allies or supporters (Correlli Barnett being a notable exception) Terraine repeated his central tenets like a mantra: the trench stalemate was due to the unavoidable conditions of the time not to the stupidity of any of the belligerents' military leaders; Britain had begun the war with a small under-equipped, volunteer Army and inexperienced senior officers but had improved steadily and, indeed, led the field with technical innovations such as the tank. By the final year of the war Haig commanded the best Army on the Western Front and by far the largest Britain had ever assembled. This Army (including the Dominions' divisions) played the principal role in securing victory on the Western Front.

In 1964 BBC Television presented the outstanding twenty-six part series *The Great War*. These programmes excelled in their all-round coverage of the war on all fronts, in their generally well-written scripts and, most importantly, for their bold use of veterans' recollections on screen. On the debit side, however, there was a bitter controversy over the extensive use of reconstructed sequences that were not clearly indicated to viewers. John Terraine and Correlli Barnett seized this opportunity to pen more nuanced, though not uncritical versions of the British Army's controversial campaigns on the Western Front. But even this moderate attempt to present a more positive presentation of the Army's role failed to offset the overwhelming power of the visual image over the spoken text. The sonorous voice-over by Sir Michael Redgrave added to the sense of sadness and melancholy. Audience research showed that the majority of viewers questioned had been most impressed by images of the appalling battlescapes with their splintered trees, water-filled craters and the corpses of men and animals. These episodes tended to confirm the already well-established opinion that combat conditions in this war were uniquely horrible, the battles badly conducted with a huge and excessive cost in lives, and all leading to an ultimately futile outcome.

So deeply entrenched had these myths become by the end of the 1960s that it became very difficult for a new generation of military historians to modify, let alone change, the mind set of even more open-minded members of the public who read serious books and watched television for enlightenment as well as entertainment. This was regrettable because the passage of time ensured that a new generation of scholars was largely free from the understandable critical attitudes and hang-ups of those who had fought in the First World War or been directly affected by it.

Outstanding among these older, critical interpreters of Britain's part in the First World War was Sir Basil Liddell Hart (who died in 1970), not only for his huge range of publications, but also for his pervasive influence on other historians (the present author included), on reviewing and publishing, television and the theatre. He had been a fierce critic of John Terraine and had resigned as an adviser to *The Great War* series because he thought the Somme episode had been too sympathetic to Haig.

The 1970s also saw the almost unrestricted opening of the official archives for the period 1914–1918, so at last it became possible for scholars to explore well beyond the limited range of sources previously available and to question all established positions on controversies and reputations.

It is not difficult to understand why scholarly revisionism (generally but not invariably favourable to Britain's role in the First World War) can make little headway when up against all the popular assumptions already outlined and to be so brilliantly exploited by the television farce *Blackadder Goes Forth* (1989), which remains as appealing now as when first shown. *Blackadder* perfectly encapsulates all the ingredients of the Western Front myth: dreadful trench conditions and asinine planning by a callous, stupid upper-class commander and his weak and servile staff who are safely ensconced in their headquarters far from the front line. Not least significant is the personification of 'everyman at war' in the scruffy, long-suffering yet humorous and ultimately heroic Tommy in the iconic character, Private Baldrick.[20]

Blackadder is perhaps the most formidable barrier to revising popular understanding of the First World War precisely because it is so entertaining, but it is far from being the only one. There are frequent revivals, for example, of the entertainment *Oh! What a Lovely War*, the film version of *All Quiet on the Western Front* and R. C. Sherriff's drama *Journey's End*. Another left-wing depiction of the war was *The Monacled Mutineer* (1986), a four-part BBC production about the disturbances at the Etaples training camp in 1917. Numerous schools have introduced generations of children to the First World War through the medium of war poetry, and especially the work of Wilfred Owen, with its power to arouse strong emotions, but likely to be seriously misleading unless offset by other literary and historical sources.

Recent growth of popular interest in what grandfather, or even great grandfather, did in the Great War, and a near obsession with surviving veterans, now all deceased, have been a mixed blessing from a historian's perspective. On the positive side, any form of interest, however limited initially, is to be welcomed if it develops into wider studies and understanding of complicated issues. Otherwise the young student is liable to take for granted the essential truths – or myths – as formulated in *Blackadder* and sanctified by Wilfred Owen's verse.

The recollections of elderly veterans, especially those of the 'last Tommies', have to be approached very warily even though this may seem heartless and ungrateful towards men who long ago risked their lives and witnessed horrific events that we can scarcely imagine. Old men notoriously forget or embroider their experiences, but it is also inevitable that they will be influenced, often unconsciously, by their own later experiences and even more by public events, such as a second world war, which have exerted an enormous effect on popular beliefs.

The late Harry Patch, who died on 26 July 2009 at the age of 111, provides an interesting example of these problems. When aged only nineteen he spent a few months on the Western Front in the Third Ypres campaign and was wounded. As a conscript he was an unwilling

[20] On the historical significance of *Blackadder* see Stephen Badsey's excellent essay in Graham Roberts and Philip M. Taylor (eds.), *The Historian, Television and History* (University of Luton Press, 2001).

soldier who returned to 'civvy street' with relief and took no further interest in the war until, in extreme old age, his very longevity made him an unlikely representative of a past generation. But, as Professor Hew Strachan has reminded us, Harry Patch looked back on his teenage years with the wisdom of hindsight and could not place those far-off events in context. 'The war of his youth was reinterpreted in light of those later events, and so too was his own understanding of that experience.'[21] In May 2012 a six-foot stone memorial to Harry Patch was unveiled on the lawn of Wells Cathedral in Somerset.

In his book *The Last Veteran: Harry Patch and the Legacy of War* (2009), Peter Parker places his subject in a much broader setting by providing an interesting survey of First World War controversies in history, literature and culture more generally. He notes, for example, that Benjamin Britten's *War Requiem*, though composed for the re-dedication of Coventry Cathedral in 1962, was inspired by the poetry of Wilfred Owen.

Parker is sympathetic towards Harry Patch as 'the last survivor', and disagrees with historians, including the present author, who challenge the view that the First World War was uniquely horrible. Where popular myths conflict with historical truth he sides with the former, believing that the First World War was 'a great national tragedy and that an entire generation was profligately and unnecessarily sacrificed'. Moreover he believes that although 'historians can usefully tell us what the war was *about* . . . what really interests us is what it was *like*'. This is surely a false dichotomy in that it is impossible to understand fully what the war was *like* unless you also understand what it was *about*.

This chapter has outlined the case for a challenge to questionable popular notions, now enjoying the status of myth, which portray Britain's role in the First World War as an almost unmitigated disaster and the Second as an almost unqualified triumph. This extreme caricature has already been modified by several historians who have viewed the two world wars as part of a continuum during which Germany's initial drive towards European domination was only temporarily checked in 1918 and then, at the second attempt, decisively defeated. From the British standpoint this approach has obvious advantages in bringing out continuities and similarities, for example in strategic planning, war readiness, mobilising resources and the conduct of operations. While

[21] Hew Strachan, 'Into History', *R.U.S.I. Journal* (August, 2009).

accepting the notion of a continuum in Anglo-German confrontations between about 1900 and 1945, this study goes further in seeking to undermine the exaggerated contrast between the First World War as failure and the Second World War as success – distortions which have become established mainly through hindsight in the decades after 1945.

2 BRITISH POLICY AND STRATEGY

In 2000 Peter Liddle and his co-editors published a two-volume study entitled *The Great World War, 1914–1945*, an interpretation which many historians would endorse for viewing the two world wars as a prolonged struggle against Germany's drive for European hegemony separated by a twenty-year truce. Britain was reluctant to enter either war but fought in both from beginning to end. Her grand strategy was essentially defensive: namely to protect the home islands, her vital sea communications and her empire.

For part of both wars France and Russia (or the Soviet Union) were her co-belligerents against Germany, and in both the USA's delayed entry was decisive in tipping the balance in Western Europe. In both conflicts Britain's fundamental assumptions about the likely length and nature of the struggle were soon completely shattered, but with sharply contrasting outcomes. Above all, the most obvious difference cannot be over-stressed. In 1914 Britain had enjoyed one hundred years of freedom from involvement in a major European war during which her industry, finance and commercial links with a worldwide empire, protected by a dominant navy, had together made her the Super Power of the era. Moreover, despite the frequent international crises of the pre-1914 decade, Europe appeared to be enjoying a period of closer communications and growing prosperity in which large-scale wars were widely viewed as unnecessary and counter-productive – indeed almost impossible to wage for more than a few months for economic and financial reasons. True, the Anglo-German naval race and invasion scares, dramatised by the press and fiction writers, had stirred up anti-German feeling (which was fully reciprocated), but in 1913–1914 there seemed little likelihood of a general European war. Where British involvement in a terrible civil war seemed a real possibility was in Ireland as the Home Rule issue, and preparations for armed resistance in Ulster, reached a crisis.

After the experience of 1914–1918 there could never, in Philip Larkin's phrase, 'be such innocence again'.[1] Memories of the Great War, enhanced and distorted by myths, cast grim shadows over the 1930s and were given shocking intimations of worse horrors to come by the Spanish Civil War. Very few citizens, at any level, cherished illusions or romantic images of another European war that, it was widely assumed, would begin with immediate and indiscriminate air attacks on British cities, employing poison gas as well as explosives. Consequently the attempt to appease Hitler (and Mussolini) received broad popular support and when this policy was clearly seen to have failed, in the summer of 1939, the approaching conflict was faced with stoicism and anxiety accompanied by escapist humour (such as Hitler being portrayed by Charlie Chaplin as a figure of fun), and a complacent certainty that whatever happened on the Continent, Britain would somehow survive and, eventually, triumph.

The Liberal government of 1914 was anything but warlike. Before the appointment of Lord Kitchener to the War Office, only Winston Churchill had seen military service, and even he, as First Lord of the Admiralty, envisaged a limited naval conflict. The other members of the Cabinet were ignorant of the realities of modern war against a major European Power. In any case there was little political hostility towards Germany when the crisis loomed in July 1914. Germany had effectively conceded defeat in the naval race in 1912 and was also a valued trading partner. An alliance with her against a combination of Britain's imperial rivals, France and Russia, had seemed a possibility until the mid-1890s when Germany's drive to become a first-class naval as well as land power created an immediate threat. Britain's *ententes* with France (1904) and Russia (1907) limited her diplomatic options, but even the close and confidential military conversations with France before 1914 were not politically binding and the latter knew this to be so.

---

[1] 'MCMXIV' in Philip Larkin, *The Whitsun Weddings* (Faber and Faber, 1964).

Consequently, as late as 29 July 1914, the Prime Minister, Asquith, could reassure the King that Britain was unlikely to be drawn into war over Belgium, and this view was shared by the majority of Cabinet members. By 2 August, however, the situation had changed drastically due to Germany's ultimatum to Belgium. While it was still hoped that Britain could remain neutral if German armies only marched through the southern tip of Belgium, Sir Edward Grey, the Foreign Minister, supported by Asquith, now feared that France might be defeated unless Britain offered her immediate support on land. Grey won over the backing of the House of Commons on 3 August, carefully mentioning Britain's obligation to France but making no reference to Russia. The Cabinet agreed to send an ultimatum to Berlin even before Belgium had asked for military support, and when it became clear, on 4 August, that Germany intended to march through the centre of Belgium the government received very strong public as well as all-party political backing. Two Cabinet ministers (Burns and Morley) resigned, but, with Lloyd George belatedly supporting intervention, the government was able to enter the war without delay, with a united Liberal government and with Unionist backing. This was a remarkable turnabout in the space of a week or so due to crass German military strategy that made gallant little Belgium a unifying popular cause as well as providing a clear diplomatic *casus belli*. On 6 August the Cabinet consented, with much less debate than Asquith had expected, to send four divisions and the cavalry division of the British Expeditionary Force (BEF, later, in 1939–1940, termed the Field Force) to France while prudently withholding two divisions in case of an attempted German invasion.

This summary has necessarily simplified a complex chain of events clouded by numerous misunderstandings, ignorance about intentions and devious manoeuvres that still arouse historical controversy. But for the British governing and professional classes, national interests and international principles were conveniently combined. They held a conviction that: 'if a Great Power were allowed to break an international agreement and to invade a small neighbour with impunity, European civilisation would sustain a blow from which it might not recover'.[2]

---

[2] Michael Brock, 'Britain Enters the War', p. 176 in R. J. W. Evans and H. P. von Strandmann (eds.), *The Coming of the First World War* (Oxford University Press, 1988).

Despite Chamberlain's ephemeral success at Munich in the autumn of 1938, another European war soon came to be viewed as imminent. Consequently, as war approached in 1939 there was an atmosphere of glum resignation among government ministers rather than the feverish uncertainty and manoeuvring of 1914. Almost to a man the Cabinet were supporters of Neville Chamberlain and therefore men of Munich. They had backed the policy of appeasement at a high cost in national honour and security in order to avoid war at almost any price. Curiously few of Chamberlain's supporters had seen military service in the First World War (Hore-Belisha at the War Office and Stanhope at the Admiralty were exceptions and the latter was about to be replaced by Churchill), whereas the war veterans, Duff Cooper Eden, Macmillan, Attlee and Churchill were mostly anti-appeasers and in opposition. Chamberlain had staked his hopes and his reputation on Hitler being a man of his word, so that the latter's occupation of Prague in March 1939 came as a terrible shock. Reacting immediately, without thinking ahead, the government offered a guarantee to Poland as a bluff or trip-wire in the hope that Hitler would understand that Britain was now prepared to go to war to resist any further act of aggression. Unfortunately Warsaw was strategically even further away than Prague and could be given no material support by Britain. France might have launched a serious diversionary attack on the Western Front, but had no intention of doing so in the short term.

Germany had been designated as Britain's ultimate enemy for defence planning and rearmament soon after Hitler's advent to power in 1933, but for several crucial years little sense of urgency was shown in preparing the Services for war. The Army, especially, was given a low priority, largely due to memories of the First World War, with the consequence that the government was reluctant to commit the small Field Force to France until February 1939. After the Munich conference top priority was given to the Air Defence of Great Britain (ADGB).

This would prove its value in the summer of 1940, but before that the emphasis on defence of 'fortress Britain' sent a negative signal to likely Continental allies, France and Belgium. Ironically, Hitler gave little thought to a possible war with Britain until 1937, and even thereafter did not instigate serious planning or the creation of air and naval forces sufficiently powerful to offer reasonable hopes of victory. This was in part due to his preoccupation with striking eastward, but also because he had formed a very low opinion of Chamberlain in the 1938 conferences and believed that he could be bullied into a climb-down. This was a serious miscalculation because even the bombshell of the Ribbentrop–Molotov Non-Aggression Pact on 23 August did not deter the British government and her even less bellicose ally France from declaring war on 3 September.

Even after the German drive into Poland was launched on 1 September Chamberlain hoped that Hitler would be willing to halt the offensive and negotiate, but at last he became convinced that this was a delusion. Throughout the following months of 'phoney war', however, he continued to hope that the conflict might wind down rather than escalate if only Germany could be convinced that she could not win.

The BEF was less well prepared for war with Germany than its predecessor in 1914, particularly as regards transport, but the first five regular divisions were dispatched to France – without losses – in September and October, and five more territorial divisions would follow by early May 1940. The soldiers were also accompanied by an Advanced Air Strike Force, but Britain was unwilling to 'take the gloves off' by launching air attacks against the Ruhr. All-out German bombing raids on British cities were expected immediately after the declaration of war and within hours of that declaration a false alarm caused panic in Whitehall. The *Luftwaffe* had acquired a fearsome reputation from the mid-1930s and this had been magnified by alarmist publications and by the destruction of Guernica. In 1939, however, the *Luftwaffe* lacked both the planning and the capacity to do serious damage to Britain without advanced bases.

Moreover, in complete contrast to 1914, the Field Force was not thrown straight into the cauldron of war but instead sat out a particularly severe winter in France interrupted by frequent false scares of imminent attack. Thus apart from German surface and submarine attacks, the British and French Services and peoples experienced eight unnerving and in some respects demoralising months of 'phoney war'.

In 1914 Asquith's Liberal government, with one exception, had no idea that it was embarking on a long and near total war in which losses, in manpower, trade and finance, were likely to be immense, whether or not Britain emerged on the winning side. Britain would embark upon a war of limited liability vis-à-vis the Continent, relying mainly on naval power to keep the sea lanes open and a blockade to bring pressure on Germany with only a modest military commitment to her allies. At home it would be essentially a matter of 'business as usual' with minimal state interference in industry, trade, commerce and, above all, manpower. The conflict might not be over by Christmas, as was widely expected, but it was scarcely conceivable that it could continue for years.

The exception to this way of thinking was Field Marshal Lord Kitchener, an imperial soldier and pro-consul with immense prestige, who was appointed to the War Office on the outbreak of war. He promptly informed his Cabinet colleagues that they must prepare for at least a three-year struggle. His persuasive strategic plan was that Britain and the Empire should build up large armies while France and Russia wore down the Central Powers' forces in a war of attrition. When the latter were exhausted Britain would bring its full weight to bear and deliver the *coup de grâce*. This would enable her to dominate the peace conference and, not least important, to hold an advantage over her recent allies, France and Russia, who were also viewed as imperial rivals.[3]

In 1939, by contrast, Britain entered the war with Germany, the bulk of whose forces were already committed to all-out war in Poland, a campaign that might drag on for months. In this eventuality Germany would be prevented from launching an early offensive in the West, giving the Allies time to strengthen their defences and build up their armies.

Britain and France had agreed that they would not risk a premature offensive but rather accepted that Germany would take the initiative at a moment that suited her. If the Allies could resist this anticipated shock attack, sheltering their armies behind the Maginot Line and fortifications extending along the Franco-Belgium frontier to the Channel, then eventually, perhaps after eighteen months or so, they could mount a carefully organised counter-offensive to expel the enemy from occupied territories in France and the Low Countries. This was, to say the least, an uninspiring strategy, risky for the troops' and civilians' morale. It also suggested depressing similarities to the static, attritional nature of the First World War. In the event an unusually severe winter caused the German offensive in the West to be repeatedly postponed, but when the blow eventually fell, on 10 May 1940, it was more devastating than anyone on the Allied side (and indeed many of the German generals) had imagined. Allied strategic assumptions had been undermined from

[3] David French, *British Strategy and War Aims 1914–1918* (Allen and Unwin, 1986).

the outset by the Nazi–Soviet Non-Aggression Pact, which permitted Germany to defeat Poland very quickly and then leave only small occupation forces in the East. Furthermore Soviet economic assistance, and German access to large areas of Eastern Europe and the Baltic, greatly reduced the prospects of an effective Allied blockade.

Thus in both world wars Britain's initial expectations and plans were speedily shattered. In 1914 the small and under-equipped BEF at once found itself in the path of the enemy's powerful right wing and was quickly entangled in the chaotic French retreat to the Marne. By the end of the year a continuous line of trenches stretched from the Swiss border to the Channel coast and the war of movement had effectively come to an end. The BEF had played a crucial role in checking the German advance in the Belgian frontier battles and later at Ypres, but in the process had suffered crippling losses.

At the end of 1914 there appeared to be a fleeting opportunity for Britain to escape from a full involvement in the war of attrition on the Western Front by launching an amphibious attack on the Ottoman Empire, an ally of the Central Powers since October. Given the power of the Royal Navy and the availability of land forces to be drawn mainly from Australia, New Zealand and India, a strategic indirect approach on the Dardanelles was feasible and attractive to a government already alarmed by the heavy demands on the Western Front. If successful and Turkey were defeated, this campaign would be no more than a diversion from the main theatre, but it would give the Allies leverage in the Balkans and, in the longer term, permit aid to be sent to Russia through the Black Sea. Although the Gallipoli operations continued from a disastrous start in March 1915 to the final withdrawal in January 1916, it quickly became clear after the failure of the landings on 25 April that this campaign also had degenerated into a trench deadlock. To the dismay of its supporters, notably Winston Churchill, this failure was widely held to show that there was no alternative to the Western Front as the decisive theatre.

In August 1915 the new Coalition government realised that France and Russia had already suffered such heavy losses that they might collapse without a much greater British contribution to the Western Front. Kitchener reluctantly accepted that the BEF would take over more of the line and would join the French in an autumn offensive. He also promised to send twenty-five new divisions before the end of the year. Moreover, the government took the first steps towards a measure that had previously seemed unthinkable – conscription – though this was not fully implemented until April 1916. The policy of 'business as usual' was also gradually abandoned as the state took control of vital components of the economy including shipping and ship building, coal production, transport and agriculture. Within two years the government had been obliged to introduce measures bringing the nation close to a 'total' war effort that had been unimaginable when hostilities began.

Although Neville Chamberlain had realised in September 1939 that Britain must be prepared for a war lasting three years, he personally continued to hope through the months of 'phoney war' that the conflict in the West would peter out rather than escalate. This delusion was based on the assumption that Hitler would come to realise that he could not win. The Prime Minister would not negotiate with the Führer but he did not rule out the possibility of a settlement with an alternative leader such as Goering. His hopes, and delusions, were shared by the Chief of the Imperial General Staff (CIGS), Sir Edmund 'Tiny' Ironside, who believed that if Germany became entangled in another war theatre, such as Scandinavia, she would lack the resources and flexibility to mount a major attack in the West. Despite the numerous German Western offensives that were ordered and then postponed, GHQ in France received accurate intelligence of enemy plans and was not deluded: the attack would come as soon as the spring weather permitted. Nevertheless there was optimism that the Allies had had sufficient time to prepare their defences so would be able to hold up the offensive. Moreover, if Hitler could be seen to have suffered a serious setback then his prestige in Germany might be fatally undermined.

In the event the German offensive against the Low Countries and France, launched on 10 May 1940, succeeded more rapidly and completely than even Hitler and many of his senior commanders, such as von Rundstedt, had thought possible. Whereas the majority of the French government and military leaders quickly accepted that the war was lost, the new British Prime Minister, Churchill, remained optimistic. He made heroic efforts to keep his ally in the war and would not acquiesce in a French request for separate peace negotiations. Among the desperate measures he took to try to keep Reynaud in office and France at war were to send a second expeditionary force to Normandy in June, and to make a quixotic and risky offer of political union between the Allies. When these guarantees failed or were rejected he still hoped France might continue to wage war from North Africa and her other overseas territories including Indo China. After France had accepted a humiliating defeat, including German occupation of the northern half of the country, Churchill widened the rift between recent allies by ordering a naval attack on the Vichy-controlled Fleet at Mers-el-Kébir and a seizure of French vessels in British ports.

This amazing transformation of the strategic and political situation had occurred between the German over-running of Denmark and Norway in April and the defeat of the Low Countries and France in May and June. With hindsight critics would discover fatal weaknesses in French society, politics and the armed services, but before the catastrophe no Jeremiah had foreseen the speed and completeness of the rout. In Britain, particularly, no British political or military leader had contemplated the nightmare scenario of a military and political collapse so shattering as to cause French withdrawal from the war. Britain had lost her Continental base and with it France's armed services and national assets. With Italy also now at war as an ally of Germany, and France's North African Empire under Vichy control, Britain's Mediterranean communications were in peril. Most dangerous of all, Germany was now in control of naval and air bases from northern Norway to the Bay of Biscay.

In these dire circumstances it is not surprising that Hitler was optimistic that Britain would give in and seek a negotiated peace. If, in the immediate aftermath of Dunkirk, Hitler had offered genuinely conciliatory peace terms, he would at the least have encouraged Churchill's numerous opponents to challenge his leadership and thereby divide public opinion. But this would have been completely out of character. By contrast, Churchill's pugnacity, patriotism and profound sense of history gave him the strength to find grounds for hope even in these darkest days. He noted, for example, that Germany had seemed to be winning in mid-1918 but then suddenly collapsed.

As the dramatic events of the summer of 1940 would show, the *Luftwaffe* and the German Navy were not as powerful as their early conquests suggested and, given Hitler's fitful, unsystematic approach to strategic planning, their higher direction was, to say the least, incoherent. Precious weeks were wasted when the British Isles were most vulnerable in the early summer of 1940.

It soon became clear that Germany would find the conquest of the British Isles very difficult, indeed virtually impossible, without thorough advance planning and total commitment to the task. Alternatively, in the longer term, Britain might be forced to negotiate by an all-out submarine and surface attack on her vital fuel and food supplies but, again, this strategy would take time to organise, making full use of the newly acquired Channel and Biscay ports. Most problematic, such a strategy would further antagonise the United States and might lead to her intervention earlier in this war than the previous one. Half American himself, Churchill placed what proved to be excessive confidence in early United States' intervention. Faith and sublime optimism are surely the key words in appraising Churchill's strategy in the fateful period between Dunkirk and Pearl Harbor. The odds seemed to be heavily stacked against Britain's survival, but the position was not quite hopeless. Churchill embodied that hope and managed to carry the vast majority of the British and Dominions' peoples with him. With all his limitations that was still a remarkable achievement.

After the strategic and political shocks of 1914 and 1940 Britain was forced to change the fundamental assumptions with which she had begun the two wars. By mid-1915 it had become evident that Kitchener's concept of allowing France and Russia to bear the brunt of attritional fighting while British and Imperial Forces steadily prepared to deal the knockout blow was not working. France and Russia had both suffered appalling losses in 1914–1915 and the latter in particular might well be defeated unless more pressure could be applied on the Western Front.

In a belated attempt to co-ordinate Allied strategy at Chantilly in December 1915 the military representatives of France, Russia, Italy and Britain undertook to launch concerted offensives in the summer of 1916. This plan, however, was fatally undermined by the German onslaught at Verdun in February, which threw the French onto the defensive and led to Haig opening the Somme offensive on 1 July before his armies were anywhere near ready. Russia attempted to fulfil her part of the plan, but Brusilov's offensive against Austria beginning on 4 June, though brilliantly successful at first, was soon halted and proved to be the last significant attack that his country would undertake. By November any hope that the Entente forces were on the brink of success on all fronts had faded. The failure at Gallipoli strengthened the convictions of Britain's military leaders that the Western Front was the vital theatre where the war would be decided and, furthermore, that Britain must play the major role there.

This was a startling departure from traditional British strategy that had sought to keep its military contribution to Continental allies as small as possible while supporting them financially and using naval supremacy to apply economic pressure on enemy ports and vulnerable overseas territories. How effectively this strategy had worked in the past was debateable, but by 1916 it was clearly in danger of failing. France and Russia were hard-pressed to resist Germany's military power; while Britain could not afford to finance her allies and was herself more vulnerable to blockade than in the past. These strategic assumptions proved to be politically costly and, as losses mounted, caused bitter controversy that has haunted the reputation of the higher conduct of the war ever since. Lloyd George had become Prime Minister in December 1916 with a clear mission to wage the war more vigorously, especially on the Western Front, but he was never wholly convinced that the generals knew what they were doing or were sufficiently careful with their soldiers' lives. Dependent on Conservative support in Parliament and lacking a military advisory committee whose judgement he could trust, Lloyd George never had confidence in his Commander-in-Chief but failed to remove him or, as attempted with serious consequences, make him subordinate to the French high command. The resultant civil-military friction severely handicapped Britain's higher direction of the war, with continuous arguments about the numbers of troops, weapons and equipment that could be spared for secondary theatres including Italy, Salonika and the Middle East.

Nevertheless British and Dominions forces did make an unprecedented contribution to Continental warfare in 1917–1918 with armies in excess of two million troops in sixty divisions, far eclipsing Britain's military effort in the Second World War. Most military historians would now agree that this commitment was necessary and eventually made a vital contribution to victory in 1918. However, what might be termed the 'Lloyd George legacy', the notion that there was a less costly alternative that would have been equally effective, continues to cast a seductive spell.

France's rapid and completely unexpected defeat in 1940 left Britain (and her Empire) in such a precarious position that many defeatists, not all of them French, anticipated that she would soon suffer the same fate. However, though in some quarters it may still be unfashionable to say so, France's withdrawal from the war proved to be a blessing in disguise for Britain. King George VI may be credited with perceiving at least part of this 'blessing' when he wrote to his mother just after the evacuation of Dunkirk that it was a relief no longer to have allies 'that we have to be polite to and pamper'.[4]

But at that time he could not know that for exactly four years (June 1940–June 1944), Britain would have no foothold in Western Europe while the greatest, most barbarous and most costly war in history raged in Eastern Europe. While it is impossible to predict in any detail what would have happened had France not collapsed in 1940, it is very likely that Britain would have increased the Field Force to around thirty divisions and suffered proportionate casualties. Of course the variables regarding what else would have happened remain matters of speculation, but it is reasonable to suggest that Hitler would have had to secure the defeat of the Western Allies before turning against the Soviet Union. Britain would then have had to bear more of the burden of the war of attrition and the Soviet Union much less.

What can be said for certain is that between 1940 and 1944 the main burden of defending the British Isles and bringing home the realities of war to the Third Reich fell to the Royal Navy and the Royal Air Force, especially Bomber Command. This is in no way intended as a slight to the vast array of civilians in uniform who largely constituted Britain's land forces. The campaigns in Burma, the Middle East, North Africa and Italy all caused terrible hardships and suffering to the combatants and, especially in Burma and Italy, were conducted in appalling conditions as bad as those of 1916 and 1917 at their worst. None of these campaigns should be viewed as pointless or without strategic meaning, but the harsh fact is that they were peripheral to the essential goal of defeating Germany, which, as in the First World War, had to be conducted in the Eastern and Western countries bordering the Third Reich.

The sequence of global events that converted Britain's desperate resistance in 1940 to a platform for eventual victory could only be dimly perceived or guessed at when Churchill uttered his defiant speeches. It was 'on the cards' that Hitler would invade the Soviet Union, but expert opinion in Britain expected the Soviet Union to be defeated in a matter of weeks. By the end of 1941 the Soviet Union was not merely resisting but counter-attacking on an impressive scale. In the same month (December 1941) Japan's attack on Pearl Harbor brought

---

[4] Brian Bond, *Britain, France and Belgium 1939–1940* (Brassey's, 1980), p. 117.

the Americans into the war, and Hitler's quixotic declaration of war on the latter gave President Roosevelt political leverage to give priority to the defeat of Germany before that of Japan.

A frequent criticism of Britain's conduct of the First World War is that the government failed to obtain a negotiated peace. It was the belief that a genuine opportunity was being ignored that prompted Siegfried Sassoon's protest in the summer of 1917, though he admitted much later that he had been mistaken. In reality war aims and convictions about acceptable peace terms were inextricably mixed and, tragically, none of the major belligerents saw a window of opportunity for an end to hostilities that suited both alliances at the same time. Britain needed a decisive victory that would ensure her survival as a Great Power. The defeat of Germany would be difficult enough, but Britain also needed a settlement that would ensure her longer-term security against states that were nominally friendly: France, Russia, Japan and even the United States.

In both world wars Britain was critically dependent on the support of allies but experienced continuous friction in trying to persuade them to accept her own plans and priorities. As David French neatly put it in *The Strategy of the Lloyd George Coalition*: 'Britain's relations with its allies (between 1914 and 1918) were distinguished by the same "competitive co-operation" that marred its relations in the Second World War'.[5] In both world wars, but especially the First, Britain's partners required *un effort du sang*, not only to wear down and eventually defeat the enemies, but also to encourage allied societies to stay in the war. These were important considerations behind the British offensives in 1916 and 1917, and when the latter failed to achieve a breakthrough Lloyd George inclined to concentrate on the defeat of Turkey while waiting for American participation in strength to win the war on the Western Front in 1919.

'War aims', as David Stevenson has reminded us, 'were necessarily hypothetical and transitory sets of options. Few entailed unconditional commitments'.[6] The rival alliances between 1914 and 1918 were too divided among themselves for peace feelers to have much chance; indeed the Central Powers saw peace feelers primarily as a

[5] David French, *The Strategy of the Lloyd George Coalition 1916–1918* (The Clarendon Press, 1995), p. 289.

[6] David Stevenson, *1914–1918: The History of the First World War* (Allen Lane, 2004), p. 150.

means of splitting their enemies. Britain had no European territorial ambitions and was not inflexibly concerned with some of the key territorial disputes, such as Alsace-Lorraine and Poland, but she did remain completely committed to the restoration of Belgian independence.

Germany had gained vital territorial advantages, both east and west, in the early part of the war and, although her war aims were imprecise, Britain was justified in believing that peace negotiations without victory would be to Germany's advantage. From mid-1916, despite heavy losses at Verdun and on the Somme, German war aims became harsher than ever. The advent of Hindenburg and Ludendorff to a virtual dictatorship resulted in more expansive war aims to be declared. Belgium's railways and economy would be placed under German control; France would cede Briey with its iron ore resources; Poland would be subordinated, and Russia would have to give up Lithuania and Courland. After the Allies rejected the German peace note of 12 December 1916 the German generals called for further annexations, and the Navy demanded control of the Baltic and Belgian coasts with a worldwide chain of bases. As Stevenson sums up: neither side desired serious discussions until it had won decisively with its alliances intact. No peace initiative in this period came close to success. By the spring of 1917, with the collapse of Russia impending and America's entry into the war, the gap between the two sides was 'wider than ever and the scope for bargaining still less'.[7]

The failure to secure a negotiated peace was not only a matter of diplomacy and *realpolitik*; at the very outset Germany's ruthless invasion of Belgium had given Britain a moral case for intervention, and thereafter Germany was its own worst enemy in the frenzied competition for the moral high ground. Whenever British moral outrage seemed to slacken Germany could be relied upon to re-stoke the fires. There were the ruthless atrocities against Belgian and French civilians; the wanton destruction of historic buildings in Louvain and elsewhere; the bombardment of British seaports; the first use of poison gas; the sinking of the Lusitania; the execution of nurse Edith Cavell; and the Zeppelin and Gotha attacks on British cities.

British propaganda exploited these opportunities to an extreme and sometimes, we may now feel, disgusting degree. The spirit of righteous anger sometimes degenerated into an atmosphere of racism and

[7] Ibid., pp. 126–127, 137, 151.

blood lust. 'An uninhibited campaign of exaggeration and vilification was launched against the "Huns" who crucified captured soldiers, raped nuns and bayoneted pregnant women.'[8] Consequently respect for the truth became the war's first casualty. An hysterical element in the public's response caused all things German, even dachshunds, to be targeted. There were demands for the Kaiser to be hanged and for reprisal bombing raids to be made on German cities. This ferocious civilian bellicosity struck many soldiers as far worse than hostilities between enemies at the front. Their alienation from militaristic civilians and sections of the press contributed to a bitter note in some of the war memoirs and poetry that were not so much 'anti-war' as expressions of disgust at the hysteria generated by propaganda on the home front.

There was a remarkable amount of idealism underpinning British war aims in both world wars. The late John Grigg was surely right to argue that there was more nobility and unselfishness in Britain's approach to the First World War than the Second if only because the former came as a shock to complacent hopes of peaceful progress and greater European co-operation, whereas by the 1930s many of these hopes had been dashed and there were ominous signs of impending disaster.[9] In 1914 H. G. Wells had published a pamphlet entitled *The War That Will End War* and subsequently campaigned for a League of Nations. Lloyd George in a House of Commons speech just after the war had ended also hoped that it had been 'a war to end all wars'; but it seems likely that this phrase only came into general use later by critics who knew the prophecy had not been realised.

Behind all the particular war aims there lay a profound desire to put an end to German, – and more specifically Prussian – militarism, but to bring about such profound political and social changes Germany would have to be completely defeated and probably occupied for some time. It became apparent, even in the 1920s, that this aim had not been achieved despite the severe limitations imposed on the size and armaments of Germany's armed forces.

What is truly surprising, however, is that throughout the Second World War Churchill frequently expressed the view that in the post-war settlement 'Prussian militarism', located in North Germany, must be eradicated forever, whereas South Germany and Austria should be

---

[8] John Bourne, *Britain and the Great War 1914–1918* (Arnold, 1989), pp. 228–232.
[9] Grigg, 'Nobility and War'.

treated more leniently.[10] Yet the Prime Minister must have known that Hitler was Austrian and that the origins of the Nazi movement were most deeply rooted in Bavaria, especially in Munich. In the event Hitler unintentionally achieved Churchill's aim by eliminating the Prussian conservative-militaristic Junker caste that had dominated politics in the Wilhelmine period, done everything possible to shorten the life of the Weimar Republic and elevated him to power in 1933. By destroying the basis of the traditional resistance to modernity and liberalism Hitler had 'left the German people with a political and social *tabula rasa* on which to create a new democratic and anti-military edifice'.[11]

It is not surprising that later critics have deplored the political leaders' failure to achieve a negotiated peace short of victory in the First World War. In reality the complex alliance systems and the enormous burdens imposed on belligerents' peoples entailed that victory would become an end in itself. So far from modifying their war aims in hopes of securing peace, both sides hardened their terms as the war dragged on.

In the Second World War there was a real and horrifying possibility that Hitler could have achieved dominance in Central and Eastern Europe by preserving good relations with the Soviet Union and either intensifying the offensive against Britain or offering her realistic peace terms that would, at least, have undermined Churchill's authority. Instead he determined to attack the Soviet Union at the earliest opportunity while doing nothing whatever to cause the British government to negotiate. In his Great Speech on 19 July 1940 he devoted only the last five minutes of a two hours and seventeen minutes harangue to vilifying Churchill, whom he sought to portray as the real barrier to amicable Anglo-German relations. He predicted that if the struggle continued it was bound to end in the complete destruction of one of the two opponents. 'Herr Churchill may think this will be Germany. I know that it will be England.'[12] He seemed to have a case at the time in that Britain lacked the power to destroy Germany, but his failure to defeat the Soviet Union in 1941, and the barbarous conduct of his

[10] Martin Gilbert, *Road to Victory: Winston S. Churchill 1941–1945* (Heinemann, 1986), pp. 575, 592, 643, 778 n2, 1,024, 1,179n.

[11] Gordon A. Craig, *Germany 1866–1945* (Oxford University Press, 1978), pp. 763–764.

[12] John Lukacs, *The Duel: Hitler Versus Churchill 10 May–31 July 1940* (The Bodley Head, 1990), pp. 189–194.

forces in the East from the outset, condemned Germany to win total victory or suffer utter defeat.

The Allies' adoption of a policy of Unconditional Surrender from January 1943 ensured that Germany's defeat would be absolute and devastating in both material and political terms. This policy has been frequently criticised ever since it was proclaimed, but it brought two great advantages that hugely outweighed the possible negative effect of stiffening German resistance. First, it determined that the Soviet commitment to the Western Allies was maintained despite Stalin's ingrained suspicions that the latter would negotiate a separate peace with Hitler, and perhaps even join the Nazis in an anti-Communist crusade. Second, it prevented another 'stab in the back' myth like that of 1918 by demonstrating beyond doubt that Germany had been utterly defeated. Had the 20 July 1944 plot succeeded in killing Hitler and removing the Nazi leadership then the Allies would have faced a dilemma, but it is difficult to conceive of any post-Nazi group that would have been acceptable to the Allies and have prevented them from pressing on to complete victory. Hitler, and the evil beliefs and practices of Nazism, had bestowed a sinister character on the German nation and its support for the war. But the harsh truth has to be faced that it was Germany and not just the Nazi Party that had to be defeated and its drive for military conquest and domination ended forever. This ambitious goal was magnificently achieved but Britain's role, particularly in the final phase, was more modest than post-war complacency and euphoria would suggest.

3 BRITISH GENERALSHIP IN THE TWO WORLD WARS

> Few groups in British history have been the subject of such
> vilification as the Western Front generals of the Great War. Their
> popular reputation remains thoroughly evil... Their professional
> competence is ridiculed, their courage impugned, their lack of
> humanity decried.[1]

Their early critics, during and just after the war, were mostly
well informed and made some valid points, but their successors in the
1960s and after were more polemical; determined to find scapegoats
and express class prejudices. In some cases lack of knowledge was no
barrier to splenetic criticisms and mockery because the writers believed
their opinions were now common knowledge. Had these authors been
required to name, say, a dozen generals and the battles in which they had
sent thousands of soldiers to pointless deaths then at least some research
would have been necessary. The grounds for angry denunciation were
the unprecedented scale of British casualties: nearly three-quarters of
a million dead and perhaps three times as many seriously wounded.
Someone or some clearly identified groups must be held responsible.
Sir Douglas Haig, Commander-in-Chief from December 1915, bore –
and continues to bear – the brunt of criticism but 'the generals', as a
privileged and mostly upper-class body are also deemed fair game.

---

[1] John Bourne, 'The BEF's Generals on 29 September 1918', in Peter Dennis and
Jeffrey Grey (eds.), *Defining Victory: 1918* (Canberra, Department of Defence,
1999) p. 97. See also Bourne's 'British Generals in the First World War', in G. D.
Sheffield (ed.), *Leadership and Command* (Brassey's, 1997).

The purpose of this chapter is not so much to provide a blanket defence of the high command, but rather to expose some of the main sources of the characteristics summarised above and then to demonstrate the complex problems that all the warring nations' military leaders had to confront. Furthermore, drawing mainly on the research of John Bourne and his colleagues at Birmingham University, it is now becoming possible to discuss the career patterns, qualities and characters of the large numbers (at least 1,255) who attained the rank of brigadier general and above on the Western Front.[2]

Although a few journalists, such as Charles Repington and Philip Gibbs, published critical reports about the high command during the war, a combination of patriotism and press censorship ensured that these were muted. Siegfried Sassoon published some savage satires, including his notorious poem 'The General', probably inspired by his corps commander, Sir Ivor Maxse, though Sir Reginald Pinney, who had provoked his troops' anger by cutting their rum rations, was another possible target for Sassoon's anger. However, these bitter effusions reached only a small readership.

It was only in the mid-1920s when widespread disillusionment with the legacies of the war, both domestically and in international relations, was setting in, that really influential criticisms began to appear. The foundations of the myth of incompetent, callous generalship were laid by Winston Churchill's *The World Crisis* (6 volumes published by Thornton Butterworth between 1923 and 1931) and particularly in Volume III (1927), which covered the battle of the Somme. Though out of office and no longer commanding a battalion on the Western Front, Churchill's critical views formed during the campaign in 1916 were never revised or placed in the wider context of the subsequent development of the war. Here, enhanced by Churchill's vivid style, were set out what would become the standard indictments: unimaginative generals, ill-planned, futile offensives, huge and unnecessary casualties in atrocious conditions. Most tellingly he berated technophobic cavalrymen for failing to exploit the war-winning potential of the tank, which he had played a crucial part in promoting early in the war. Serialisation in *The Times*, and frequent reprinting of *The World Crisis* in abridged popular editions, served to keep Churchill's polemical interpretations before the public. Although he had briefly (November 1915–May 1916)

[2] Ibid., p. 97.

commanded a battalion there, Churchill showed little understanding of the reality of trench warfare in 1916 or of the tactical skills and moral commitment required to fight and win this pivotal battle of attrition.

Lloyd George published his *Memoirs*, also in six volumes, between 1933 and 1936, followed by a cheaper two-volume edition in 1938.[3] As Prime Minister from December 1916 he had had no confidence in the Commander-in-Chief, Sir Douglas Haig, or in the CIGS, Sir William Robertson, who tended to support his fellow-soldier in his obstinate, laconic style. Believing that he lacked the political support necessary to dismiss Haig, the Prime Minister attempted, and failed, to subordinate him to the French command in February 1917. Later he tried, again without success, to find a senior general who would take Haig's place. After the war Lloyd George was stung by criticism from the generals' supporters and cited this as a justification for writing with brutal frankness about soldiers (notably Haig) no longer alive and so unable to respond.

Even after so long a lapse in time the bitterness suffusing Lloyd George's *Memoirs* seems sensational and shocking. He, after all, had held political responsibility throughout the Third Ypres offensive in 1917, and if he felt so strongly that the operations were being criminally mismanaged then his duty was to halt the offensive, sack Haig if he refused and, as a last resort, threaten to resign himself. Since he did none of these things, but let the campaign drag on into its final muddy denouement in November, it seems curious that he could later stand aloof in his savage denunciation of Haig and the high command.

A few passages will suffice to capture the tone of Lloyd George's impassioned polemic. In the foreword to the new edition in 1938 he wrote that he aimed to tell 'the naked truth about the War as I saw it from the conning-tower at Downing Street. I saw how the incredible heroism of the common man was being squandered to repair the incompetence of the trained inexperts [*sic*]... in the narrow, selfish and unimaginative strategy and in the ghastly butchery of a succession of vain and insane offensives'. During this campaign, he alleged, 'reports of success became rosier and ruddier'. 'GHQ could not capture the Passchendaele Ridge, but it was determined to storm Fleet Street and here strategy and tactics were superb.' While this 'triumphal crawl through the mud was proceeding', the Germans were able to send

[3] Lloyd George, *The War Memoirs of David Lloyd George* (Odhams Press, 1938).

divisions to reinforce the Russian and Italian fronts. On the next page he referred to the 'bovine and brutal game of attrition on the Western Front'. In examining the consequences of the operations he wrote that 'No soldier of any intelligence now defends this senseless campaign; certainly not one who is not implicated by some share of responsibility for it'. While Haig was insisting on the need for replacements for the men he had sent to die in the mud, the campaign culminated in the 'insane egotism of Passchendaele'. This campaign was 'indeed one of the greatest disasters of the War, and I never think of it without feeling grateful for the combination of seamanship and luck which enabled us to survive and repair its unutterable folly'.

The index in the two-volume edition contains five columns of references to Haig, nearly all derogatory and vitriolic but nevertheless genuine. Here are just a few examples of entries under 'Military mind': 'narrowness of, stubbornness of, does not seem to understand arithmetic, obsessed with the North-West frontier of India, impossibility of trusting, regards thinking as a form of mutiny'. The final reference to Haig reflects badly on Lloyd George: 'No conspicuous officer better suited to high command than'.[4]

Lloyd George had enlisted expert help and advice in making the chapter on Passchendaele as damning an indictment of Haig and the high command as he possibly could because he saw this section as crucial to the British peoples' memory of the Great War. As was to be expected there were some strong adverse reactions, notably from Sir Frederick Maurice, who had sacrificed his military career in a vain attempt to convict Lloyd George of lying about military manpower statistics, the official historian Sir James Edmonds and Haig's biographer, Duff Cooper. The majority of reviewers were, however, sympathetic to Lloyd George, who had succeeded in stigmatising indelibly in popular memory the role of the military elite in the war. More recently, notably since the anniversary in 1966, the Somme has tended to overshadow Third Ypres in the popular mind as the greatest catastrophe of the war, mainly due to the obsessive interest focused on its disastrous first day: 1 July 1916.

A young but already influential journalist and historian who vetted the *Memoirs* in draft and helped Lloyd George to elaborate his critical chapters on the attritional battles of the Western Front was

---

[4] Ibid., Vol. II (Odhams Press, 1938). See especially Chapter 62, pp. 2,073–2,076.

Captain B. H. (created Sir Basil in 1965) Liddell Hart who was military correspondent of *The Daily Telegraph* from 1925 to 1935 and defence correspondent of *The Times* from 1935 to 1939. In the long term Liddell Hart was probably the most important critic of Haig and the high command because his influence was so varied, pervasive and enduring. In addition to the direct effects of his own numerous publications he exerted a remarkable indirect influence through skilful help and advice to other authors, reviewers and the media.

As an infantry subaltern Basil Hart had experienced three brief tours on the Western Front culminating in July 1916 when he was wounded and badly gassed. He remained in the Army until 1924 but saw no further active service. His personal experience therefore ended just before significant developments, now loosely termed 'the learning curve', began to take effect, and long before the final victorious advance in 1918. Perhaps in consequence, like many critics of British generalship and attrition, he never properly grappled with the improvements implemented after the Somme experience, or explained how Haig and the other 'donkeys' had achieved their remarkable victory.[5]

As a young subaltern Hart was a naïve admirer of the British high command, and general staff, but, fortunately for his later reputation as a radical critic, his fulsome essay written during convalescence in 1916 was not published in his lifetime, indeed not until very recently.[6]

Why then did the young Basil Hart, who morphed into 'Captain B. H. Liddell Hart', only in 1920, become ever more critical of Haig, the high command and the strategic priority given to the Western Front? Several different kinds of explanation may be offered. Had he remained in the Army his critical bent would have been strictly confined, but as a leading defence journalist there was every incentive to adopt a critical stance. He also claimed that the post-1918 outpouring of self-justifying generals' memoirs, notably the posthumously published *Life and Diaries of Field Marshal Sir Henry Wilson* (two volumes, Cassell, 1927), shattered his earlier faith in their honesty and integrity. Lastly, as he came to know several senior officers personally, and to hear informed gossip about their shortcomings, he began to think that they were not as intelligent as he had believed during the war, even, it

---

[5] For a perceptive critique of Liddell Hart's interpretation of the First World War see Hew Strachan's essay 'The Real War' in Brian Bond (ed.), *The First World War and British Military History* (Clarendon Press, 1991).

[6] Brian Bond (ed.), *Liddell Hart's Western Front* (Tom Donovan, 2010).

may be suggested, not in the same league as himself as a military intellectual.

Liddell Hart's first significant publication about the recent conflict was *The Real War* (1927), later expanded and revised as *The First World War* and with several other book-length studies. His notion of what constituted the 'real war' seems strange to modern readers since he was not much concerned with battlefield conditions or the experience of front-line soldiers. His approach was always inclined to the didactic; the main purpose of writing about war was to expose errors, learn lessons and disseminate them. He believed profoundly in the continuing relevance of 'Great Captains' in deciding the outcome; hence his disapproval of the distant, managerial style adopted by Haig and other senior commanders and his fascination with the scholar-cum-guerrilla leader, T. E. Lawrence. By arguing that Britain's commitment to all-out war on the Western Front had been a political and strategic aberration, and underplaying the steady improvements achieved in both strategy and tactics, he was able to make a plausible case that British commanders had not matched up to the standards of the great Continental armies – and never would. The nation should reject the Western Front as a model and revert to the historically successful 'British Way in Warfare' relying essentially on naval power to enforce blockade and participate in small-scale amphibious operations. This strategic concept exerted a very seductive political appeal in the inter-war decades. Although Liddell Hart's notion of what constituted the 'real war' on the Western front was anachronistic in underplaying the vast problems posed by mass warfare in the industrial age, he was nevertheless remarkably successful in establishing the restricted parameters in which much of the controversy about Western Front generalship would take place until some years after his death in 1970.[7]

In the 1950s and 1960s Liddell Hart bestrode the world of twentieth-century military history studies like a Colossus. He continued to publish prolifically and, despite the lack of a university chair, contrived to influence a younger generation of scholars including Ronald Lewin, Alistair Horne, Alan Clark and Paul Kennedy. Though open-minded and tolerant of differing opinions in conversation, he became increasingly unsympathetic towards publications that took a different line to his own on the British conduct of war on the Western Front.

[7] Brian Bond, *Liddell Hart: A Study of his Military Thought* (Cassell, 1977).

For example, he indulged in something approaching a vendetta against John Terraine in 1963 over his biography *Haig: The Educated Soldier*.

Liddell Hart's tireless efforts to exert an indirect influence on the portrayal of the First World War in the media, notably in publications, film and the theatre, need only be briefly touched on here. He was, for example, editor-in-chief of *Purnell's* very successful part-works on the *History of the First and Second World Wars* in the 1960s. He was an adviser for the film *Lawrence of Arabia* and took part in several public controversies in defence of his hero. He was a principal adviser to the outstanding BBC television series *The Great War* until he resigned over the script for the Somme episode, which he regarded as too favourable to Haig. Perhaps most influential of all, he was an adviser, indeed an inspiration, behind the stage entertainment *Oh! What a Lovely War*. One of the three principal creators of the improvised drama, Raymond Fletcher, described his three-hour harangue to the actors as 'one part me, one part Liddell Hart, the rest Lenin'.[8]

Although some authors entirely escaped or rejected Liddell Hart's help and his pervasive influence (enhanced by his enormous archive, which was unrivalled until the Fifty Year Rule governing access to official documents was relaxed), his imprimatur was widely sought and his pre-eminence as the guru of military history broadly acknowledged.

Gradually, in the 1970s and 1980s a new generation of scholars without the 'hang-ups' of the First World War generation, and with a much wider range of sources to draw upon, began to examine the conflict afresh and from many different perspectives. Without ignoring the many faults and failings in Britain's conduct of the war, a more positive, or less damning interpretation of her role on the Western Front began to emerge, emphasising the revolutionary developments that took place between 1914 and 1918, and confirming the significant role that Haig's enormous armies played in achieving victory.

However, there is still a considerable gap between scholarly revisionism and more traditional popular criticism where Liddell Hart's influence may still be detected. For example, John Laffin's angry and careless polemic *British Butchers and Bunglers of the Western Front* (1988) is only a more extreme version of the Liddell Hart line. The splendid, if historically flawed, television series *Blackadder Goes Forth*

[8] See Bond, 'Oh! What a Lovely War'.

(1989) also depends on public belief in the incompetence and callousness of British generals and their staffs in a futile conflict where only the victimised other ranks retain their dignified and even heroic status.

It must be stressed that although revisionist scholars are generally more sympathetic towards the problems confronting all the armies on the Western Front and more favourable to the BEF's performance, particularly in 1916–1918, none is blind to the latter's limitations and failings. The BEF was slow to adapt to static siege warfare. Too many lives were squandered in trench raids and in repeating attacks that had clearly failed. In the attritional warfare of 1916 and 1917 the projected advances were too ambitious, and campaigns were prolonged in over-optimistic expectations of a dramatic breakthrough. Tactical innovations and the training necessary to ensure that they were implemented 'across the board' were only belatedly co-ordinated and formally promulgated as official doctrine. Strained relations between GHQ in France and the government in Whitehall, not to mention differences with allies, added greatly to the unavoidable friction on the battlefield. Given the long chain of command and the cumbersome means of communication available, senior headquarters were necessarily distant from the front line, but nevertheless a critical impression became firmly established that the generals were too physically and socially remote from the troops and, as a corollary, that they were not as concerned about heavy casualties and dreadful conditions as they should have been.

However, the more severe critics of British generalship on the Western Front, ranging from Fuller and Liddell Hart to A. J. P. Taylor, Alan Clark, John Laffin and Denis Winter are themselves open to the charge of underestimating the enormous problems that had to be tackled and, eventually, overcome. The original BEF of fewer than 200,000 troops expanded quite rapidly to two million. To the regular soldiers and territorial reservists of 1914 were soon added the huge Kitchener volunteer armies followed, from mid-1916, by conscripts who increasingly filled the ranks. The challenges presented by this unprecedented expansion were daunting. At the outset only a handful of generals had commanded a division (and those nearly all in peace time), let alone a corps or an army. There were scarcely sufficient trained staff officers for the original BEF and even these were thinly spread. There were far too few suitable officers and NCOs to train the influx of volunteers in the autumn of 1914, hence the resort to 'dug-outs' recalled from retirement, to makeshift uniforms and imitation firearms. Critics have tended to skip over the tremendous feats of production and logistics required to clothe, feed, equip and transport these huge forces to the Continent and, once there, meet all the administrative demands equivalent to those of a great city.

The original BEF consisted of a well-trained infantry component, a cavalry division, mainly employed in reconnaissance, and field artillery prepared for mobile warfare. Even before the largely static siege warfare set in at the end of 1914 it was obvious that the supply of shells, based on the rate of expenditure in the South African War, was completely inadequate. The worst of the shell shortage crisis was overcome by 1916, but even after that too many shells proved to be defective or of the wrong type; namely shrapnel rather than the high explosive needed. In these unforeseen circumstances, with inexperienced commanders at all levels learning on the battlefield, disasters like the whole battle of Loos and the first day of the Somme campaign, were to be expected. Historians confront a problem of what standards to apply in evaluating the BEF's performance, especially in the first two years of the war. Should they be in the main sympathetic or censorious? Castigating the generals as 'donkeys' and lauding the other ranks as 'lions' does not seem helpful in explaining how an unmilitary nation painfully adapted to the demands of the first 'total' war of the industrial age.

It soon became apparent that in the unexpected siege conditions, with an unbroken line of trenches and fortifications stretching from the Channel coast to Switzerland, it would be extremely difficult to achieve surprise on a strategic level sufficient to secure a breakthrough into open country. Furthermore in the battle zone the means of mobility, mainly horse-drawn wagons and men on foot, were completely outclassed by the protected defenders and their weapons – machine guns, mortars and artillery.

Crucially, this was the only modern war where commanders were unable to use 'voice control', falling as it did between the tradition of personal leadership in or near the front line and later reliance on wireless and 'walkie-talkies'. In the First World War the principal means of communications were telephones, fixed instruments at the end of complicated masses of wire that were frequently destroyed by enemy action. Commanders of divisions and higher formations faced the dilemma of whether to stay in their headquarters comparatively remote from the changing events on the battlefield, or move nearer to the front in the hope of being able to exercise some control of chaotic events, but thereby in effect disrupting the chain of command. In any case the brutal reality was that the communication system on the ground did not extend beyond the front trench. Once an attack was launched the troops entered both a real and metaphorical 'fog of war' that even battalion commanders could seldom penetrate.

Perhaps most important of all, British generals were facing a most formidable opponent whose leaders and staff officers were equipped for siege warfare, and enjoying the strategic advantage of occupying strong defensive positions deep in enemy territory. German commanders also showed themselves to be professional at all levels and resourceful in developing complex measures for defence in depth, so that even when the Allies began to improve their offensive capabilities, for example by the employment of tanks from 15 September 1916, success in converting a break-in to a breakthrough remained very hard to achieve.

Recent research, particularly by John Bourne,[9] is at last providing the statistical information that will enable historians to rebut some of the sweeping charges against the 'generals', while other criticisms will be shown to be not proven. Above all this research is demonstrating the variety of the generals' characters, careers, ages on appointment and styles of command. Of course, adverse anecdotal instances will persist, but as this evidence is disseminated and discussed it should undermine, if not banish, some time-worn generalisations and clichés such as 'lions led by donkeys', and 'butchers and bunglers'.

A persistent canard is that senior commanders deliberately avoided personal risk and enjoyed lives of luxury far from the front. Seven divisional commanders were killed in action, three died of wounds and nine were wounded. Thirty brigadiers were killed in action, eight died of wounds and a further seventy-two were wounded. Some châteaux were clearly built too close to the front line.

In the early months of the war some staff officers at higher headquarters felt that senior staff officers were not keeping in close enough touch with the front, but later 'trench walking' was overdone, thereby risking lives, interfering with daily routines and wasting time that could have been better devoted to planning. Earl Stanhope, then a

---

[9] See, for example, his essay, 'British Generals in the First World War', pp. 93–116. See also Mark Mortimer, 'The Snobbery of Chronology: In Defence of the Generals on the Western Front', *The Historian* (Spring 2009).

junior staff officer, cites the case of General Sir Walter Congreve (GOC XIII Corps), who was wounded as a consequence of taking unnecessary risks:

> General Sir Walter Congreve, ailing but indomitable, insisted on exploring the Somme battlefield near Beaumont Hamel without consideration of the danger to which he was exposing himself and his staff. When eventually Stanhope pointed out they were almost on the enemy wire Congreve retorted 'then why don't they shoot' to which he replied 'God knows'. Congreve returned very pleased, having walked practically the whole of his Corps front.[10]

It is easy to understand how the legend of luxury-loving châteaux generals became popular. In the eyes of dirty, cold and exhausted soldiers returning from front-line duty, the appearance of immaculate red-tabbed generals, their staffs and aides-de-camp must sometimes have seemed provocative and hard to bear. Parades, especially, could readily be linked with the unnecessary deaths from 'friendly fire' or precise enemy shelling. While a few senior commanders may have given too high a priority to personal safety and comfort, the necessity for a clear and lengthy chain of command with the limited means of communications available surely gave the majority of generals little choice. Châteaux were usually large and convenient but not invariably comfortable. Haig's headquarters were concentrated in Montreuil but he personally occupied one of two modest houses and made frequent and assiduous tours of the front areas. Also, contrary to popular myth, he led a sober and abstemious life, much to the Prime Minister 'Squiff' Asquith's disappointment. Herbert Plumer, as corps and then army commander, occupied a series of modest and sometimes quite spartan buildings, such as school rooms and town halls, in the Ypres sector. Indeed Plumer hated being confined to his headquarters and insisted, even while battle raged, on moving up every day to a forward report centre where he was some 2,000 yards in advance of two of his three divisional headquarters. This was a nuisance for his staff, who had to take up all his paperwork in the morning and bring it back at night.

[10] Brian Bond (ed.), *War Memoirs of Earl Stanhope 1914–1918* (Pen and Sword, 2005), pp. 106–107, and pp. ix, 28, 39 for Plumer's hatred of being confined to his headquarters.

Admonished both by Sir John French and Sir William Robertson for endangering his staff, Plumer reluctantly curtailed the daily routine, but made frequent, unheralded visits to the trenches early in the morning so as to avoid all the fuss associated with high-level inspection. Hubert Gough too hated to be confined to Fifth Army HQ, where he also led a spartan existence. It should also be noted that many staff officers, men as different in character as Earl Stanhope and Edmund Blunden, hated the routines and boredom of higher headquarters and made repeated efforts to return to their battalions; Blunden successfully after he told his commander that the war was 'stupid and inhuman' and that, but for the accident of birth, he would have been on the German side.[11] Lastly, on this topic, it should be recalled that senior commanders in the Second World War often occupied large and comfortable residences distant from the front without provoking comparable criticism. During the months of 'phoney war' in 1939 and 1940, for example, Lord Gort, Commander of the Field Force, occupied a small château west of Arras, but any senior officer less inclined to a comfortable lifestyle would be hard to imagine. Ever conscious of his public image, Montgomery immediately on appointment to command the Eighth Army in 1942 moved his personal headquarters close up behind the front at El Alamein, but unavoidably the vast array of headquarters, officers' clubs, depots and hospitals remained in Cairo.

One of the most persistent myths is that all First World War generals were cavalrymen, with the further assumptions that all were stupid, opposed to technical change and profligate with their soldiers' lives. The myth has an element of truth in that French, Haig, Gough and Edmund Allenby all came from that arm. Moreover five out of the eleven who held Army commands were also from the cavalry, two of whom, Julian Byng and William Birdwood were still in office in September 1918. But on a wider view the picture is quite different. By the end of the war only one corps commander (Sir Beauvoir de Lisle) was a cavalryman, and he had spent his early career in the infantry. At the same date only six out of fifty divisional commanders were cavalrymen and only seventeen out of 155 commanded brigades. Sir John French may have favoured promising young officers from his own

[11] Brian Bond, *Survivors of a Kind: Memoirs of the Western Front* (Continuum, 2008), p. 38.

arm, but if Haig had any preference it was for gunners: he did not surround himself with cavalrymen at GHQ.[12]

A preference that may be held against Haig was that he favoured 'thrusters' – bold, aggressive commanders – such as Gough – over more cautious generals such as Plumer. Some commanders who incurred heavy casualties but remained in office, such as Richard Haking and Aylmer Hunter-Weston, may have owed their survival, at least in part, to their hard-driving reputations. However, one must be cautious about judging First World War generals from their appearance in photographs. Haig's Army commanders in 1918 might almost be mistaken for geriatric survivors of the Crimean War yet Plumer, the most 'Blimpish' looking of all, was in reality energetic, well-informed, an exponent of careful planning and, by common consent, a complete professional. He was not, however, sanguine about the prospect of ambitious offensives.

It is another popular misconception that most First World War generals were elderly and unable to cope with new challenges. Haig was only 56 when the war ended. By the last year of the war senior officers were younger and fitter than their predecessors in 1914. The average age of divisional commanders on appointment fell by approximately nine years, from 55.2 years in 1914 to 45.9 in 1918. In the latter year no fewer than sixteen were under 45, the youngest being the 35-year-old Keppel Bethell, who used ruthless methods to galvanise and re-equip the 66th (2nd East Lancashire Division) after it had suffered heavy losses and disorganisation in the March 1918 retreat.[13] Bethell was two years younger than the youngest divisional commander of the Second World War, Major General (later Sir) Richard Hull, who took over 1st Armoured Division in 1944 aged 37. The youngest brigade commander in either war was R. B. 'Boy' Bradford VC, who was only 25 when appointed and had risen from the rank of lieutenant in 1914.

The final myth to be challenged here is that British generals were reactionary and hostile to technical innovations. On the contrary the British Army in France embraced new technology more readily

[12] See Bourne's essays 'The BEF's Generals' and 'British Generals in the First World War' and the same author's 'British Divisional Commanders during the Great War', in *Gun Fire: A Journal of First World War History*, 29 (nd).

[13] On Bethell's dynamic personality and ruthless methods see Brian Bond and Simon Robbins (eds.), *Staff Officer: The Diaries of Lord Moyne 1914–1918* (Leo Cooper, 1987).

than did the Germans. Though not an innovator himself, Haig was interested in any developments that would enhance his forces' fighting capacity.[14] Reactionaries would not have been tolerated on his staff or among senior officers. Haig was a strong supporter of the Royal Flying Corps (RFC), which, combined with the Royal Naval Air Service in 1918, became the world's first independent air force. He also welcomed the arrival of the first tanks in France and, despite the new machines' disappointing debut on 15 September 1916, never lost faith in their potential, which was amply demonstrated at Cambrai the following year. By contrast, Germany constructed only about twenty experimental tanks in the whole war. Much more important than tanks, artillery dominated the battlefield on the Western Front. Here again the British Army excelled: by 1918 the Royal Artillery was larger in personnel than the whole BEF of 1914. The gunners' impressive developments included creeping barrages, sound ranging, flash spotting and aerial gun control. The overall effect was revolutionary and, by 1918, constituted a key component in the advent of the modern style of war.

In the first half of the war rapid expansion beyond what any of the planners at the War Office thought possible caused enormous difficulties for the selection of senior commanders (and staff) for divisions, corps and armies. Stress and insufficiently robust health took their toll, while others were sent home because they had displayed lack of 'grip' or drive in action. But from the battle of the Somme onwards such was the competition and the ambition of young 'thrusters' that very few duds or time-servers could survive. By the final year of the war Haig had assembled a large team of youngish generals with efficient staffs who brought to their commands the training and experience of regimental officers. Their virtues included personal courage, a high sense of duty and professional attention to detail. Indeed the higher ranks of the Army were more genuinely open to talent than ever before. In the well-organised Army that won a remarkable victory in the final 'One Hundred Days' in 1918 there were very few donkeys, butchers or bunglers. Critics who employ such derogatory terms should be obliged to name names.

The British Army was treated as the 'Cinderella Service' in the inter-war decades, with the result that in September 1939 the

---

[14] Gary Sheffield and John Bourne (eds.), *Douglas Haig: War Diaries and Letters 1914–1918* (Weidenfeld & Nicolson, 2005).

expeditionary force available at the outset was smaller, less well equipped and much less well trained than the BEF of 1914. Even after the breathing space of the 'phoney war' months the British forces proved to be no match for the *Wehrmacht* in modern, mobile ground–air operations.[15] The Commander-in-Chief of the Field Force, Lord Gort, and some senior officers, paid the price for this unpreparedness and were not given another field command.

This debacle could be partly excused by the poor performance of unreliable allies France and Belgium, but Britain then endured a series of shocking defeats at German hands: Norway, Greece, Crete, the Dieppe Raid and the loss of Tobruk, not to dwell on the even more humiliating disasters inflicted by the Japanese in Hong Kong, Malaya and Burma. These defeats taken together, and the plunging trajectory of the war as a whole for Britain in 1940–1942, were at least as bad, if not worse, than those suffered in the First World War, including Gallipoli, and Kut. Yet no Joan Littlewood, Richard Attenborough, Alan Clark or Ben Elton has come forward to pillory or ridicule the generals responsible. Why has the historical legacy and myth been so harsh on the military leaders who won the First World War, yet comparatively gentle on those who performed badly until rescued by Hitler's folly in invading the Soviet Union and Japan's suicidal recklessness in attacking Pearl Harbor?

The 'graveyard' of dismissed generals was certainly becoming over-crowded in the first half of the war, those sacked or transferred included Archibald Wavell and Claude Auchinleck (both from the Middle East Command), Alan Cunningham and Neil Ritchie (both Eighth Army), Eric Dorman-Smith (Deputy Chief of Staff, Middle East), Herbert Lumsden (X Corps), Alexander ('Alec') Gatehouse (10th Armoured Division) and Alfred Godwin-Austen (XIII Corps). Few of these names, and there were many more, will resonate with the general public today; indeed probably only one 'fallen star' has remained notorious, the unfortunate General Percival, who surrendered Singapore, and he of course was taken prisoner not sacked. Why then, on the positive side, has only one commander, Bernard Montgomery, remained famous from the war against Germany and Italy and only William ('Bill') Slim and Orde Wingate, from the war against Japan?

[15] Brian Bond, *British Military Policy between the Two World Wars* (Clarendon Press, 1980).

For most people the immediate answer is likely to be that although these generals were deemed to have failed they incurred far fewer casualties than their predecessors did between 1914 and 1918: approximately 300,000 military fatalities as against nearly three-quarters of a million in the earlier war. This reasoning is true up to a point but does not provide a full explanation. There were no equivalents of the Somme and Third Ypres in the later war because Britain fortunately escaped long attritional campaigns in the main theatre. But in Italy in 1943–1945 and North-West Europe in 1944–1945 losses were as severe as in 1916–1918 in proportion to the number of front-line combatants. More important, surely, is the fact that virtually all the senior commanders in the Second World War had been field officers in the earlier war and knew that they could not afford to be profligate with their soldiers' lives; partly for humanitarian reasons, but also because limited manpower resources were tautly stretched over the other Services and the vital requirements of a whole nation mobilised for war.

Another legacy of the First World War was that officers were drawn from a wider range of social backgrounds and had a more sympathetic rapport with their troops, who were mostly citizens in uniform, not hardened regulars or idealistic volunteers. Senior commanders were determined not to appear so remote from their men as had Haig and his generals. As Sir Michael Howard reflected from personal experience of the war in Italy:

> Attacks were always carefully prepared, fully supported with firepower, and – perhaps most important – we were always told why they were taking place and what they were expected to achieve. Even at the lowest levels of command we felt that we were being treated as intelligent human beings, and were expected to treat those under our own command accordingly.[16]

Another valuable lesson learnt by some senior commanders lay in their attitude to the Press and to public relations more broadly. Haig and some of his generals had displayed an aloof and frosty attitude to the Press that had its origins long before 1914. In May 1915, for example, Haig flatly declined to hold an interview with Colonel Repington of *The*

---

[16] Michael Howard, 'Leadership in the British Army in the Second World War', in Sheffield, *Leadership and Command*, pp. 189–190.

Times, stating that 'Neither I nor my staff had the authority to see any newspaper correspondents'.[17] Haig's power base depended essentially on the political and social elite, including the King, and he disapproved of those like Lloyd George who sought Press and popular attention. He also took care to put nothing in his own handwriting that could be quoted. Near the end of the war he wrote sharply in reply to a congratulatory message from the new CIGS, Sir Henry Wilson, that he was not and never would be a 'famous general'. 'For that, must we not have pandered to Repington and the Gutter Press?' This remark, as Stephen Badsey notes, 'could serve as his professional epitaph'.[18]

In sharp contrast, Montgomery displayed a genius for public relations; the promotion of his own reputation and his Army's image: those of us of a certain age still recall our association, however tenuous, with the 'Desert Rats'. He realised, as did Mountbatten and Wingate in Burma, and his own suave and charming corps commander Sir Brian Horrocks, that publicity could be a precious asset. Decades before the advent of the television 'sound bite' Montgomery displayed a mastery of the common touch and the memorable phrase such as 'knocking Rommel for six right out of Africa'. He also exploited his distinctive appearance, mannerisms and uniform to full advantage in a manner that Haig would have found extremely distasteful. Sir John Smyth commented on these traits and affectations:

> Monty adopted a distinctive form of dress. He was the first British General to appear on all occasions in public in a beret and battledress instead of in the regulation red-banded cap and khaki tunic. When others followed his example Monty went several jumps ahead of them by adopting a mufti battle costume of corduroy trousers, high-necked polo sweater and rainproof shooting coat, with only the beret, and sometimes one medal, to mark the costume as bearing any resemblance to military uniform . . . He believed always in speaking to as many of the men as often as possible. These little impromptu talks were never meant to be recorded or written down. It was not what he said that mattered but how he said it and the general atmosphere in which he spoke. He cultivated certain tricks of oratory such as the

[17] Stephen Badsey, 'Haig and the Press', in Brian Bond and Nigel Cave (eds.), *Haig: A Reappraisal 80 Years On* (Leo Cooper, 1999), pp. 179–190.
[18] Ibid., p. 190.

repetition of sentences to add emphasis to his remarks ... To many people Montgomery's publicity methods appeared theatrical, un-British and altogether distasteful. But the fact remains that he captured the imagination and gained the confidence of his troops and of the British public as no other military leader has ever done before.[19]

Needless to say, this blatant showmanship would not have worked had not Montgomery won a critical victory at a vital time in the war for Britain, and demonstrated to a wider public that he was a thoroughly professional soldier with exceptional qualities of command and leadership.

In the Second World War few British generals had the opportunity to command formations (corps and armies) and even then their tenure was often brief, as shown earlier by the rapid turnover of many senior commanders in North Africa. Nevertheless, at divisional level, especially in the fluid, small-scale operations in the Western Desert, there was scope for charismatic leaders to make an impressive impact. Commanders such as Herbert Lumsden (1st Armoured), John Harding (7th Armoured), Douglas Wimberley (51st Highland) and Francis Tuker (4th Indian) expressed their strong personalities through such idiosyncrasies as double cap badges (much favoured by Montgomery), silk scarves and showy desert boots, thereby helping to sustain the troops' morale.

These, however, were exceptional leaders in exceptional circumstances. In the war as a whole there was a dearth of officers suitable for high command, largely the consequence of the Army's failure to train for large-scale operations in the inter-war decades. As the new CIGS, Sir Alan Brooke, noted early in 1942: 'Half our Corps and Divisional commanders are totally unfit for their appointments, and yet if I were to sack them I could find no better! They lack character, imagination, drive and power of leadership'.[20] Ironically, training for the command of higher formations was not taken seriously until the late twentieth century, in the Higher Command and Staff Course, by which time it was highly unlikely that Britain would ever again mobilise a mass army.

[19] Sir John Smyth VC, *Leadership in War 1939–1945* (David and Charles, 1974), p. 191.
[20] David Fraser, *Alanbrooke* (Collins, 1982), p. 297.

Another contributory explanation as to why British generals were not later held responsible for the run of defeats in the first years of the war was that after the *Wehrmacht*'s brilliant performances in Norway, France, Greece and Crete (perhaps most importantly in inflicting the demoralising experience of Dunkirk), the public realised that British civilians in uniform were up against highly trained and ideologically motivated warriors. Public admiration for Rommel 'the Desert Fox', which the author remembers as a schoolboy, was symptomatic of this respect, though SS atrocities in France added the elements of fear and loathing. With these exceptions, the *Wehrmacht* in its campaigns in Western Europe and North Africa earned grudging admiration for its outstanding professionalism. German units from different arms and regiments co-operated more easily than their more individualistic British equivalents; they were more expert at all-arms tactics; quick to seize the initiative in attack; and stubborn in defence, even when outnumbered, short of supplies and lacking in air support. From the beginning of hostilities until the final days in May 1945 there were no easy victories against the *Wehrmacht*.

A different kind of explanation for the post-war lack of hostility towards defeated British commanders, Percival excepted, was the correct public perception that political leaders, above all Churchill, as First Lord of the Admiralty and then Prime Minister from May 1940, bore a heavy burden of responsibility for these disasters. But since he was widely regarded as the saviour of the nation who skilfully obscured his numerous strategic miscalculations and blunders in his magisterial history of the Second World War, his failings simply had to be accepted as the price for avoiding defeat and eventually finishing on the winning side. This last consideration was surely the most important. For all the disasters, destruction suffered and loss of lives, the British people were persuaded that they had won the war. With every passing year after 1945 the positive, patriotic side of the war effort was extolled. Moreover, as the horrific nature of Nazi barbarity was revealed in more and more detail it was easy to believe that the war had been fought not only in self-defence but also as a crusade to save the Jews and other persecuted groups. Given this perception of a noble and victorious struggle it would have seemed churlish to criticise the generals.

Consequently, in sharp contrast to the bitter denunciation heaped on Haig and his commanders, the generals of the Second World War have largely escaped censure. Before El Alamein, it was suggested, there had been no victories on land but, after Montgomery's triumph, no more defeats. Montgomery's reputation was established as the all-conquering general while Churchill was lauded as the heroic statesman who had led the British and Commonwealth peoples from the slough of despair to the broad sunlit uplands. Truly, all was well that had ended so well in emphatic victory over Nazi (and Japanese) militarism and tyranny.

4 AT THE SHARP END: COMBAT EXPERIENCE IN THE TWO WORLD WARS

The unique awfulness and 'horror' of the First World War has become so deeply entrenched in British folk memory that it may seem almost blasphemous to suggest that combat conditions in other modern conflicts have been equally dreadful or, in some particular cases, even worse. Yet contemporary historians, including John Ellis, John Bourne and Gary Sheffield, have shown that modern industrialised war is always horrific for soldiers 'at the sharp end', that is in close proximity to the enemy. Why then has the First World War, and above all the Western Front, retained and even increased its reputation for unique dreadfulness and futility?

Here are some of the answers. Before 1914 the nature of modern war had not been properly understood by the British public. Romantic illusions flourished about a limited, chivalrous and exciting conflict that might well be 'over by Christmas'. Rupert Brooke, in his poem 'Peace' (1914), touched on another appealing theme with his line about 'swimmers into cleanness leaping',[1] while Philip Larkin would much later allude nostalgically to the spirit of innocence prevalent in 1914 but soon to disappear forever.

In reality the small British Expeditionary Force, though extremely well trained, was not technically or tactically prepared for the conditions of siege warfare that would soon set in. Consequently, as Lord Kitchener, recently appointed Secretary of State for War, promptly realised, unless the Entente Powers were quickly defeated, it was likely

---

[1] Rupert Brooke, *Peace* (1914).

to be a long attritional struggle requiring an unprecedented mobilisation of national resources.

By early 1915 it was clear that an unexpected and largely static siege war had developed along the whole of the Western Front between the Channel coast and the Swiss frontier. A complex network of trenches protected by strongpoints and barbed wire entanglements became virtually impossible to break through with the technology available at the start. The phrase 'the horror of the trenches' has become shorthand for conditions generally on the Western front, but it is misleading. The trenches could indeed become hellish if waterlogged, infested by rats and littered with unburied corpses; but their essential function was to act as shields and sanctuaries against artillery and machine-gun fire. It was when men *left* the trenches to attack or were driven from their defences that most casualties occurred. This was true even in a successful offensive. In the autumn of 1918 more mobile operations, as the Allies advanced to victory, did not necessarily mean that casualties would be light.[2]

For the civil population the heavy losses and the Entente's failure to deliver a knockout blow imposed ever increasing strain. The first great British offensive, beginning on the Somme on 1 July 1916, was widely expected, in home propaganda, to deliver this blow so that its costly failure was extraordinarily disappointing, establishing a grim landmark whose resonance has grown with the years. It needs to be stressed that with France suffering huge losses on her own soil and Russia sliding towards collapse, the possibility of victory on the Western Front was hard to envisage through 1916, 1917 and, above all, in the first half of 1918. Only in August 1918 did some British generals, notably Sir Douglas Haig, begin to believe that victory might be achieved that year. By contrast, in the Second World War, Germany appeared doomed to defeat from mid-1943. This made the prolongation of the war in both Europe and Asia until 1945 deeply frustrating for Western leaders and their war-weary peoples. Finally, in recent decades especially, the media (novels, plays, film and television) have seldom found anything positive to say about the Western Front, focusing on the failures and disasters such as Loos, the first day on the Somme and the Third Ypres campaign (now always referred to by its final dismal phase as 'Passchendaele') where, contrary to received wisdom, the

---

[2] Gary Sheffield, *Forgotten Victory*, p. 204.

month of September was generally sunny and dry. Successful set-piece battles such as Messines in June 1917 or Hamel in July 1918, and the spectacular advance east of Amiens from 8 August 1918, are seldom mentioned, let alone commemorated. Shortly before this was written (in November 2011) an episode in the ITV television series *Downton Abbey* depicted the start of this victorious offensive as though it were the first day of the Somme. This obsession with one disastrous day obscures the fact that the nature of war was transformed – even revolutionised – between 1914 and 1918. Had Napoleon been present in August 1914 he would have been reasonably familiar with the uniforms, weapons, formations and approach to battle, but he would have been 'out of his depth' if confronted with the 'high tech' war of 1918, encompassing the advent of tanks, aircraft and much more sophisticated artillery methods. He would also have been bewildered by the apparently empty battlefield in which vast numbers of troops were sheltered below ground.

It must now be shown in more detail why the First World War was not 'hellish' all the time on all sectors or, at any given time, for a large component of what became a huge manifestation of the nation in arms. It is a popular misconception that all the soldiers sent to France served 'in the trenches', and that whole battalions were herded into the front line and left there for weeks or months until killed, wounded or utterly exhausted. In reality, given the variety and geographical depth of support services that made up the line of communications troops, railway and road maintenance staff, ammunition, food and forage depots, rest and training facilities, signallers, farriers and many other support services, it is clear that 'the tail' outnumbered the front-line combatants by at least four to one.

Moreover, only a little reflection is required to realise that prolonged duty in the front-line trenches would rapidly lead to physical and mental exhaustion and the disintegration of whole units. Conditions in the first two lines – the fire trench and travel trench – were indeed spartan, but more comforts were possible in the support trench, some hundreds of yards to the rear. In the latter could be found kitchens, stores and above all dug-outs, which provided havens mostly, but not exclusively, for officers.[3]

---

[3] Denis Winter, *Death's Men: Soldiers of the Great War* (Allen Lane, 1978) remains an excellent source for conditions on the Western Front. I have drawn on it extensively here.

Individuals served in the front trenches relatively rarely. Of the 20,000 or so soldiers in a division, only about 2,000 were likely to be in the forward zone at any moment. A typical infantryman's month might consist of four days in the front line, four in support, eight further back in reserve, in case of emergency, and the remainder out of the combat area 'in rest'; often a euphemism for fatigues, training and inspections. Charles Carrington, an infantry officer with the Royal Warwicks, calculated from his diary that in 1916 he was under fire for 101 days (65 in the front line), with 120 in reserve and 73 in rest; the remainder spent in travelling, on courses and on leave.[4]

The sector where a man served was crucial. Anywhere near Ypres was always dangerous; consistently worse than the Somme except in 1916. But the sector of the 1915 battles – Neuve Chapelle, Aubers Ridge, Festubert and Loos – was mostly quiet after that. Incredibly, given the popular image of unceasing hell, there were periods of leisure and peace to decorate and beautify the front area. In the autumn of 1917, while battle raged at Ypres and Cambrai, no-man's-land north of Bapaume was a mile wide and Alec Waugh's company suffered not a single casualty in a month. In the autumn of 1915 before the battle of the Somme, the whole area was as green and peaceful as the South Downs, and it returned to relative tranquillity in 1917.

Some regiments considered to be 'elite', that is disciplined, efficient and aggressive, such as the Guards, the Royal Welch Fusiliers, and some of the Scottish battalions, were repeatedly thrown into battle and suffered heavy losses whereas others were more fortunate. Between June 1915 and January 1918, for example, the Royal Sussex served in twenty-one sectors of which sixteen were quiet.

It is fairly well known that the famous 'Christmas Truce' of December 1914 was only an early and much publicised version of a practice that became quite widespread and was termed the 'live and let live system'.[5] The nature of trench routine, usually inactive by day but hectically busy by night, provided opportunities for mutual agreement to relax hostilities to allow both sides time for relative security, freedom to emerge above ground and even to exchange pleasantries. Inevitably, these were fragile arrangements that could easily be broken by the

[4] Charles Carrington (pseud. Charles Edmonds), *A Subaltern's War* (Peter Davies, 1929), pp. 120–121.
[5] Tony Ashworth, *Trench Warfare 1914–1918: The Live and Let Live System* (Macmillan, 1980).

arrival of new battalions (Saxons quiescent and co-operative, Prussians less so); unintentional breach of the informal rules by nervous outposts; or intentional hostility from mortars and guns stationed further back. Evidently the high command and staff could only turn a blind eye to such relaxation of hostilities in certain circumstances, and the practice was anathema to elite units on either side whose constant policy was to harass the enemy and dominate no-man's-land. As John Ellis remarks perceptively:

> One reason for this was that the soldiers were stuck in their respective trenches for weeks on end, only actually going after the enemy head on during one of the big offensives. In between times the enemy front-line soldier contributed little to one's discomfort – this was all done by the weather and his artillery – and it was possible to sympathise with him, knowing he was suffering just as much from the climate and one's own big guns.[6]

It is not surprising that post-war accounts by soldier-authors, such as Robert Graves, Siegfried Sassoon and E. M. Remarque (though not the outstanding portrayer of actual soldiering, Frederic Manning), tended to emphasise the dramatic and horrific episodes in their service – a tradition that has understandably been followed by playwrights, film-makers and television producers. Unfortunately for historical accuracy, this trend has had the distorting effort of underplaying the long periods of training, rest, sport and entertainments, and marching from one dreary village to another.

Marching out of the battle zone into rest and in the peace-ful French countryside could bring rapid, almost miraculous healing effects. Soldiers felt as though 'born again' and could again hope for survival. Fortunate men would march into quiet villages free from shell-fire, constant fear and the debris of the battle zone. Domestic billets in French farms or houses offered contact with women, children and animals, reminding the soldiers that they were themselves civilians tem-porarily in uniform. But we should not sentimentalise these intervals: low pay limited amusements open to other ranks, and French civilians were often mercenary and hostile.[7]

We must also be wary of interpreting the military notion of 'rest' as allowing the ranks to loll about at leisure, smoking, drinking,

[6] Ellis, *The Sharp End*, p. 317.   [7] Winter, *Death's Men*, p. 143.

reading newspapers and playing a gramophone. The Army then held and perhaps still does, dark suspicions about what the soldiers would get up to if left to their own devices for more than an hour or two. A rigid routine was consequently enforced: typically reveille at 6 am followed by roll call and breakfast; inspection, drill and training from 9 am to lunch at 1 pm; then a further two hours of training up to 4 pm, with supper at 7 pm.

Periods of rest were also blighted by the crippling burden of fatigues that were particularly onerous in the forward sectors within a few miles of the front line. Men were therefore compelled to undertake all the carrying that needed to be done. Pit props, duckboards, coils of barbed wire, two petrol tins of water per man linked with belts, dixies of stew and boxes of bombs all went up by hand. These articles gathered weight progressively on the way, while no sagging telephone wire, no uncovered sump, no worn duckboard, no unexpected projection would be missed.

Denis Winter comments that the men deeply resented losing their rest periods for hard manual labour, worst of all the gruesomeness, fear and danger involved in burial fatigues and wiring parties. Nevertheless the Army provided a good deal of genuine entertainment. Country sports, such as hunting and shooting, were generally only available to officers, but the other ranks enjoyed athletic events, boxing matches and swimming galas. Football was universally popular, with the officers sometimes joining in, and anarchic games with as many as one hundred per side were played. 'The battalion concert epitomised all that was best in the leisure of rest-relaxation proportionate to the release of tension after front-line duty, magnificent companionship and the reassertion of civilian habits.'[8]

There were also regular film shows and entertainments, the latter often organised and performed at short notice by the officers for their men. Denis Winter refers to a show put on in less than a week in 1917 that was so popular that it was repeated on four successive nights. Officers dressed as attractive young women, displaying expertise at dancing or imitating popular music hall stars showed their human side and, however briefly, narrowed the gulf between themselves and the other ranks. When the latter were allowed to put on a show, individuals often displayed remarkable talents and, through satirical sketches, were able to poke fun at military regulations, brass hats and politicians.

[8] Ibid., pp. 157–159.

Contrary to the impression conveyed by media emphasis on the 'horrors of the trenches', the main problem for most of the soldiers most of the time was boredom. This resulted from endless marching, fatigues, drilling, inspections and, perhaps most dramatically of all, uncertainty exacerbated by rumours, and lack of regular sleep. For example, Frederic Manning's battalion (7th King's Shropshire Light Infantry) moved at least thirteen times between the very costly action at Bazentin Le Grand in July and the disastrous attack at Serre on 14 November in which 214 other ranks were killed, wounded or missing. As Sir Michael Howard comments in his introduction to Manning's wonderful book *The Middle Parts of Fortune*, this is an account of soldiering rather than fighting: 'about the scrounging, drilling, yarning, gossiping, gambling, drinking and womanising which has always constituted the great bulk of military experience'.[9]

It is also very important to record, to offset the popular image of unending hardship and misery, that many survivors recalled the happiness they had found in the comradeship of the section and the platoon, while some went well beyond that to admit to feelings of excitement and even ecstasy in battle. Fighting side by side, Carrington wrote 'created a sense of being initiated, of a shared inner life'.[10] For him the special bond of comradeship was richer and stronger in war than he had ever known since. Another memoir writer, Guy Chapman, could never share the warrior's enjoyment of combat, but he did experience the compelling fascination of war and analysed his feelings in a remarkably honest paragraph on its bewitching powers.[11] Sidney Rogerson was another veteran of the Western Front who testified to the war years as the happiest period of his life, as it was for 'vast numbers of his comrades'.[12] Maurice Bowra, later famous as a classical scholar and Master of Wadham College, Oxford, hated war but on 8 August 1918 advanced into battle laughing and joking in an ecstatic mood that he could not recapture or explain afterwards.

Gary Sheffield succinctly challenges the popular misconception regarding the two world wars as being totally different: namely that in the First World War the armies endured static trench warfare whereas

---

[9] See my chapter on Manning in *Survivors of a Kind*. Michael Howard's introduction to Frederic Manning, *The Middle Parts of Fortune* (Peter Davies, 1977), p. VIII.

[10] Carrington in Bond, *Survivors of a Kind*, p. 15.

[11] Guy Chapman in Bond, *Survivors of a Kind*, p. 34.

[12] Winter, *Death's Men*, pp. 55, 180–181.

in the Second 'free-flowing mobile warfare predominated'.[13] True, in the later war better communications at all levels and a more effective instrument of exploitation (the tank specifically and armoured forces more broadly) made breakthroughs and rapid penetration possible. But mobile or *Blitzkrieg* operations were by no means characteristic of the Second World War where slow, attritional advances, already evident from 1916 onwards, predominated. Even in the Western Desert where vast barren spaces and logistical problems led at times to mobile operations of dizzying speed and complexity, there were still attritional phases, notably in the siege of Tobruk and the protracted struggle at Second Alamein before Montgomery eventually achieved a breakthrough. In other theatres, including Italy and North-West Europe, slow-moving attritional warfare was the norm. Nor is this merely the impression of later historians: combatants in these campaigns recorded their hardships and suffering in vivid detail. Unfortunately for historical balance, their recollections are far less well remembered now than the more sensational memoirs about the First World War.

The historian who has most thoroughly studied the experience of front-line soldiers in both world wars, John Ellis, originally assumed that combatants in the First World War had had a far harder time than their successors, but was forced by the evidence to change his mind. It took some time to convince a publisher that this was a worthwhile approach likely to appeal to a wide readership.[14]

In 1997 he summarised his conclusions about 'the sharp end of war' in terms that had still not gained general acceptance. He contended that the front-line soldier in the Second World War spent almost as much time in holes in the ground as his predecessors between 1914 and 1918; that movement was so hazardous that casualties among front-line troops were of the same order as in the First War; and that the appalling conditions in the First World War were matched by those in North Africa, Italy and North-West Europe. Though outside the scope of this study, conditions in the war in Burma against the Japanese were generally worse than in either world war in Europe.

Ellis also showed that the psychological strains so apparent in what was labelled 'shellshock' on the Western Front were not specific

---

[13] Sheffield, 'The Shadow of the Somme', pp. 34–36.
[14] John Ellis, 'Reflections on the Sharp End of War', in Addison and Calder (eds.), *Time to Kill*, pp. 12–18.

to that war but were an unavoidable element in all modern conflicts. War at the sharp end remained an intimate affair of very small groups where only fierce loyalty and mutual dependence could keep individuals from breaking down. Finally, Ellis asserted that despite spectacular achievements of armoured formations in 1940 and 1941, tanks did not continue to constitute a war-winning instrument. The Second World War proved once again to be essentially an infantry man's and a gunner's conflict.

Some of these points need elaboration to demonstrate the similarity of the two world wars 'at the sharp end'. Although trench systems were never so elaborate or so static in the Second World War as on the Western Front, soldiers in the former spent much of their time hastily digging fox-holes and burrowing into the ground. These precarious shelters were impermanent so that new entrenchments were essential after each advance. Every theatre suffered from the curse of mud, observers recording the uniqueness of their own brand, ranging from the notorious Flanders mud, experienced again in 1940, the grey soil of Tunisia rapidly forming a 'witches' brew' in rain, and the infamous mud in Italy, which at the worst effectively prevented any movement.

The concept of *Blitzkrieg*, due to its dramatic speed and potential to decide a campaign, has received far more attention from historians and pundits than it deserves as a characteristic feature of the Second World War. Most Allied attacks encountered formidable defensive, heavily fortified networks that might consist of trenches, deep bunkers, minefields and booby traps, supported by machine guns, mortars and artillery. Even in the Western Desert the Allies were often forced to attack formidable entrenchments surrounded by extensive minefields. In sum, this later war was for the most part 'a bloody slogging match in which mobility was only occasionally of real significance . . . In the last analysis, men and the weapons that they could carry with them were what counted'.[15]

The one aspect in which critics of the First World War in comparison with the Second appear to have a trump card is in the matter of casualties. It is undeniable that the British and Dominion armies suffered nearly a million fatalities in the First World War compared

---

[15] John Ellis, *The Sharp End of War: The Fighting Man in World War II* (David and Charles, 1980), pp. 72–76.

with about 300,000 in the Second. Critics might concede that the First World War was a labour-intensive conflict in which lethal weapons dominated the battlefields in relation to inferior means of communication and mobility. But they might also contend that generals were often spendthrift with soldiers' lives and sometimes persisted with offensives that had clearly stalled.

However, two further considerations must be borne in mind. First, the British Army did not fight in Western Europe between June 1940 and June 1944 and raised far fewer divisions than in the earlier war. Had the Allied defences held in May 1940 then it is easy to envisage the re-emergence of static warfare with heavy casualties. Secondly, in the later war there was a much longer 'tail' of support services and far fewer 'teeth' in the form of front-line infantry. In the British and Commonwealth armies as many as two-thirds of the soldiers were engaged in maintaining one-third in the forward areas.

Another important factor in reducing battle casualties in the Second World War lay in the great advances in medicine. The powerful antibiotic penicillin became available in quantities during the campaign in Sicily in 1943 and was routinely used thereafter. Sulpha-drugs were also developed to combat infections that were not suitable for penicillin. Blood transfusion was another vital innovation, made possible for use in battle by the ability to store both liquid blood and powdered plasma. From 1943 onwards blood transfusion became standard procedure on all Allied fronts. Consequently, thousands of severely wounded men were saved who would certainly have died in the First World War. An obstacle to saving wounded men that in some theatres, notably Italy, was greater than on the Western Front was in carrying casualties from where they had been hit to the nearest dressing station. If this could be accomplished then air evacuation, in general use by the end of the war, went far to ensure survival and recovery.[16]

Many British generals of the Second World War had served as junior officers in the First. Some of them, notably Montgomery and Horrocks, deliberately displayed showmanship in order to reduce the earlier gulf between senior officers and their men, and virtually all had learnt the lesson that they must not be reckless with soldiers' lives. This was partly due to humane considerations but also because trained manpower, especially for the teeth arms, became critically lacking in

[16] Ibid., p. 174.

the last years of the war. As a consequence there was far less bitter recrimination after the Second World War on the score that the high command had been callous in their attitude to the other ranks.

It is easy, but dangerous, to assume from the far lower army fatalities in the Second World War that the fighting was easier and the loss of life comparatively economical. But in proportion to the numbers involved in units serving in the combat zone casualties could be equally or even more severe.

British and Canadian battalions suffered about 100 casualties a month on average on the Western Front in the First World War. In the 1944–1945 North-West European campaign, battalions suffered a minimum of 100 per month but 175 per month was not uncommon. The daily casualty rate of Allied forces in Normandy actually exceeded that of the BEF, including RFC, at Passchendaele in 1917. In the North African and Italian campaigns of the Second World War the figures were about seventy casualties per battalion per month, but on some occasions casualty rates matched anything in Normandy.[17] To give a specific example, the 2nd Battalion Scots Guards suffered more casualties in the Second than the First World War: 113 officers and 1,246 other ranks killed or wounded.[18]

Beyond all the obstacles posed by weather, terrain and logistics the British forces faced a most formidable enemy in the *Wehrmacht*: operationally and tactically outstanding; defending every fortified line and natural obstacle with remarkably accurate artillery and mortar fire; and fighting tenaciously even when greatly outnumbered and bereft of air cover. Sir Michael Howard, who experienced these enemy skills in Italy and, while convalescing, made an intensive study of the German Army, was mystified as to why it was so *bloody good*, a question that still puzzled him half a century later.[19]

The contention that combat conditions in the Second World War, though more varied, were certainly no less stressful, exhausting and horrific than the First, will be illustrated by a brief survey of the main campaigns.

[17] Sheffield, 'The Shadow of the Somme', p. 35.
[18] W. A. Elliott, *Esprit de Corps: A Scots Guards Officer on Active Service 1943–1945* (Michael Russell, 1996), p. 147.
[19] Michael Howard, *Captain Professor: A Life in War and Peace* (Continuum, 2006), p. 89.

The small Field Force that was sent to France after the outbreak of war in September 1939 was less well trained and less materially prepared than the BEF of 1914. Unlike the latter, however, it unexpectedly had eight months of general inactivity ('the phoney war') in which to dig in and await the enemy offensive. 'Dig in' is the appropriate term because the Field Force dug trenches and built pill boxes along its sector of the French–Belgian border in preparation for linear defence before an eventual methodical offensive. For many senior officers who had served in the same area in the First World War there was an eerie sense of *déjà vu*. It was to be a war of the trenches all over again. Before these assumptions were shattered in May 1940 the troops experienced a very stressful winter. It was one of the coldest for many years and dreadful conditions in the forward zone were exacerbated by a dozen false alarms causing movement from their shelters to the trenches in expectation of imminent enemy attack. These experiences had a bad effect on Allied morale.

When the German offensive was launched on 10 May 1940 the Field Force advanced efficiently into Belgium and fought well for a few days in an attempt to check the enemy on the frontier. Then, after the French collapse further south, the British forces began a disorderly retreat towards the coast that was rendered chaotic in parts by lack of transport and a clear command structure. The troops suffered from heat and thirst and from constant harassment from the *Luftwaffe*. Although the survivors felt that they had not been defeated in battle – casualties were light – they, and the senior officers especially, had been sharply reminded of German military power and professional excellence. Though Gort, Brooke, Sir Henry Pownall (Gort's Chief of Staff 1939–1940) and others expressed themselves guardedly it was evident to them that the *Wehrmacht* was in 'a different league' in land and air operations.

It is easy to underestimate the ghastliness of warfare in the Western Desert. Newsreels intended mainly to boost home morale portrayed officers in flamboyant, irregular uniforms and soldiers bathing happily in the Mediterranean. This, in short, seemed to be a relatively humane war in a warm and healthy area against a sporting opponent. Understandably there was less emphasis on the failed offensives and demoralising retreats, the sandstorms and extremes of heat and cold, or what happened when a tank was hit and 'brewed up'.

Lieutenant Colonel Cyril Joly served in tanks and armoured formations throughout the Desert War, winning a Military Cross and Bar and writing an outstanding account of these campaigns in *Take These Men*. He is excellent on the drawbacks of war in the desert. Flies were an ever present menace:

> Whatever we did . . . wherever we went during these first two weeks of July, we were followed by the sickly sweet pungent, musty odour of decomposing bodies and hounded by the flies, which grew in size each day, gorged by their beastly feeding on the dead, coming to renew their appetites or satisfy the curious cravings of their palates by nibbling at our fresher diet. So gross were they that they refused to be disturbed from where they had settled, and we had to cover carefully each morsel as we moved it into our mouths, or we took a bite of flies as well.[20]

The ferocious heat of the sun was appalling, particularly the glare reflected and magnified by the sand. The thick armour plate of the tanks became painful to touch while the crew had to huddle inside in stifling air made worse by oil, petrol and gun fumes. At the worst there was not a breath of air – no breeze – no light stirring of wind. In the winter months, in sharp contrast, the cold caused acute discomfort. On the move, wind lashed their eyes and faces, hence in part the unorthodox garb of balaclava helmets and scarves. Troops left in the open at night found it hard to sleep.

The worst natural enemy was the *khamsin*, a dry, oven-hot searing wind of tremendous heat. This would usually be followed by sandstorms so severe that they interrupted all military activity for several days. 'For about three days we would be enveloped in a fog of sand, a tangible fog which clogged the eyes and nostrils, entered the most closely sealed boxes and cases, covered the tables and chairs and beds, and mixed with our food and water'.[21]

Digging was an oppressive daily chore at sundown even after units had been on the move. A battalion would dig a perimeter square of about 1,000 yards per side, then within it pits for Bren guns and slit trenches for riflemen. The men then had to dig holes for sleeping, about six feet square and 'as deep as the digger's patience'. Everything went

---

[20] Cyril Joly, *Take These Men* (Constable, 1955), p. 323.   [21] Ibid. p. 279.

below the surface. It was a nightly matter of 'digging in case of bombs, digging to save your skin, digging through sand and even through rock. Digging for victory.'[22]

The weight of equipment carried into action also imposed a fearful burden:

> The assault troops at Alamein, for example, wore steel helmets and web equipment, carried a rifle, grenades, Bren magazines, water-bottle and entrenching tool, while two bandoliers of ammunition were crammed in the front pouches and in the back-pack were rations for one day, an emergency ration, mess tin, groundsheet, sacks for conversion into sandbags, and a pick or shovel strapped to the top of the pack.[23]

Keith Douglas, one of the best poets of the Second World War, served in the desert as a tank commander in the Notts Sherwood Rangers Yeomanry from 1941 and took part in the battle of Alamein. He was killed in Normandy in June 1944 at the age of 24. His posthumously published memoir *Alamein to Zem Zem* provides a brilliant account of combat with reflections on the nature of war in the desert. After describing some fleeting comforts and pleasures he admits that time spent inactive in the desert was tedious for someone like himself given to imaginative speculations about the future. It was a strain to live entirely in the present, with the same companions and very little in the way of entertainment. The featureless terrain caused a particular form of weariness. Sensory stimulation was totally lacking, the days monotonous and the future uncertain.[24]

When, however, battle did occur the brutality of combat could be as horrific as at 'the sharp end' anywhere. When tanks were hit and shells penetrated, the effects were always sickening. Douglas examined one of his tanks that had been hit and two of the crew killed, the driver outside eating nonchalantly out of a tin. The shells in the rack were thickly splashed with blood and empty cases lay in an inch-deep pool of blood on the floor. 'Bit mucky in the turret' was the driver's laconic comment. On another occasion, on looking into a derelict Italian tank, he encountered a gruesome sight:

[22] Ellis, *The Sharp End*, pp. 38–39.   [23] Ibid., p. 98.
[24] Keith Douglas, *Alamein to Zem Zem* (Penguin, 1969), pp. 49, 65, 109–111, 137, 156–157.

> The crew were, so to speak, distributed around the turret. At first it was difficult to work out how the limbs were arranged. They lay in a clumsy embrace, their white faces whiter, as those of dead men in the desert always were, for the light powdering of dust on them. One with a six-inch hole in his head, the whole skull smashed in behind the remains of an ear – the other covered with his own and a friend's blood, held up by the blue steel mechanism of a machine gun, his legs twisting among the dully gleaming gear levers.[25]

When Joly's tank was hit he survived, though shocked and burnt, because he was standing in the cupola, but inside there was a shambles.

> The shot had penetrated the front of the turret just in front of King, the loader. It had twisted the machine-gun out of its mounting. It, or a jagged piece of the torn turret, had then hit the round that King had been holding ready – had set it on fire. The explosion had wrecked the wireless, torn King's head and shoulders from the rest of his body and started a fire among the machine-gun boxes stowed on the floor.[26]

A second shell hit the turret, and the driver, trapped in his seat, was killed instantly. Joly, trying to escape, saw all three tanks of a friend's troop ablaze. Only one dazed figure emerged and stumbled towards the enemy.

Even outside the great battles, like Operation Crusader, Tobruk and Alamein there was a steady stream of casualties, especially among tank crews. As Joly recalled, 'new tanks and new crews arrived and were lost almost before the men were known by name'.[27] It was nerve-wracking to be trapped all day beside a crippled tank with the dead crew lying round it. The bodies were decayed beyond recognition but on turning away Joly noticed the letters ESH on an officer's bedroll – it was that of a close friend, Chesham.[28]

Already near breaking point, Joly was sickened and furious when his gunner 'Rogers' machine-gunned fourteen Italian prisoners only yards from his tank. This was in revenge for his parents' death in the Blitz. Early in 1942 Joly lamented the need once again to memorise the names and faces of a new batch of officers. Only the commander,

[25] Ibid.   [26] Joly, *Take These Men*, p. 143.   [27] Ibid., p. 145.   [28] Ibid., p. 219.

the doctor, the padre and the quartermaster remained at regimental headquarters: very similar to survivors in front-line battalions in the First World War. In his own squadron all but one of the officers was new and of the troops little more than a tenth remained from their stay at the same camp six months earlier. Some were missing, but a large number had been killed and of the survivors many were so badly wounded that they would never lead a full life again.[29]

Twenty-first-century readers must dismiss from their minds the pictures of Italy conjured up by films, tourist brochures and, perhaps, their own sun-drenched holidays there. Apart from Burma and the Pacific theatre generally, Italy posed some of the worst conditions that the Allies encountered anywhere. A glance at topography shows that fighting up the spine of the country from the southern tip to the north-east frontier in face of rivers and mountain chains, quite apart from a determined enemy resisting every advance, was a strategist's nightmare. Even these natural obstacles were eclipsed in many combatants' minds by another factor – the weather.

The Allies struggled northwards through two appalling bleak winters: that of 1943–1944 marked by almost continuous rain and freezing temperatures – with the following winter the worst Italy had suffered in twenty years. A very wet autumn was followed by lasting snow and sub-zero temperatures. Soldiers in the front line were permanently cold, soaked and exposed to enemy shellfire and sniping. Some combatants recorded their opinion that physical conditions caused more misery than the fear of shooting, shelling and booby traps.

Many accounts described the debilitating and dangerous slog lasting several hours to reach the forward positions on mountainous ridges where they would shelter as best they could in shallow sangars, trenches being impossible to dig, and at best covered by a tarpaulin. Relief procedures were very like those of the First World War followed by a hazardous journey back to reserve and rest in pitch darkness. The men were short of sleep, only three or four hours a day was common, and utterly exhausted by their duties in the front line. Ellis quotes a diary description of such a nightmare march: 'Officers, British and Gurkha, shouted at, scolded, cajoled, assisted men as they collapsed. At times we had no alternative but to strike soldiers who just gave up interest in anything, including the desire to live.'[30]

[29] Ibid., pp. 228–229, 273.   [30] Ellis, *The Sharp End*, p. 45.

In the days following the Salerno landings there were frequent close-quarter encounters in the effort to defend and expand the precarious bridgehead. Walter Elliott graphically describes such a clash of patrols at night in the vicinity of the tobacco factory. All hell broke loose and everyone started yelling. Elliott shot point blank a German refusing to surrender. A similar incident occurred in September 1944 when his battalion was trying to capture a German-held ridge on Monte Croche. A combination of frustration and fear caused the officers to lose control, indeed they joined in the mayhem:

> There was no withstanding the company once its blood was up.
> Our shouts of 'come out and fight you bastards' could even be
> heard by battalion headquarters up the hill; but any Germans
> who did so were promptly bayoneted. I never saw the troops in so
> ferocious a mood. It was as if all the pent-up fury at the shelling,
> the casualties and not being able to get one's own back was at last
> to have its vengeance.[31]

After crossing the Garigliano early in 1944 Elliott's battalion occupied a line in low-lying country very close to the enemy. They held the position for six weeks with an average of seven days in the line and three days rest. They seldom saw a German but endured perpetual rain and constant shelling. When they took over from the Cameronians near Mount Natale conditions were even worse. The slit trenches were literally filled to the top with water. So the troops were simply standing in darkness beside them.

> We baled out these two-man slit trenches all through the night
> with our mess tins or steel helmets, for we had to stay
> underground all day as we were under observation on a forward
> slope...The mud was so sodden that our slit trench soon filled up
> again, while we sat on branches suspended halfway up the
> sides...I spent three days like this soaked to the skin. It seemed
> worse than the 1914–1918 war when deep trenches were all
> inter-connected and there were also communal dug outs.[32]

The three battles for Monte Cassino have come to represent the hardship and horrors of the Italian campaign much as the Somme and

---

[31] Elliott, *Esprit de Corps*, pp. 35, 73.   [32] Ibid., pp. 95–96.

Passchendaele stand for the worst fighting conditions on the Western Front. Fred Majdalany recounts how his battalion was overlooked by the monastery from the front and by Monte Cairo from the rear. Consequently any movement by daylight in the forward areas was out of the question. There was no water on the heights, so like food and ammunition it had to be carried by mules from the dump at San Michele six miles to the rear and then humped by porters – mostly Indian – up to the front lines. Medical evacuation posed enormous problems. There were stretcher bearer posts every 200 yards or so with a dressing station at the foot of the mountain. On wet nights it might take eight hours or more to reach the dressing station, with the high risk of wounded soldiers being dropped. In Majdalany's words 'It was ours... a cemetery for the living'.[33] When a company was relieved after doing six or seven days on the ridge the men's limbs were so stiff that they often had difficulty in climbing out of their sangars, even though a period of rest was awaiting them in the valley.

In his classic account *Cassino: Portrait of a Battle* Majdalany described the extraordinary ordeal of 1st/9th Gurkhas on Hangman's Hill. For eight days and nights they held an exposed shoulder of the mountain close to the monastery on a steep slope protected only by clefts in the rock or by stone breastworks. Acute supply problems meant that greatcoats and blankets had to be left behind. For the whole time they were obliged to exist on this exposed cliff-face, in mid-winter, without even a coat to protect them against icy winds and rain in temperatures that barely rose above freezing point. For most of the time they existed entirely on American K rations, an emergency pack of dried food that worked out at two rations between four men per day. When the survivors were eventually withdrawn by night only 8 officers and 177 other ranks out of the 400 who had taken up the position stumbled to safety.[34]

Conditions were equally hellish for the Germans. A machine-gunner who moved into the Cassino sector at the beginning of the battle recorded, 'I'm sure I can maintain that the Somme battlefield did not look worse. It is fearful, and horror overcomes you as you wonder when this misery will stop.' In March, now back in the hills behind Cassino he wrote, 'What we are going through here is beyond description. I never

[33] Fred Majdalany, *The Monastery* (Boderly Head, 1945), pp. 19–23.
[34] Fred Majdalany, *Cassino: Portrait of a Battle* (Corgi, 1959), pp. 218–223.

experienced anything like this in Russia, not even a second's peace, only the dreadful thunder of guns and mortars', with Allied planes dominant in the skies above.[35]

The exceptional nature of the three battles for Cassino: the proximity of the lines, the acute problems of bringing in food and water and, above all, extreme hazards of treating and evacuating the wounded, provided unusual circumstances in which mutual restraint, even chivalry, could occur in an informal 'live and let live' situation. Both sides permitted Red Cross orderlies to move about in daylight tending the wounded and bringing in the dead. The front-line soldiers developed a strange kinship in these extreme conditions. A British medical officer with a party of orderlies even made three daylight trips to the crest to bring down wounded men, but after the third he was warned that it must be his last.[36] British and German troops displayed a good deal of professional courtesies and respect, and the Poles also behaved well despite their visceral hatred of the enemy. There was, however, little evidence of any chivalry on the eastern side of the Apennines where conditions, for example in the area of the river Sangro, were as horrendous as any in the west. Mutual hatred was exacerbated by German atrocities against civilians and the increasing activity of partisans.[37]

At Anzio the terrain differed markedly from the river crossings and mountain barriers described above. Once the high command had failed to seize the fleeting opportunity available after the unopposed landing in January 1944, the Allies were trapped for four months in a narrow beachhead in filthy weather and under constant bombardment. The journalist Wynford Vaughan-Thomas wrote that these conditions bore a close resemblance to the Somme or Ypres in 1916–1917.[38] Soldiers had to think in terms of communication trenches, barbed wire in no-man's-land and all the paraphernalia of the Western Front. But there was at least one grim analogy with Cassino: it was seldom possible to evacuate the wounded in daylight.

In his classic account, *The Fortress*, Raleigh Trevelyan described his harsh initiation into combat in the Anzio bridgehead with a three-day stint in 'The Fortress', a strongly defended obstacle at the

---

[35] Ibid., p. 229.   [36] Ibid., p. 226.

[37] Denis Forman, *To Reason Why* (Andre Deutsch, 1991). This is a vital source for the training and operations of 'Wigforce', a combination of British troops and partisans led by Lionel Wigram. See in particular pp. 102–107, 190.

[38] Ellis, *The Sharp End*, pp. 42–43.

northern tip of the Allied perimeter. He shared a slit trench with his bat-man close to the enemy, who could be heard talking and eating. Their trench was waterlogged so they had to sit on ration boxes, occasionally easing their joints by sticking out their feet onto each other's knees. It rained all the time they were at the front. The men looked purple from the cold, and it needed willpower to stop one's teeth from chattering.

Later, in May, in Cicada Valley, Trevelyan's battalion occupied a wadi where two British battalions had been massacred by German tanks. Corpses and bits of bodies lay all around. He thought the place a natural setting for a battlefield of the 1917 vintage: 'shattered farm-houses...scrolls of rusted dannert wire, abandoned weapons of all kinds...the brooding dark shapes of the burnt-out lorries, all in a waste land of churned up earth and craters'.[39] His platoon bombed a German working party only a few feet away and listened to their sob-bing and moaning for at least an hour. Although the cries haunted him, he shortly afterwards shot a German between the eyes at close range. He was worried that he found it so easy to be callous. 'I kill with as much detachment as if I were a robot. Except that a robot wouldn't enjoy killing.'[40]

The major episodes of the British Army's role in the conquest of North-West Europe between June 1944 and early May 1945 are well known, notably from films and documentaries. The D-Day landings and the long struggle to gain a break-out; the daring but unsuccessful attempt to end the European war in 1944 by a thrust into the Ruhr from Arnhem; and the Allied defeat of the last German offensive through the Ardennes: all had a strong attritional element and all caused massive destruction and loss of life. In the final months of the war, however, there is a popular belief, sometimes openly stated on television, that the advance into Germany was relatively easy and painless, something of a 'mopping up operation'. This delusion, which needs correction, probably stems from the assumption that mobile warfare against an enemy who was clearly losing and in retreat could not have been grim, relentless and costly.

The late David Holbrook vividly depicts the hell of the Normandy battlefield in the days after the successful landings. The

---

[39] Raleigh Trevelyan, *The Fortress* (Collins, 1956), pp. 16–17, 83. Ellis, pp. 42–43. See also Howard, *Captain Professor*, pp. 61–119.

[40] Raleigh Trevelyan, *The Fortress*, pp. 93–96.

countryside 'stank of dead cattle and dead men, of burning tanks and stores, of stale cordite fumes, of phosphorus and other chemical stenches and of human hatred.'[41]

John Ellis reminds us that much of the infantry fighting in Normandy was waged by men living as much as possible below ground. An artillery officer wrote home to his parents 'this stabilised Front area is just like Flanders must have been – every building a pile of rubble, every field a showpiece of a soldier's desire to get underground if he's stopping five minutes'.[42] In the dogged defence of the Normandy *bocage*, narrow sunken roads sheltered by high dense hedgerows, the enemy displayed determination and small group fieldcraft of the highest order. Charles Farrell describes how a neighbouring squadron lost thirteen out of sixteen tanks in a few minutes, destroyed at close range by two Panther self-propelled guns. The squadron commander, a close friend, and his crew were so completely incinerated that not even their identity discs could be found.[43] Though justified by eventual victory, the battle for Normandy was extremely costly. For example the 3rd Division, which had landed on D-Day, suffered 7,100 casualties, nearly one thousand of whom had been killed. Over a shorter period 15th Division lost 5,345 men killed or wounded.

As his title makes clear, Martin Lindsay's published diaries and reflections, *So Few Got Through*, is a lament for the officers and men of the Gordon Highlanders killed between mid-July 1944 and the end of April 1945.[44] Lindsay, then aged 39, joined as second in command of the 1st Battalion and later commanded the 5th/7th Battalion. His terse diary entries chronicle the fierce resistance his troops encountered from the first day to the last, with few periods of rest and a steady stream of casualties. At St Sylvain, for example, on 12 August his brigade suffered a heavy mortar attack with sixty-five casualties, including seven officers. Further south that day a Canadian tank regiment lost fifty-three out of its sixty-five tanks. One regiment lost its commander and all its squadron leaders. In the breakthrough to Lisieux between 8 and 23 August Lindsay's battalion lost fifteen officers and 150 other ranks. The remnants of the four rifle companies were amalgamated into one

[41] David Holbrook, *Flesh Wounds* (Buchan & Enright, 1987), pp. 225, 233–235.

[42] Ellis, pp. 45–46, 168.

[43] Charles Farrell, *Reflections 1939–1945* (The Pentland Press, 2000), pp. 82–84.

[44] Martin Lindsay, *So Few Got Through* (Collins, 1946), pp. 47, 51, 67, 126, 162, 212, 217, 225, 242, 266–268.

and the Pipe Band, pioneers, spare drivers and clerks were summoned to the front.

These soldiers, heavily burdened and grim faced, and the officers leading them, were the true heroes. The average life of a platoon commander was about a month – not much better than the previous war. At the end of the year Lindsay recorded that losses in the four rifle companies had been appalling. From the established officer strength of twenty (and replacements), nine had been killed and thirty wounded. In the other ranks the total of killed and wounded precisely matched the ration strength – 500.

Suffering the effects of 'friendly fire' was a frequent hazard. In February 1945 in Goch, Lindsay's battalion was bombarded by their own medium artillery and, a few days later, bombed by the RAF in broad daylight and perfect visibility. He nevertheless accepted that overall the Army owed the RAF a deep debt of gratitude.

Even after the Rhine had been crossed, with light casualties, Lindsay found enemy resistance as stubborn as ever. He described German parachutists holding the town of Rees against heavy odds as 'incredibly tough'. They defended the town street by street, exacting heavy casualties. In mid-April, only twenty miles from Bremen, his battalion was held up by an obstinate rearguard action that was remarkable given that the defenders must have known that the war was lost.

After the war Lindsay found from the files on officers' service that since D-Day no fewer than fifty-five officers had commanded the twelve rifle platoons with an average service time of thirty-eight days: 77 per cent had been killed or wounded. He concluded by listing the names of officers and other ranks whose deaths had affected him deeply. Sadness at the extinction of their joyous personalities would always remain with him. 'It is as if some spring deep down inside me has run down.'[45]

If the foregoing extracts have not convinced the reader that the Second World War was at least as stressful, harsh and horrific at the sharp end as the First then a remarkable account of combat in North-West Europe in 1944–1945, *With the Jocks*, should clinch the matter.[46]

[45] Lindsay, 'It is as if some spring', p. 275.

[46] Peter White, *With the Jocks: A Soldier's Struggle for Europe 1944–1945* (The History Press, 2009). See especially pp. 44–45, 68–69, 77–79, 109, 117–120, 304 and 455 for the author's final tribute to his men.

This book, the work of Peter White, was typed up soon after the war from daily notes describing the ordeals and incredible endurance of 4th Battalion King's Own Scottish Borderers. White was a most unusual man to command a troop of 'Jocks'. Coming from an upper-class, religious family, he was brought up in southern England and began to study at the Royal Academy of Arts in October 1939 (his brilliant sketches of people and places illustrate the book). But an even greater surprise is that White was a teetotaller inclined to pacifism; hardly traits likely to endear him initially to his tough territorial soldiers. Yet he clearly overcame his scruples about killing, and anxiety about his leadership ability, to become a brave and popular officer. White died in 1985 with his work unpublished and it eventually appeared only in 2001. Nevertheless the book has achieved several reprints in a paperback edition; it is beautifully written and merits all the plaudits quoted on the covers.

White's narrative needs to be read in full because it is the cumulative effect of the daily endurance and bravery of ordinary soldiers in appalling weather, lack of sleep, a monotonous diet and constant danger that make such a powerful impression. The following episodes should convey a strong sense of the sheer awfulness of this campaign and banish any notion that the final months of the European war were a walk-over against a beaten and dispirited enemy.

Early in 1945 the Jocks were holding a line on the Dutch–German border. It was an exceptionally cold winter with deep snow lying. Sleep was almost impossible in the frozen mud with only sodden straw in the slit trenches. Cold or tepid meals with scalding tea laced with Hexamine tablets were snatched at odd intervals. White and his men slept fully dressed with boots and equipment ready for immediate action. Orders were frequently changed at very short notice. After a brief respite at Meersum, the Jocks left the defensive line to take part in an offensive towards Geilenkirchen. In mid-January they encountered nine days of the coldest weather of the whole winter with blizzards and 20 degrees of frost. As they were to travel lightly in company with Canadian Kangaroos (turretless tanks) they were not issued with blankets or great coats. They endured several days of this misery and uncertainty before suddenly coming under intense fire from an enemy on three sides of the wood they occupied.

As with Lindsay's troops, the worst of their ordeals was to be fired on by their own side. Advancing in broad daylight along a straight road on the Dutch–German border there was little cover for the thirty Jocks outlined against the snow. Although White had warned a Canadian tank commander close behind them about their patrol and its direction they were duly fired on by the same tank, being spattered with earth and snow but this time suffering no casualties. The ashen and speechless Canadian officer was subjected to a torrent of abuse.

A truly horrific incident was to occur on 23 January as they advanced towards Heinsberg. It was bitterly cold, they were short of sleep and had gone for thirty-five hours without food. Already under fire from German guns they attempted to dig slit trenches in frozen bogland but struck water only a few inches below the surface. While thus wretchedly exposed, they were subjected to a concentrated barrage from their own twenty-five-pounders firing 350 yards short of their target. Company headquarters was wiped out because the commander had been unable to get in touch with the gunners on his radio link. Already near to complete collapse from fear and lack of food and sleep, the Jocks were pinned into freezing immobility for a further ten hours.

Any notion that resistance slackened as the Allies thrust into Germany and the war neared its end is banished by the experience of the Jocks. As late in the war as 3 April some 300 SS cadets from a training school near Hanover held up the bulk of two armoured divisions and supporting infantry for several days. White had to admire the desperate stand these young men put up with such limited numbers and in a hopeless position.

Soon after this the Jocks suffered their worst disaster. The farm where they were resting, with no enemy nearby, was suddenly pounded into a heap of smoking rubble. Those inside were all killed or badly wounded. Moreover, the pathetic forms of twenty-two other men were scattered about the farm, bloodstained, mutilated bodies of messy khaki. The culprits were three seventeen-pounder self-propelled guns firing directly at the farm at a range of only 350 yards. The commander, who had the wrong building marked on his map, collapsed when he realised what he had done. White comments that this officer was mercifully killed by a mine a few hours later.

The battalion took part in the attack on Bremen and as late as 7 May they were still encountering opposition. By then there was a growing unwillingness to take risks, and as hostilities at last petered out, a terrible tiredness engulfed all the survivors.

White concluded with a moving tribute to his men: unlike the officers they could have had little sense of any plan or continuity in the succession of confused orders and resultant shambles that dominated their lives.

This chapter has tried to show that there were no easy victories against the *Wehrmacht*, and that the contrast between combat at the sharp end in the two world wars has been exaggerated. Even with Allied dominance in the air and in material and manpower, much of the combat took on a slow attritional character against a stubborn unyielding enemy. Moreover, with the exception of the rapid Allied advance from Normandy to the Belgian frontier, high mobility was not the norm. Even during periods of mobility casualties remained high. In proportion to numbers in the front line – the poor bloody infantry of both wars – British casualties in the two world wars were approximately equal. Stalemate in the trenches in 1914–1918 even had some advantages. Relatively static warfare made an informal system of 'live and let live' possible in quiet times and on quiet sectors; while rest and medical centres could be established quite close to the front in towns such as Amiens, Armentières and Poperinghe.

With the exception of the Ardennes offensive in December 1944 the Germans were generally on the defensive, though capable to the end of launching spirited counter-attacks on a small scale. As in the earlier war, but perhaps with even more fanaticism and professional skill, the Germans showed themselves to be masters of the tactical defensive, holding up the Allied advance from fortified positions and relying on mortars, artillery, machine guns and powerful tanks to take a heavy toll on infantry in the open.

The weather and the terrain often favoured the defender. Conditions in the two winters of the Italian campaign and the exceptionally severe weather in the early months of 1945 created hardships and misery comparable to the worst experiences on the Western Front. A number of vivid writers, such as Graves and Blunden, succeeded in etching the 'horrors of the Western Front' so deeply in national folklore that they appear impervious to challenges as to their uniqueness by mere historians. Yet the Second World War was equally savage at the sharp end, and writers such as Cyril Joly, Fred Majdalany, Denis Forman, Raleigh Trevelyan, Peter White and many others have shown this to be so. That they have not had a comparable impact on public opinion remains a mystery. Perhaps combatants in the later war have inadvertently contributed to the myth by convincing themselves that none of the dreadful conditions, hardships and miseries they experienced were comparable to what their fathers had endured in the trenches between 1914 and 1918.

5 ATTRITION IN THE FIRST WORLD WAR: THE NAVAL BLOCKADE

In both world wars Britain pursued harsh attritional strategies towards Germany. Naval blockade in the First World War and strategic bombing in the Second were both effective in causing serious damage to the enemy's infrastructure, economy and morale, but neither was in itself decisive. The naval blockade caused hardship, bordering on starvation, for the civil population, particularly women, children and the elderly, but was not much criticised in Britain, either at the time or later. In sharp contrast, strategic bombing, though generally popular during the war, has been subjected to bitter criticism in recent decades, even to the extent of being labelled a war crime. This chapter examines the development and impact of the strategy of blockade in the broad context of deciding the outcome of the First World War, and seeks to explain the contrasting reactions of public opinion.

Historically naval blockade had been a key element in British naval power with the aim of denying seaborne commerce to Continental enemies. The policy and strategy of blockade remained very attractive to the government and the Royal Navy before 1914 and had an influential spokesperson in Maurice Hankey, Secretary of the Committee of Imperial Defence. This exercise of superior naval power would be much cheaper and more popular than raising a large army and, in addition to its economic effects, would have the equally important consequence of forcing the German High Seas Fleet to seek a decisive battle in the North Sea.

In 1914, however, there appeared to be serious legal and practical obstacles to a strategy of blockade. As recently as 1907 the

British-sponsored Declaration of London had restricted the concept of blockade to the 'close blockade' of enemy ports and had narrowly defined the terms of contraband. Thanks to opposition in the House of Lords Britain had not ratified the Declaration, but even so had to be wary of alienating neutral opinion, not only the European maritime trading nations but most importantly in the United States of America.

There were also formidable practical problems. By the early twentieth century technological developments – notably the magnetic mine, the torpedo, the submarine and powerful coastal guns – were collectively making close blockade virtually impossible. This left Britain with the hazardous and untried alternative of distant blockade, which entailed leaving the main fleet in northern harbours such as Scapa Flow and Rosyth, mining Germany's exits through the Channel and the North Sea and intercepting enemy and neutral shipping by cruiser patrols. This was in effect a strategy of 'contraband control' rather than a true blockade and was in principle severely constrained by strict definitions of contraband and the trading rights of neutrals. From the outset, however, the Royal Navy, with government backing, did its best to overcome these restrictions, causing critics to comment that Britannia not only 'rules the waves', but also 'waives the rules'. Even so the sensibilities of neutral European nations such as Norway, Denmark, Sweden and, above all, the Netherlands had to be handled carefully, while American opinion and naval power simply had to be appeased.

Wider economic and financial considerations also militated against a rapid success for the British blockade of Germany. The latter was far less vulnerable to blockade than Britain's enemies in earlier centuries. Her colonies were prestige symbols but, on balance, a drain on national resources, so their seizure would not constitute a valuable coup for Britain. Only a modest income was derived from Germany's extra-European exports, and overseas investment contributed only 2 per cent to her national income. Loss of essential raw materials would soon in theory have a crippling effect, but the Central Powers possessed, or soon took over, vast resources such as Romanian wheat and oil, and continued to receive significant supplies from neutral neighbours such as the Netherlands, Switzerland and, above all, Sweden.[1]

[1] Paul M. Kennedy, *The Rise and Fall of British Naval Mastery* (Allen Lane, 1976), Chapter 9.

On the other hand, Britain herself had become dangerously vulnerable to economic warfare. Whereas during the Napoleonic Wars she had been largely self-sufficient in food, by 1914 she imported four-fifths of her wheat, two-thirds of her bacon and all of her sugar from abroad. Germany was able to exploit this weakness through her submarine campaigns, bringing Britain close to starvation in 1917 but, in consequence of her unrestricted attacks on neutral as well as enemy shipping, caused the fatal intervention of the United States against her.[2]

Despite Britain's tightening of the blockade with more stringent definitions of contraband and the stricter implementation of the arrest and searching (in port) of neutral vessels, Germany did not appear to be seriously affected by the middle of the war. She could still import Swedish iron ore, Norwegian pyrites, Romanian oil and food from Switzerland, Denmark and Holland. Switzerland and Holland established independent companies that could trade with Germany without compromising their government's neutrality. Germany did, however, feel the pinch from the confiscations of its merchant fleet and loss of its overseas trade so that without exporting it could not earn foreign exchange. Consequently, in the later war years, Germany incurred huge debts to the Netherlands and lesser amounts to its other neighbours. 'As the Reichbank's gold reserves dwindled, Germany found it harder not only to secure its imports, but also to subsidise its allies.' Millions of Germans, working-class as well as middle-class investors, gambled their savings on a German victory.[3]

From mid-1916 the German home front began to experience serious food shortages caused by its expanding war effort, the blockade and declining agricultural production. With priority given to manning, equipping and transporting the Army, the costs and suffering were inexorably passed on to the home front. The blockade closed the ports and reduced traffic on the railways; loss of manpower and the extension of military fronts reduced the railways' capacity and these shortcomings were exacerbated by lack of lubricants and inferior coal. Consequently by 1917 the transport system was virtually paralysed. Moreover after the two disastrous winters of 1916–1917 ('the turnip winter') and 1917–1918 there was an acute shortage of both food and fuels.

[2] Bourne, *Britain and the Great War*, p. 137.
[3] David Stevenson, *With Our Backs to the Wall: Victory and Defeat in 1918* (Allen Lane, 2011), pp. 421–422.

The German home front suffered most directly and severely from the crisis in agricultural production. About two-fifths of farm workers were called up, leaving the same percentage of farms to be run by women. Even the employment of some 900,000 prisoners of war on the land did not solve the shortfall; nor were Germany's allies or the occupied territories of much help. More than one million draft horses were called up by the Army and those that remained were increasingly short of food. The blockade exerted a direct effect in the loss of farm machinery and, even more important, fertilisers. Germany had relied more heavily on fertilisers than other large economies such as France, and the halving of available nitrates and phosphates caused a dramatic war-time decline in the yields of wheat, rye, oats and potatoes. Moreover, the area under cultivation for these crops fell by some 15 per cent. In view of the government's award of first priority to the soldiers and its inept measures to control the food available and ensure that it was fairly distributed – particularly between rural areas and the cities – the problem of maintaining civilian food supply eventually proved to be insoluble.[4]

America's entry into the war against the Central Powers in April 1917 clinched the success of the Allied blockade. Until the resumption of German unrestricted submarine warfare in February 1917, American collaboration could not have been assumed. Woodrow Wilson had striven to maintain her neutrality and this policy had prevailed despite the German sinking of the *Lusitania* in May 1915 with the loss of 128 American lives, and subsequent interference with American vessels. Indeed Britain's similar activities had caused the proclamation of several formal American protests and there was even the possibility the Americans would side openly with Germany.

After April 1917 Britain and America could now enforce restrictions on neutrals without regard for diplomatic niceties. American officials now endorsed what they had previously condemned as flagrant violations of international law. Whereas it had taken Britain three years to reach this point, a State Department official told Arthur Balfour 'it will take us only three months to become as great criminals as you are'.[5] Although the neutrals protested about the ruthless enforcement of the

---

[4] Ibid., pp. 431–433.

[5] Nigel Hawkins, *The Starvation Blockades: Naval Blockades of World War I* (Leo Cooper, Pen and Sword, 2002), pp. 231–232.

blockade, and achieved some concessions, they were in a weak bargaining position. If they would not consent to send their agreed quotas of produce to the Allies they would receive no coal from Britain or other supplies promised by the United States. As Nigel Hawkins neatly puts it, they were 'caught between the devil and the dark North Sea'. By the end of 1917 all the neutrals concerned, including Switzerland (under French pressure), had imposed rationing on bread and other goods. America's entry into the war as an Allied co-belligerent also had the vital consequence of offsetting the overthrow of the Tsar's regime in February–March 1917 with its clear signs of impending collapse and withdrawal from the war. As regards the blockade, these two events settled the fate of Sweden as a close trading partner, and even a possible ally of Germany. Sweden's freedom to supply goods to Germany was in large part due to her ports providing the only effective trading link with Russia. Consequently in 1915 Sweden had negotiated a transhipment agreement whereby for every ton of goods that crossed her territory for Russia, Sweden could export a similar amount to Germany. With Russia now taking a much lower priority, the Allies tightened their blockade of exports from Russia to Sweden and thereby virtually ended her ability to assist Germany.[6]

The British blockade of Germany between August 1914 and April 1917 had certainly not been a complete failure: it had disrupted the enemy's economy; exacerbated shortages of food and some war materials; and provoked domestic unrest that had already led to food riots. But with the intervention of the United States' Navy and full access to American economic and financial resources, the blockade now began to exert a stranglehold that was a significant factor in causing the collapse of the Central Powers.[7]

There is abundant evidence that the German home front suffered increasing deprivation and hardships as the war dragged on. Although civilian sacrifices and stoical endurance kept the armies supplied with weapons, munitions and basic food, virtually all essential commodities became scarce at home. What chiefly kept the civilian population dutiful and loyal was confident belief in eventual victory on land and sea. When hopes in both war theatres were shattered

---

[6] B. J. C. McKercher, 'Economic Warfare', in Hew Strachan (ed.), *The Oxford Illustrated History of the First World War* (Oxford University Press, 1998), pp. 129–132.

[7] Ibid., p. 132.

between spring and autumn 1918 the domestic collapse was all the more widespread and dramatic because illusory hopes had persisted for so long. To give just a few examples of the shortages: cotton textiles were widely replaced by paper fabric; train carriages were cut up by passengers desperately seeking leather; even new shoes had wooden soles and cardboard uppers; milk was rationed and limited to a litre a week, and even that was frequently watered down.

Distress at home affected soldiers on leave and their depressing experiences were carried back to the trenches. Millions of Allied propaganda leaflets dropped by balloon over enemy lines rubbed in the failure of the U-boat campaign and the hopelessness of continuing the struggle against the huge numbers of fresh American troops arriving in France every month. As regards supplies of vital foodstuffs, the civilian population never fully recovered from the appalling 'turnip winter' of 1916–1917 in which persistent rain caused the annual potato yield to fall by nearly 60 per cent. The bread ration was also drastically cut and supplies remained precarious until the harvest of 1917. Another terrible winter followed in which meat and fat rations were further reduced. Perhaps the worst effect of these shortages was the social tensions caused by the manifest unfairness of the allocation and distribution system where, for example, some areas and cities (such as Berlin) were treated more generously than others, and whence in some cases, city dwellers did not always receive the meagre rations to which they were entitled. In David Stevenson's words 'food shortages created a war of all against all, exacerbating tensions between the workers and the wealthy, between town and countryside, and between west and east'.[8]

There can be no doubt that acute food shortages and deteriorating living conditions were a prime cause of the growing civilian death rate during the war. By 1917 the female death rate was 23 per cent higher than before the war. In the seventy largest cities the overall death rate was 37 per cent higher than in 1913. In the worst-hit areas starvation was not simply threatening but a social reality. Reports spoke grimly of people dropping dead in the streets.[9]

It is clearly impossible to draw a precise line between civilian deaths due to privations caused by the war effort in the widest sense, including incompetent administration by the home authorities, and the specific effects of the blockade. One authority states

[8] Stevenson, *With Our Backs to the Wall*, p. 435.
[9] Ibid. Hawkins, *The Starvation Blockades*, pp. 236–238.

confidently that three-quarters of a million people died of starvation in Germany between 1914 and 1918. Another source suggests that by 1918 the total of civilian deaths had climbed to 293,000, but this must be treated with caution. A London-based analyst, Max Müller, calculated in 1918 that Germany would certainly face famine if the war lasted another twelve months. David Stevenson concluded that 'mass starvation was not imminent when the Reich sued for an armistice'.[10] But on the industrial front it faced disaster within a few months, and from the loss of its allies even before then. While accepting that the German civil population suffered from severe food shortages and were often cold and hungry, Avner Offer concludes robustly that 'whatever their complaints, Germany did not starve'.[11] He also contends that the German economy held up much better than the British planners supposed. 'Blockade alone was not sufficient to defeat her';[12] rather it was the series of futile offensives that drained her manpower and resources and directly caused collapse.[13]

In the last year or so of the war front-line soldiers also began to suffer the effects of shortages already experienced at home. Their bread and meat supplies were reduced and of inferior quality. Even their uniforms and footwear were put together from poor ersatz materials. It is frequently mentioned that the final German offensives beginning in March 1918 were affected in two ways by these material disadvantages: the discovery of ample supplies of food and wine behind the enemy front lines resulted in disorderly binges that delayed the advance; and the realisation that the enemy troops were well supplied dealt a serious blow to propaganda about the effectiveness of the German submarine campaign.

However, the hardships increasingly suffered by the troops did not mean that Germany faced a crisis in armaments production. On the contrary, to the very end the large armies were generally well equipped. In 1916 Germany produced three times as many rifles as Britain and in the following year some 115,000 machine guns to Britain's 80,000. Adequate artillery and infantry weapons were produced for trench

[10] Stevenson, *With Our Backs to the Wall*, p. 437.
[11] Avner Offer, *The First World War: An Agrarian Interpretation* (Oxford University Press, 1991), pp. 53, 76.
[12] Ibid.
[13] See also Loewenberg, 'Germany, the Home Front (1)' and Jackson, 'Germany, the Home Front (2)', in Hugh Cecil and Peter H. Liddle (eds.), *Facing Armageddon*, pp. 554–576.

warfare, and Germany was not far behind Britain and France in the quality and quantity of its aircraft. Germany probably erred in deciding not to produce more than a few tanks, but a more serious handicap in the renewal of offensive operations in early 1918 was its relative lack of mobility due to the shortage of horses especially and also lorries. Indeed, it needs to be stressed that in the main armaments Germany enjoyed such a surplus that it was able to make huge contributions to its principal allies, Austria-Hungary, Bulgaria and Turkey. Austria-Hungary, for example, received more than 400 aircraft, 182,000 rifles, more than 600 machine guns and more than 400 artillery pieces.[14]

It seems clear that the German Army was not so short of weapons and military supplies in general that it was forced to sue for peace in the autumn of 1918; indeed but for Ludendorff's temporary loss of nerve (caused by the collapse of Bulgaria) in calling for an armistice on 4 October, the war could probably have continued well into 1919. In reality Ludendorff's nervous collapse ensured that military morale at the front was fatally undermined and, with the Armistice accepted by Germany, civilian disaffection and the signs of imminent revolution entailed that the war could not be resumed.[15]

The severity, or as its critics would say, brutality, of the Allied strategy of blockade was evident in the fact that it was not relaxed with the Armistice but rigorously maintained until Germany had signed the Treaty of Versailles, and was only terminated on 12 July 1919. Maintaining the blockade was the vital factor in forcing the enemy to accept the severe peace terms because with the end of open hostilities in November 1918 it was far from certain that the Anglo-French land forces would be sufficiently large and determined enough to march deep into Germany.

The blockade was not merely continued, but extended into the Baltic to coerce Germany into surrendering her merchant fleet to the Allies. An American study of the effects of the blockade after the Armistice, published in 1942, concluded that the suffering of German civilians was even more severe than before November 1918. Tuberculosis, especially among children, and rickets were manifested on a previously unknown scale. A British observer noted, 'If suffering were a communicable experience, another such blockade would be impossible.'[16]

---

[14] Stevenson, *With Our Backs to the Wall*, p. 437.

[15] Ibid., p. 424. Offer, *The First World War*, p. 77.

[16] Loewenberg, 'Germany, the Home Front (1)' and Jackson, 'Germany, the Home Front (2)'.

Contrary to what some critics have alleged, however, there was some relaxation in Anglo-American arrangements to allow the importation of foodstuffs into Germany and the neighbouring neutral nations. Mainly at the instigation of President Wilson, as A. C. Bell revealed in his official history, better rations were made available to most German towns by early December 1918, and plans were made to allow the German merchant service to help transport supplies under Allied control. These proposals were eventually agreed upon at a conference with German representatives in Brussels in mid-March 1919. Germany was now allowed to import 370,000 tons of foodstuffs, forage and fats per month, and could resume exports to bordering neutrals excluding only bullion and arms, and coastal trade between Germany, Holland and Scandinavia was to be freed of all restraints. On 22 April a further significant relaxation was agreed by every Allied government: namely that all black lists and enemy trading regulations should cease. The fact remains that although the Treaty of Versailles was signed on 28 June 1919 the Allied blockade was not formally ended until 12 July.[17]

It may seem surprising, in retrospect, that there was little criticism in Britain of this harsh instrument of total war or what Hawkins has bluntly termed 'The Starvation Blockades'. The following considerations have to be taken into account. Close blockade of enemy ports and interference with neutral shipping had been a traditional instrument of British naval power, most notably during the Napoleonic Wars. Enemy civilians, especially the poorest and most vulnerable, would inevitably suffer from a prolonged economic stranglehold, but they were not *seen* to suffer. In the First World War the horrific battlefield conditions and huge casualty tolls made a much more dramatic impact on the public than shortages at home. In this war, also, propaganda reached new levels in range, intensity and sheer virulence against the enemy. Some aspects of Allied propaganda against 'the Hun' would in retrospect come to appear regrettable, even shameful, but Germany displayed such ruthlessness and lack of humanitarian consideration across the board as to forfeit any claims to the moral high ground. It was, above all, difficult for the British public to feel any sympathy for German civilians

---

[17] Hawkins, *The Starvation Blockades*, p. 247. Douglas Newton, *British Policy and the Weimar Republic 1918–1919* (Clarendon Press, 1997) is a severe critic of the continuation of the blockade after the Armistice, but A. C. Bell's compilation *A History of the Blockade of Germany 1914–1918* (HMSO, 1937), especially pp. 705–708, shows that the United States and Britain did relax the regulations early in 1919 to mitigate civilian suffering.

suffering the effects of blockade when they had had to endure the more ghastly effects of unrestricted submarine warfare that did not merely interfere with Allied and neutral shipping, but also sunk thousands of ships, most of them unarmed, and drowned their crews. In comparison, the privations resulting from the Allied blockade appeared not merely acceptable but also a legitimate and comparatively humane means of bringing pressure to bear on an enemy without the destruction and loss of life unavoidable in land warfare.

Failure to end the war quickly gradually caused strategies of economic warfare on both sides to become more rigorously formulated and more stringently enforced. In this relentless aspect of total war Britain and, eventually, the United States proved more successful in their creation of new ministries to deal with the international ramifications of contraband and blockade policies; their use of naval and commercial intelligence; their defeat of the U-boat offensive; and their diplomatic handling of the most important neutral states, such as the Netherlands and Sweden. Starting from a far less favourable position, in geographic, commercial and financial terms, Germany resorted to ruthless submarine warfare as early as February 1915 and, after a pause in the attempt to mollify the United States, again resorted to unrestricted submarine warfare two years later.

This was not only ultimately responsible for bringing about the United States' intervention, but also weakened relations with friendly neutrals like Sweden, and added to privations on the home front. The Allied blockade was by no means solely responsible for the collapse of the Central Powers, but it proved to be a harsh economic instrument in the waging of modern 'total war' in which the civil population was widely accepted as being a legitimate target.[18]

In post-war discussions about the blockade the influential historian, journalist and polemicist Captain B. H. Liddell Hart took a most positive view. This resulted less from a careful analysis of the blockade than from a conviction that the British Army had been unwisely committed to Continental warfare and had not played a decisive part on the Western Front due to poor leadership. Britain was, he contended, inherently unsuited to wage large-scale Continental war. In his book *A History of the World War 1914–1918* he wrote that the Navy 'was to

---

[18] Hawkins, *The Starvation Blockades*, pp. 246–247, Loewenberg, 'Germany, the Home Front (1)', p. 557, Jackson, 'Germany, the Home Front (2)', p. 573, McKercher, 'Economic Warfare', p. 133.

do more than any other factor towards winning the war for the Allies. For the Navy was the instrument of the blockade . . . which is seen to be more and more clearly the decisive agency in the struggle.'[19] In his Epilogue he allowed that there had been other important factors or 'claims', but still insisted that 'the blockade ranks first and began first'.[20]

In sharp contrast, a modern scholar, Paul Kennedy, boldly asserted that Liddell Hart had been mistaken in placing so much emphasis on the blockade as a successful application of the so-called 'British Way in Warfare'. Germany had not been critically dependent on overseas trade or investments. Blockade could only become effective in conjunction with a successful land blockade. 'Not only did the bloody wars of attrition on the eastern and western fronts sap the manpower, economy and morale of the Central Powers at a far higher rate than the maritime blockade ever did, but the latter could be easily neutralised by a German victory in either theatre'. Kennedy concludes that Britain had no choice 'but to commit an ever-increasing share of her resources to the land struggle'.[21]

A. J. P. Taylor took a similarly sceptical view in discussing the legacy of the blockade strategy in the inter-war decades. In post-war propaganda Germany used the blockade in an attempt to conceal the fact that her armies had been defeated. Britain exaggerated the role of blockade in deciding the war in the widespread but illusory belief that under League of Nations terminology 'economic sanctions' would be a cheap alternative to unpopular armaments in resolving international crises. In short 'peace would be maintained without effort. Blockade would stop any aggressor in his tracks'.[22] As Taylor goes on to show, the naïvety behind this thinking was quickly exposed in the League's failure to apply sanctions effectively in either the Manchurian or Abyssinian crises.[23]

Considering the severity of its regulations on contraband and neutral shipping, and their draconian enforcement, Britain's blockade of the Central Powers was subjected to little heart-searching or ethical

---

[19] Liddell Hart, *A History of the World War 1914–1918* (Faber and Faber, 1934), pp. 587–588.

[20] Ibid., p. 592.

[21] Kennedy, *Rise and Fall*, pp. 254–255.

[22] A. J. P. Taylor, *English History 1914–1945* (Oxford University Press, 1965), pp. 369–372.

[23] Ibid., pp. 369–372.

debate at home after 1919. British strategy appeared to be relatively humane compared with Germany's unrestricted submarine campaign, which deliberately targeted and killed seamen and civilians, neutral as well as belligerents. Britain certainly flouted neutral rights, whereas Germany violated the rights of humanity. Germany had confounded pre-1914 naval beliefs that no power would risk the odium of sinking a merchant ship with all its crew, and had thereby contributed to the twentieth-century advent of total war.[24]

When a new war with Germany loomed in the 1930s British politicians and planners tended to exaggerate the contribution that blockade had made to victory in the First World War and to underplay the difficulties it had caused with neutrals, especially the United States. Consequently, before 1939, considerable emphasis was placed upon Germany's assumed dependence on imported war materials whose interdiction would, at the very least, put pressure upon the government. In particular during the 'phoney war' between September 1939 and April 1940 great hopes were placed on the consequences of denying Swedish iron ore to Germany. The latter's rapid conquest of Norway shattered these illusions, and her expansion in Eastern Europe and the Balkans, abetted by the profitable trade agreement with the Soviet Union between August 1939 and June 1941, demonstrated that Germany was not seriously at risk from naval blockade. By contrast, Britain was much more vulnerable to the interruption of her imports than in the First World War, especially when the enemy secured submarine bases from the north of Norway to the Bay of Biscay, and with Italy also posing a naval–air threat in the Mediterranean. Britain therefore turned increasingly to the alternative instrument of attrition; namely the destruction of Germany's war industry at its source by means of strategic bombing.

[24] On the larger humanitarian and political aspects see Geoffrey Best, *Humanity in Warfare: The Modern History of International Law and Armed Conflicts* (Weidenfeld & Nicolson, 1980), pp. 244–261.

6 ATTRITION IN THE SECOND WORLD WAR: THE STRATEGIC BOMBING OF GERMANY

The changing attitudes to the British bomber offensive against Germany provide a clear example of distortion in hindsight. There were a few pacifist or near pacifist critics during the war but in general the campaign received public support. In the immediate post-war years there was some criticism, mostly on operational grounds, but also a strong show of resentment at the way Bomber Command and Sir Arthur Harris had been slighted in post-war commemorations and honours. Since the 1960s, however, there has been widespread condemnation of the campaign for a complex and sometimes muddled combination of moral, strategic and political reasons. In principle a critical reappraisal is entirely legitimate, but in some cases there has been a marked lack of historical understanding and empathy, both as regards the fraught conditions in which decisions were made and the operational problems in implementing them. There is a certain irony in the tendency to exaggerate Britain's contribution to the defeat of Germany, in comparison to those of the United States and the Soviet Union, while underrating, and even condemning, Britain's principal offensive achievement: namely the strategic bombing campaign against Germany.

British opinion at all levels has been deeply affected by the pervasive arguments propagated in the inter-war decades about the omnipotence of the bomber and fear that the next major war would begin with immediate cataclysmic bombing of cities with high explosives and poison gas. British governments, and more especially the Royal Air Force as the interested Service struggling to maintain its independent status, had placed great emphasis on Bomber Command, primarily as a deterrent to enemy air attack, but also as a counter-weapon should deterrence fail. In the late 1930s, however, a much higher priority was given to fighter aircraft for home defence, and little thought was given to the huge problems involved in penetrating distant enemy defences, locating legitimate targets and hitting them with sufficiently heavy bombs to inflict significant damage. Consequently when war came Bomber Command was completely unprepared to carry out its offensive role; but in any case Neville Chamberlain's government during the months of 'phoney war' proved unwilling to initiate the bombing of Germany ('taking the gloves off' in the idiom of the day) for fear of provoking enemy retaliation. Britain and France generally observed these self-imposed restrictions on bombing, which were confined to clearly defined and specific military targets. However, Hitler flagrantly ignored them, first in Poland and then in his Western conquests of April–May 1940.

Churchill too was remarkably reluctant to abandon his moderate stance that British actions should be confined to purely military targets and that there should be no spirit of hatred or retaliation towards Germany or enemy personnel. But in late August 1940 Churchill broke the tacit truce with Hitler by ordering a token raid on Berlin after the *Luftwaffe* had accidentally bombed London. He became more belligerent from mid-September 1940 when the *Luftwaffe* began to drop 500-kilogram aerial mines on London and other cities, including the shocking destruction of Coventry in November.[1]

Even before Churchill's conversion to an all-out bombing campaign, from May 1940 onwards, Bomber Command dropped between 1,500 and 6,000 tons per month on Germany, targeting oil installations on moonlit nights and urban areas when visibility was poor. Even in clear weather it was difficult to locate precise targets so in practice the aircraft had to bomb blind or abandon their mission. In reality, while many of the airmen believed they were finding and hitting their targets as well as providing reassuring propaganda for the public, in practice the best hope was to inflict collateral damage in the broadly defined target area, and to undermine civilian morale. Though never openly admitted by the War Cabinet, there was a shift in strategy towards bombing urban areas because they were the only realistic targets.

---

[1] Michael Burleigh, *Moral Combat: A History of World War II* (Harper Press, 2010), pp. 164–165.

Critics have lambasted British bombing strategy in this early phase (1940–1941) when Bomber Command was lucky to hit anything at all, carried only modest payloads and suffered heavy losses. But the counter-arguments are weighty. Bombing was Britain's only way of hitting Germany directly after Dunkirk, the Battle of Britain, the Blitz and a series of disasters from Norway to Singapore and Tobruk. It was vital to home morale to believe that Bomber Command, night after night, was inflicting heavy damage on Germany's war industry; to impress the United States with Britain's indomitable determination to stay in the war; and, after June 1941, to show Stalin that his new ally was doing something, however inadequate, to offset Russia's staggering losses in manpower and territory. Three further considerations should be added to the balance. Even in this largely ineffective phase, British bombing was showing the German people that the Nazis' boast of guaranteeing complete immunity to air attack was false. Secondly, scarce enemy resources, notably 88-mm anti-aircraft guns, had to be diverted for home defence. Lastly, and most important for later critics to understand, only by persisting with the development of Bomber Command – its numbers, optimum aircraft type, direction finding and bombing aids – could a powerful strategic instrument eventually be created. The RAF went to war in 1939 with stop-gap bombers: Hampdens, Blenheims, Whitleys, Wellingtons and, most lethal of all for its crews, the Battle.[2]

Needless to say these arguments in favour of a high priority for the bombing strategy were by no means universally accepted, or that the immense resources committed to bombing after 1941 were inevitable. The other Services understandably competed fiercely for a greater share of available aircraft and for more concentration on close co-operation in maritime and land warfare. The Air Staff itself was far from unanimous in its support of strategic bombing, particularly after Sir Arthur Harris was appointed Commander-in-Chief in February 1942.

A period of great uncertainty began in August 1941 when the RAF's extravagant claims about the effects of strategic bombing were subjected to statistical analysis by a civil servant in the War Cabinet secretariat, David Butt. He demonstrated from a study of bomb damage photos that only one aircraft in three got within five miles of its target,

[2] Ibid., pp. 484–487. Max Hastings, *Bomber Command* (Pan, 1979), pp. 58, 420.

and even this fell to one in ten when smog enveloped the Ruhr. Nearly half the bombs dropped between May 1940 and May 1941 had fallen on open country.[3]

Sir Charles Portal (Chief of the Air Staff) and the Air Staff were obliged to modify their claims regarding precision bombing, but successfully counter-attacked the other Services' efforts to downgrade the priority and therefore the resources devoted to Bomber Command. Portal still insisted that with a bomber force of 4,000 aircraft he could win the war in six months. In face of Churchill's scepticism he modified these claims to the belief that bombing would so weaken Germany that the Allied forces would be able to invade and occupy Western Europe without serious opposition.

Professor Lindemann (Lord Cherwell) produced dubious statistics to support the Air Staff's argument that the de-housing of workers could seriously undermine enemy war production, and his influence prevailed against the more sceptical views of other eminent scientists, including Sir Patrick Blackett (chief scientist of the Royal Navy) and Sir Henry Tizard (Rector of Imperial College London). Portal reminded the Prime Minister that he had thus far strongly supported the bombing strategy and that future production plans were heavily committed to it. If the strategy was to be changed the War Cabinet would need to take a prompt decision.[4]

The Chief of the Air Staff was probably right to argue that commitment of resources had gone too far for a sudden change of priorities. Churchill increased the Air Ministry's funding for 1943 by a third more than it had requested, while Portal issued a stream of directives stressing that the morale and health of German workers were as important to target as attacks on factories and the transport infrastructure. A fresh directive embodying the above ideas, which effectively entailed area bombing, was issued in February 1942, shortly before Sir Arthur Harris was appointed the new Chief of Bomber Command. Harris thus inherited the broad strategy of the area bombing of German cities and did not originate it. Nevertheless, through his single-minded and even obsessive pursuit of this directive, he would become famous (or notorious) as the personification of the strategy intended to destroy German cities as Bomber Command's overriding concern. Standing on the Air Ministry roof during a

---

[3] Burleigh, *Moral Combat*, p. 489.   [4] Ibid., pp. 490–491.

Luftwaffe raid, Harris famously remarked to Portal, 'Well they are sowing the wind, and they will reap the whirlwind'. He, more than any other individual, ensured that this would happen though it must be added that this ultra-aggressive attitude accorded well with Churchill's offensive spirit and he gave Harris invaluable backing until very late in the war.

The crucial decision in February 1942 to build up a huge force of the newly available and much more effective Lancaster bombers was taken despite the powerful competing claims of the other Services.[5] Moreover, despite the practical and statistical criticisms of the eminent scientists already mentioned, the decision appears to have been taken entirely on political and strategic grounds: namely that area bombing would be welcomed by Stalin and would wear down German resistance by attrition leading to the enemy's collapse or, at worst, to greatly reduce the opposition to an eventual Allied landing. By this stage of the war, ethical qualms or reservations do not appear to have weighed heavily in reaching decisions that, decades later, would be deplored and even condemned on moral grounds.

Under Harris' dynamic leadership Bomber Command achieved a series of remarkable successes in 1942 and 1943 that raised morale among the crews and secured support for further expansion from the government. In March 1942, for example, some 200 acres of the medieval city of Lübeck were destroyed by a combination of high explosives and incendiary bombs.

A year later, however, between 5 March and the end of July, Bomber Command had acquired adequate numbers of aircraft (mainly Lancasters), better target location by means of the OBOE electronic guidance system and improved marking by the Pathfinder Force to carry out a sustained and devastating campaign against all the main industrial cities in the battle of the Ruhr. The destruction of a significant amount of the Ruhr's coking coal and steel, and many intermediate components of war production, disrupted Albert Speer's programme for increased armaments at a crucial time. Speer himself admitted that Allied bombing of the Ruhr had seriously negated his plans, particularly for the output of aircraft. In Adam Tooze's authoritative judgement, 'Bomber Command had stopped Speer's armaments miracle in its tracks'. As

[5] Hastings, *Bomber Command*, pp. 182–184.

Tooze also comments, this was a turning point in the history of the German war economy 'which has been grossly underestimated by post-war accounts'.[6]

This phase of the offensive culminated in the destruction of Hamburg, later to be condemned by some critics on the Allied side as infamous due to the firestorm that killed more than 40,000 people. In four concentrated night attacks, complemented by equally powerful American attacks by day, more than 3,000 sorties were flown and some 9,000 tons of bombs dropped. Nearly a million survivors fled the city and this great port and dockyard never recovered full production. It was Hamburg's devastation that caused Speer to declare that six more actions of this magnitude would cause Germany to collapse.[7]

In late 1943 and early 1944, however, Bomber Command suffered a serious setback in its raids on Berlin. Between 18 November 1943 and the end of March 1944 there were sixteen major attacks upon the capital involving more than 9,000 sorties, more than 7,000 of them flown by Lancasters. Berlin was well beyond the range of Bomber Command's radar (OBOE), and the city's sprawling expanse of built-up areas made individual targets almost impossible to identify. Consequently, the concentration of bombing was considerably less than achieved in the Ruhr towns or Hamburg. The capital was ferociously defended by searchlights, ack-ack and fighters, causing Bomber Command to suffer a casualty rate that could not be maintained. In these months over 1,000 British bombers failed to return. Contrary to Stanley Baldwin's celebrated remark, Berlin was a clear case where the bomber did not always get through. Indeed at the end of this offensive phase on 30 March 1944 Bomber Command suffered its worst disaster when ninety six of the 795 aircraft sent to Nuremberg were shot down and a further dozen fatally damaged. This operation contrasted sharply with the later over-bombing of Dresden in that a combination of poor planning and clear conditions gave a decisive advantage to the defenders. More broadly, Bomber Command's losses over Berlin and other targets deep in Germany underline the point that the offensive was far from being one-sided bullying of defenceless civilians, but rather a fiercely contended struggle for most of the war. In sum by 1944

---

[6] Adam Tooze, *The Wages of Destruction: Making and Breaking of Nazi Germany* (Penguin Books, 2007), pp. 597–598, 621.

[7] Tooze, *Wages of Destruction*, p. 601. Burleigh, *Moral Combat*, p. 499.

the German air defences had achieved a clear advantage over the night bombers. Only in the closing months when the Allies, and especially the Americans, had achieved dominance in the skies over Germany through employment of long-range fighters (the P51 Mustang) could they sometimes bomb their targets almost at will and with minimal interference.[8]

In the spring of 1944 Bomber Command was facing another crisis as its losses mounted and its exaggerated undertakings to bring about Germany's collapse seemed no nearer to achievement. Though opposed by Harris, Bomber Command's diversion to help prepare the way for Overlord, and then to assist the break-out from Normandy, proved a blessing in disguise. It provided a respite of nearly six months in which to re-group and develop improved methods for detecting and hitting targets.

Despite Speer's pessimistic remark after the disaster in Hamburg, it had become clear that hopes that intensive bombing of German cities would soon bring about the surrender were mistaken. Bombing *had* caused a decline in the German workers' morale and growing pessimism due to the Nazis' inability to protect them, but ruthless suppression of any dissent in a police state made open protest impossible. Even had Hitler and leading Nazi henchmen been removed, the most likely course for a successor would have been to try to achieve a truce in the West so as to continue the life and death struggle with the Soviet Union. In other words, no matter how successful the Allied bombing offensive might be in strategic terms, it could not by itself secure the political termination of the war.

By mid-1943, specially trained bomber squadrons employing the multipurpose Mosquito fighter-bomber were able to hit certain well-defined 'precision targets' in good weather that did not require deep penetration into enemy territory. For example Amiens and Copenhagen were less strongly defended than targets inside Germany. The Dam Busters raid by Lancasters of 617 Squadron on 16 May was probably the most brilliant 'pin-point' attack in the whole of the war. The Mohne and Sorpe dams were thought to be the key to the Ruhr's water supplies. The former was successfully breached, but then Guy Gibson's crews used their remaining bouncing mines to wreck the Eder dam, which was much less significant. The raid achieved considerable but

---

[8] Hastings, *Bomber Command*, pp. 310, 318.

temporary flooding, drowning nearly 500 Germans, more than 700 foreign workers and over 1,000 cattle, but did not inflict lasting damage on the German economy. The raid was also costly: eight of the nineteen Lancasters were lost. The raid has been lauded ever since as an outstanding combination of scientific innovation, courage and very-low-flying skills, but this was precisely its immediate and lasting value – as propaganda.[9]

Other low-level raids on special targets were delivered with spectacular accuracy but usually at high cost and with mixed results. In February 1944, for example, at the request of the French resistance, the Gestapo prison at Amiens was attacked in an effort to save prisoners awaiting execution. The walls were smashed but 100 prisoners were killed and the majority of the 250 who escaped were recaptured and shot. Subsequently a Mosquito force also successfully destroyed the Gestapo headquarters in Copenhagen but one of the bombers crashed into a nearby infants' school. These and other similar cases show that precision bombing was possible in 1943 by specially trained crews at very high cost. This was not an option for the main force of Bomber Command.[10]

The diversion of Bomber Command from the destruction of German cities to prepare the way for the Allied landings in Normandy and then to assist in the break-out from the beachheads and the drive across France is generally regarded as a great success.

These operations should not, however, be used as a reason to castigate Harris for once again giving priority to area bombing when command of the force was restored to him in September 1944. In some crucial respects conditions were more favourable for attacking the transport infrastructure in France than in Germany. In the former, German air and ground defences were much more thinly spread; it was impossible to guard the vast network of roads, railways, bridges, marshalling yards and other bottlenecks; and resistance activity made repair work more hazardous. Above all, the bombers were operating over short distances and in the long summer days were better able to locate specific targets in daylight. Tremendous improvements were made in the accuracy of bombing targets in France, especially by 5 and

[9] Ibid., p. 271. Denis Richards, *Royal Air Force 1939–1945*, Vol. II (HMSO, 1954), pp. 294–296.
[10] Burleigh, *Moral Combat*, p. 456.

8 Groups, between which there was intense rivalry. The key to success lay primarily in accurate marking from very low levels, which was 5 Group's speciality. Number 8 Group used OBOE to place its markers and this necessitated flying much higher because it relied on signals from England. Leonard Cheshire, for example, had marked an engines factory at Limoges in February from a height of 200 feet, and won his VC in April for a roof-level marking in Munich. The main hazards were the necessity for clear visibility and for the bombers to linger over the target until the Master Bomber was sufficiently satisfied to issue orders by radio-telephone. As a pilot in 617 Squadron remarked, 'it seemed to work well enough against no opposition, but I decided it might not be such fun against a heavily defended German target'. Indeed lingering around a target for accurate visual marking could be fatal. On 3 May 1944 forty-two out of 362 aircraft were lost to night fighters in a raid on Mailly-Le-Camp, and a week later twelve out of eighty-nine Lancasters were lost in an attack on Lille.[11]

In their role of assisting the Allied advance across France the British and American bomber forces were often a blunt instrument. Charles Carrington, who was the senior Army liaison officer at Bomber Command, issued a scathing report on the Command's failings in the needless destruction of Caen and the subsequent request that Allied troops be withdrawn to a distance of 2,000 yards from the aiming points to avoid casualties from friendly fire in what the bombers termed 'cratering'. The American air blitz in support of the break-out at St Lô was badly bungled with the result that many of their own troops, including a general, were killed. In early August American Fortresses, bombing in daylight, dropped three sticks of bombs five miles short and scored three bull's-eyes: on the headquarters of the 3rd Canadian Division; on a British gun-park; and on the main British ammunition dump. A Bomber Command attack on the Falaise pocket on 14 August showed that no lessons in close air–ground liaison had been learnt from previous mistakes. The bomb line was not precisely indicated; there was no liaison with the Pathfinders; and no ground to air signals. Seven per cent of bombs fell on Allied forces that day including the headquarters of the Army Group Royal Artillery, and the wretched Canadian infantry were pulverised again by Allied aircraft. This latter disaster was rendered even more tragic by the Canadians' correct use of

---

[11] Hastings, *Bomber Command*, pp. 339–342.

yellow flares to indicate their position while the Pathfinders were using similar coloured flares as markers.[12]

Bombing was clearly more hazardous when the ground forces were advancing in close contact with the enemy. For example, as the Gordon Highlanders advanced across northern France and into Belgium they were frequently strafed by Typhoons. As Colonel Lindsay noted, 'everybody is scared stiff of the RAF'. He heard his commander telling the general on the phone. 'The one thing I cannot afford is to have the RAF operating anywhere within fifty miles of me'.[13] When the battalion was approaching the river Rhine they were bombed by the RAF at Goch in broad daylight and perfect visibility. The commanding officer of the Royal Engineers was seriously wounded, the Argylls suffered a dozen casualties and one company's transport was destroyed. The survivors naturally cursed the RAF for its carelessness, but Lindsay was remarkably dispassionate in recording the Army's deep gratitude to Bomber Command for almost banishing the *Luftwaffe* from the skies.[14]

It was hardly surprising that Harris, after these bombing errors and the more serious blunders committed in the Caen–Falaise operations, was confirmed in his opinion 'that the Heavy Bomber blitz was unsuitable for giving close support to infantry on the battlefield'.[15]

The most important phase for the Allied strategic bombing of Germany fell between September 1944 and April 1945. Direction-finding aids and the ability to mark and hit specific targets had improved greatly during the previous year, and the enemy's air defence system (radar chain and network of airfields) had been weakened by the Allied advance towards the German homeland. Perhaps most significant of all, the remarkable P51 Mustang was now in full operational use with its amazing dual capability – the range of a heavy bomber and the performance of an interceptor fighter.

The Mustang could outmanoeuvre and outpace the opposition's aircraft in nearly every respect (speed, height, diving power and manoeuvrability), while its long-range fuel tanks gave it a reach of nearly 1,500 miles. By the end of the war nearly 14,000 of these outstanding aircraft had been produced. By March 1944, thanks largely to

[12] Charles Carrington, *Soldier at Bomber Command* (Leo Cooper, Pen and Sword, 1987), pp. 158–166.
[13] Lindsay, *So Few Got Through*, pp. 57, 217.   [14] Ibid., p. 217.
[15] Carrington, *Soldier at Bomber Command*, p. 164.

the American air strategy of using the Mustangs to hunt down German fighters, rather than serve as bomber escorts, the *Luftwaffe* had lost command of the air in daylight.[16]

Britain produced no long-range fighter equivalent to the Mustang. The Mosquito operated as a long-range night fighter later in the war, though in limited numbers. The success rate was disappointing, mainly due to inadequate radar, but the Mosquitos did have some success against the German night fighters, particularly by lurking near the enemy airfields to catch the aircraft as they tried to land. There is evidence that morale among the German night fighter pilots suffered as a result of these increased losses.[17]

Nevertheless Bomber Command, operating at night, benefited considerably from the American dominance in daylight. Morale among *Luftwaffe* pilots declined and their training was dislocated, and practice flying-time reduced. The Allied attacks on oil through the summer of 1944 produced a petrol famine. The German withdrawal from France entailed the loss of a vital section of the early warning radar chain.

Thus in the final months of the war the *Luftwaffe* and the ground defence forces could offer only sporadic resistance. The worst enemy to successful bombing remained the weather, which tended to favour the defenders during the winter months. Bomber Command now possessed a vast force of four-engined bombers and, at its peak, could operate more than a thousand Lancasters in a single night, carrying a formidable payload ranging from the 22,000-pound Grand Slam to the 4-pound incendiary cluster bombs. Although Allied bomber forces secured the destruction of the German war machine by April 1945 some critics, including one of the official historians, Noble Frankland, have argued that victory could have been won earlier but for division over priorities in the RAF high command.[18]

Harris, in particular, has been severely criticised in the final phase of the war for devoting far too high a percentage of attacks to destroying cities, and too low a percentage on precision targets, especially oil. For example, Max Hastings, in his influential book *Bomber Command*, writes that 'the cost of Harris's stubbornness to the Allied

---

[16] Noble Frankland, *The Bombing Offensive Against Germany* (Faber, 1965), pp. 81–83.

[17] Ibid., p. 85 and information supplied by Sebastian Cox, Head of the Air Historical Branch.

[18] Frankland, *Bombing Offensive*, pp. 88–89.

war effort at this last stage was almost certainly grievous. The oil plan will be remembered by history as one of the Allies' great missed opportunities.'[19] Hastings added that, 'It was impossible to believe that Harris was applying himself to the September Directive'. Was it true that even after receiving favourable weather reports Harris 'again and again came down in favour of attacking a city rather than oil plants'?[20]

While it is certainly true that Harris was unenthusiastic about attacking oil installations, which he included in his dismissive phrase 'panacea targets', this indictment needs considerable modification. The first qualification is that many of the oil targets were in Central or Eastern Europe where they were beyond the Bombers' direction-finding instrument OBOE. Also, although low-level marking techniques had now been tried and tested they were only viable in good weather, which could not be relied upon in the autumn and winter months. Moreover, low-level marking techniques, though usually accurate, still remained more effective as aids to the area bombing of cities, as would be demonstrated in the raids on Dresden.

Secondly, it is simply not true that Harris ignored favourable weather reports on several occasions due to his obsession with area bombing. A post-war study by the Chiefs of Staff on oil as a factor in the German war effort revealed that in the three critical months – October to December 1944 – there were only seven nights and three days when weather conditions meant that oil targets could have been attacked but were not. Furthermore after a dispute with Portal, Harris did significantly increase his attacks against oil targets in the remaining months of the war. Lastly, on this point, the American official history of Allied bombing, not generally favourable to Harris, makes the remarkable statement that by the end of November 1944 'all of the RAF's synthetic oil targets were suspended because they were no longer operating'.[21]

Thirdly, in a detailed analysis, the Head of Air Historical Branch, Sebastian Cox, has demonstrated that much more caution

---

[19] Hastings, *Bomber Command*, p. 403.   [20] Ibid., pp. 394–416 passim.
[21] Sebastian Cox, 'A Loose Cannon who Should Have Been Fired? Sir Arthur Harris and the Bomber Offensive September 1944–April 1945'. An unpublished paper, especially pp. 10–12. Most of the information cited can be read in Sebastian Cox, 'Sir Arthur Harris and Some Myths and Controversies of the Bomber Offensive', *Royal Air Force Historical Journal*, 47, 2010, pp. 6–33.

needs to be exercised in using percentages of raids on specific categories of bombing targets as a stick with which to beat Harris. The British official historians' warning on this point has too often been ignored: namely that tactical and strategic bombing operations could easily be confused and, moreover, it was often difficult to make clear distinctions between different target systems. Cox cites as an example area attacks on towns in the Ruhr where substantial damage was done to benzol plants, which belong to the oil plan. Indeed much of Germany's fuel in the autumn of 1944 was produced from coal or as a by-product of coke ovens, mainly located in the Ruhr. Directions received by Harris in October and November 1944 required him to attack 'the undamaged parts of the major industrial cities of the Ruhr',[22] and these would clearly include targets relating to fuel.

Criticism based on percentages of raids on different types of target could easily be misinterpreted in another respect. Target systems, particularly communications, were rarely isolated or physically distinct in urban areas. For example, raids on railways were usually given two aiming points: the main railway station and the centre of town. The devastation of the latter would add to the difficulty of repairing the railway. The official historians concluded that it would be 'entirely misleading to judge the bomber effort against communications by the statistics recorded under that heading'. As a final comment on this point, Air Vice-Marshal SO Bufton, who had been a persistent critic of Harris' bombing priorities during the war, wrote in 1959 that, 'The difference between the air staff and the C-in-C was not as great as the amount of paper absorbed in the discussion would indicate. The C-in-C attacked many precise targets with astonishing skill and accuracy. Reasonably good weather was essential for such precision attacks... The balance of effort would still, in bad weather, have gone on area targets.'[23]

The severest charge against Harris and Bomber Command is that the British forces persisted to the end of the war in area bombing whereas, in sharp contrast, the American bomber forces operating in Europe carried out precision bombing throughout their operation. The contrast is almost completely invalid and it is astonishing that the myth has persisted for so long. Critics have either not read or, worse, deliberately ignored the authoritative demolition of the myth in 1995 by

---

[22] Cox, 'Sir Arthur Harris and Some Myths and Controversies', pp. 10–11.
[23] Ibid., p. 12.

W. Hays Parks, an attorney in the American Department of Defense specialising in political-legal issues relating to air power. Parks shows that from the outset the USAAF leadership was anxious to distance itself from Bomber Command's area offensive, and succeeded brilliantly by obfuscating the definitions of 'precision' and 'accuracy'. In principle the American heavy bomber daylight raids on Germany were based on a strategy of selected targeting against military and industrial installations thought to be contributing directly to the enemy's war effort. In practice, however, the combination of formidable enemy defences and poor weather frequently forced the Americans to 'bomb blind' using radar techniques in which they were less well-trained and less experienced than Bomber Command. Consequently, despite the myth successfully promulgated, their bombing was seldom 'precise', 'pickle barrel' or 'pin-point'; indeed towards the end of the war 'when both were operating mature, full-strength forces – the RAF Bomber Command was more successful in placing its bombs on target than the Americans'.[24]

Whereas Bomber Command had been forced to accept the strictures of the Butt Report and strive to improve accuracy, the Americans continued to define accuracy more loosely (for example, to include bombs that fell within 1,000 feet of the aiming point but caused no damage), while 'mission failures' and 'gross errors' were omitted from any analysis of accuracy. The numerous devices introduced in both bomber forces in 1942 and 1943 improved navigation and target location and succeeded in placing a much higher percentage of bombs dropped within three miles of their aiming point, but in normal conditions of weather and enemy interference none proved adequate for the precision bombing that American publicity claimed.

The US Strategic Bombing Survey was later candid about the 'spin' placed on targeting by its bomber forces; if the declared intention of a particular attack had been a precise target then it was recorded as such even if in reality it had resembled an area attack on the city. As the biographer of General Carl Spaatz, Commander of US Eighth Air Force, concluded, 'Marshalling yards was a USAAF euphemism for city areas'.[25] As late as December 1943 bad weather had resulted in blind-bombing missions in which only 5 per cent of American bombs

---

[24] W. Hays Parks, 'Precision and Area Bombing: Who Did Which and When?', *The Journal of Strategic Studies*, 18, March 1995, pp. 145–174.

[25] Ibid., p. 154.

had fallen within five miles of the aiming point. Later still, on 29 April 1944, Eighth Air Force attacked specific railway facilities in Berlin but only one of the eleven combat wings placed its bombs within five miles of the target. By this stage in the war Bomber Command's practice of each crew flying its own mission once over the target was proving much more effective than the Americans' reliance on a group leader. Consequently, while many American raids were listed in the records as directed at selective targets, adverse weather and the high altitudes from which the Americans preferred to operate were, in reality, general area attacks. Parks concludes that, 'Given American blind bombing accuracy, it is difficult to distinguish between Bomber Command's general area offensive and the USAAF's blind [area] bombing of selected targets'.[26]

A significant point is that in a post-war American report on oil targets, German employees and defence personnel were almost unanimous in reporting that RAF attacks were more damaging due to each RAF bombardier sighting his bombs independently (as opposed to American formation bombing on the leader), and because the RAF used a single as against multiple American aiming points. But even more important was the fact that Bomber Command aircraft could carry a heavier load of high explosives, which did fearsome damage to the oil plants and consequently took longer to repair.[27]

In recent years critics of Bomber Command have focused so obsessively on the destruction of Dresden between 13 and 15 February 1945 that it is easy, but erroneous, to view this particular raid as the culmination of Harris' area bombing obsession and a mission with unique characteristics that caused it to be regarded as infamous, an atrocity or war crime. Unjustly, Harris has borne the brunt of responsibility and blame while Churchill's reputation has escaped largely unscathed, suggesting comparisons with Haig taking most of the blame for British losses in 1917 and 1918 when the Prime Minister, Lloyd George, was ultimately responsible. The analogy may be pressed further in that both Haig and Harris were taciturn, deficient in charm and charisma and deeply suspicious of political guile and skulduggery. But, in his defence, Harris showed an intense devotion to his men and was very popular

[26] Ibid., p. 162.
[27] Ibid. and his note 48. See also W. Hays Parks, 'Air War and the Laws of War', in Horst Boog (ed.), *The Conduct of the Air War in the Second World War* (Berg, 1992).

with them. Also, like Haig, he displayed absolute tenacity of purpose and great strength of character to cope with the daily tensions and the heavy losses sustained by his Command.

Dresden became a probable Allied bombing target early in 1945 for several reasons. It was still hoped that a truly devastating raid on a major German city might hasten the Nazis' downfall. Berlin had been heavily bombed without achieving this aim but Dresden along with Chemnitz and Leipzig were largely unscathed and now within reach of Allied bombers. Perhaps most important was the notion of impeding German reinforcements to the ever shrinking Eastern Front through this important rail centre and so assist the advancing Soviet forces. Stalin had not called for such an attack but welcomed it when informed at the Yalta Conference that it was impending.[28]

On the night of Tuesday 14 February an advance group of Lancasters dropped green markers to illuminate the general target area, followed by low-flying Mosquitos, which dropped canisters with red target indicators. After checking that the markers were clearly visible, the Master Bomber ordered the first attack by a force of 240 Lancasters flying at about only 12,000 feet. The total bomb load of some 808 tons consisted of 57 per cent high explosive and 43 per cent incendiaries. Fires, which were visible fifty miles away, engulfed the centre of the city and into this conflagration the second wave of 535 bombers hit the central area in the early hours of the morning. At noon that day a huge force of American B-17 bombers, nominally targeting the marshalling yards, added to the physical devastation and pandemonium among the survivors. As if this were not enough in over-destruction another American force, diverted from bombing oil installations at Böhlen, jettisoned its bombs over Dresden. The centre of the city was reduced to smoking, blackened ruins, and considerable damage was done to the arms factories, though some escaped lightly because they were based in the suburbs. The vital railway system was badly damaged but was quickly repaired.[29]

Estimates of the casualty figures varied greatly, and hugely exaggerated totals were immediately used by Goebbels for propaganda purposes. It is now thought that between 25,000 and 35,000 citizens

[28] An outstanding recent study is Frederick Taylor, *Dresden: Tuesday 13 February 1945* (Bloomsbury, 2005). See also Hastings, *Bomber Command*, p. 412 and Burleigh, *Moral Combat*, p. 512.

[29] Burleigh, *Moral Combat*, pp. 512–513.

died, some directly from the bombing but many vaporised in the resultant firestorms or asphyxiated in the cellars. The fact that the raids were more devastating than expected owed much to the weather being near perfect with visibility over the target area excellent. It is seldom remarked that on the very next night a large Bomber Command raid on Chemnitz largely failed due to thick cloud cover.[30]

The raid had also been very carefully planned with a circuitous approach route to avoid German radar and with small-scale feints on other cities further north. There was also a large-scale attack on the important synthetic oil works at Böhlen, showing that Harris was keen to raid oil targets whenever possible. There were hardly any ground or air defences to protect Dresden, and the river Elbe provided a first-class navigational aid. Not least important as regards the high casualty levels, civil defences had been badly neglected, and the Gauleiter responsible, Martin Mutschmann, compounded this neglect by fleeing the city shortly before the raids began.[31]

The Dresden raid at once became and remained a political and propaganda issue in Germany. Goebbels exploited the event effectively as proof of the Allies' employment of deliberate 'terror bombing' and after the war the Communists promptly took over the theme of Western imperialism against East Germany. Their estimate of casualties fluctuated in accord with the highs and lows of the Cold War, but were always higher than the actual figures, dreadful though these were.[32]

In Britain political reactions to the raid were at first muted. On 6 March Richard Stokes, a Labour back-bencher, launched a strong attack on the government in the House of Commons for its indiscriminate bombing of cities, reading into the record the entire dispatch of a journalist's uncensored report, published in the United States, which had used the emotive term 'terror bombing'. Government spokesmen could only attempt damage limitation by denying that it had ever been a deliberate aim to kill women and children. Other prominent figures, including Violet Bonham Carter, openly expressed their disquiet but the controversy did not become a major public issue at the time. Things might have been different had Churchill's deplorable letter to the Air

---

[30] Taylor, *Dresden*, pp. 389–390.

[31] Ibid., pp. 468–469. See also Sebastian Cox, 'The Dresden Raids: Why and How', in Paul Addison and Jeremy A. Crang (eds.), *Firestorm. The Bombing of Dresden, 1945* (Pimlico, 2006).

[32] Taylor, *Dresden*, pp. 412–414.

Staff at the end of March, attempting to distance himself from the 'terror bombing', been made public. In the event the letter remained confidential until the publication of the official history of strategic bombing in 1961. It was clear, however, in the immediate aftermath of the war that Bomber Command was not in political favour. Harris received only a belated baronetcy in 1953, and Churchill gave the Command's exploits only a passing mention in his history of the war.[33] Eventually Harris was honoured by a statue outside St Clement Danes Church on the Strand and a memorial to Bomber Command was at last opened in Green Park in London on 28 June 2012.

What really made Dresden an immediate and lasting controversy was the publication of David Irving's book *The Destruction of Dresden* in 1963. Irving, openly sympathetic towards Hitler and a Holocaust denier, stressed the horrors experienced by the city's population and estimated the death toll at 135,000. The book was widely regarded as authoritative and made a huge impact at the time on anti-war and anti-establishment sentiments. The inflated death toll was the revelation that reviewers found most shocking: it was thought to be worse than the two atomic bombs dropped on Japan and three times the number of British deaths from all the German air raids together. In 1966 Irving publicly accepted that his estimate was much too high and the more likely figure was 35,000, but he later reverted to his original total, even at times raising it to as high as 250,000. His argument, widely accepted ever since, was that this was a deliberate atrocity of exceptional callousness, which demonstrated that the Western Democracies were not at all morally superior to their enemies. Most military historians reject the notions that the raid was somehow different from Bomber Command's other operations or that it marked a new plunge into barbarism, but they have failed to convince a broad sector of public opinion. As Paul Addison comments: this was 'a terrible event by any reckoning, but it would have never bulked so large in the consciousness of the post-war world but for the legends that accumulated around it'.[34]

What were these 'legends' that have given Irving and later critics such ammunition to fire against Harris, Bomber Command and by implication Churchill and the government? The following four points

---

[33] Hastings, *Bomber Command*, pp. 413–419.
[34] Paul Addison, 'Retrospective', in Addison and Crang (eds.), *Firestorm*. See also Richard Overy, 'The Post-War Debate', in the same volume.

are repeatedly made. First, Dresden was a beautiful city famous for its architecture, culture and porcelain, and had largely escaped the ravages of war until February 1945. Many upper-class Britons cherished fond memories of the city from being students or tourists there. Second, it was believed to be a purely cultural centre making no significant contribution to the war effort and somehow untainted with Nazism. Thirdly, it seemed in retrospect that the war was nearly over, so why go to such trouble to inflict gratuitous damage and deaths on an unnecessary target. Lastly, it was clear even to staunch supporters of Allied bombing that Dresden had been over-bombed; the initial RAF attack had effectively blitzed the city centre and the subsequent British and American attacks had resulted in a massive overkill, serving to stoke up the firestorms and expand the inferno.

It has already been mentioned that Dresden was far from being detached from the Nazi war effort. On the contrary its distance from the front and relative safety from air attack made it a popular centre for dispersed war work. It contained about 130 war-related factories, the most important being the Zeiss Ikon plants famous for their optical-precision engineering works. Moreover, by the later stages of the war, all the main factories had been converted to war work including the camera firms that now produced most of the *Luftwaffe*'s gauges. Even the famous porcelain centre at Meissen had been converted to war work, making telex terminals for the *Wehrmacht*. The principal Dresden factories also relied heavily upon forced Jewish workers and thousands of imported slave labourers. The effects of the raids on armaments production was massive. Many factories were seriously damaged, twenty-one reporting a 100 per cent stoppage of work, and some had not returned to full production when the war ended. The disruption of the labour force was even more significant: deaths of key workers, destruction of housing and the chaos caused to the city's transport system all contributed to drastic reduction in productivity.[35]

The retrospective, post-war arguments that Dresden should not have been attacked because 'the war was nearly over' are completely unconvincing. The failure at Arnhem, which really had raised hopes that the European war could be ended in 1944, and the titanic battle of the Ardennes, only won after a tremendous Allied commitment of resources, in January 1945, suggested that the enemy was still full of

[35] Taylor, *Dresden*, pp. 410–414, 474–475.

fight; and anxieties for the future were exacerbated by fears that Hitler was developing new terror weapons. No one knew when the war would end. Allied combatants, prisoners, slave labourers and civilians in occupied countries were dying every day. The fact that Germany's leaders insisted on prolonging the struggle long after defeat was inevitable probably 'hardened the hearts of a war-weary, embittered Allied public'. More than 400 British bombers were lost between the Dresden raid and the end of the war; and the last V2 rocket fell on Whitechapel in East London as late in the war as 27 March, killing 134 civilians, many of them Jewish.[36]

Lastly, it needs to be mentioned that although Dresden doubtless contained many humane, non-Nazi citizens, its population in general was far from innocent of the regime's barbarous doctrines and practices. Victor Klemperer, a former professor who lost his appointment and only survived because he had an Aryan wife, chronicled in obsessive detail the humiliations, torment and eventual deportation of Dresden's Jews to the death camps, which few of their fellow-citizens did anything to obviate. Only about 100 of the city's 7,000 Jews survived the war and most of these, including Klemperer, owed their fortuitous escape to the chaos caused by the bombing.[37]

In Frederick Taylor's telling phrase the raids on Dresden went 'horribly right'. It was one of a sequence of massive raids that for various reasons caused most casualties, though proportionally the smaller city of Pforzheim experienced worse; on 23–24 February losing 17,600 citizens and 83 per cent of its built-up area. Dresden's destruction became notorious but it was not a special case in the context of the war. On the following night the unattractive industrial city of Chemnitz was attacked but, due to poor weather, little damage was inflicted. The two cities were part of the same system. As Michael Burleigh concludes, Dresden was not a war crime and should not be equated with Nazi crimes against humanity.[38]

It was to be expected, and entirely legitimate, that there should have been opponents and critics of strategic bombing. Some, including Bishop Bell and Vera Brittain, took a consistent near pacifist line that

[36] Ibid., p. 429, 460–461.
[37] Jeremy A. Crang, 'Victor Klemperer's Dresden', in Addison and Crang (eds.) *Firestorm* and Klemperer's, *To The Bitter End* (Weidenfeld & Nicolson, 1999), pp. 389ff.
[38] Taylor, *Dresden*, pp. 463, 475. Burleigh, *Moral Combat*, pp. 512–514.

the strategy of bombing non-combatants was morally wrong; and there were politicians on both the right and the left, such as Lord Salisbury and Richard Stokes, who should be placed in the same category. Scientists like A. V. Hill, Sir Henry Tizard and Sir Patrick Blackett were sceptical about the statistical and practical claims of the bombing supporters. Captain B. H. Liddell Hart, an influential journalist and author, completely changed his position, from believing that strategic bombing would be brief, brutal and decisive, to one of fierce opposition. This was based partly on moral grounds, but also on his realisation that if Germany were to be turned into a wasteland, Britain would be put to enormous expense in helping her rebuild.[39]

Historians cannot avoid hindsight, particularly in this case, in knowing when and how the war was won and how later revelations and controversies had developed. But in dealing with such an emotional and divisive topic as strategic bombing critics need to show understanding regarding the enormous stresses and uncertainties affecting decision-makers, who seldom had time for detached reflection about urgent decisions or what later generations might think. There is also the crucial question of personalities. It is hard to believe that either Neville Chamberlain or Lord Halifax would have persisted with an all-out bombing offensive. Indeed it is quite possible that under another leader Britain might have sought a negotiated peace with Germany. By contrast, this aggressive form of carrying the war to enemy homeland perfectly suited Churchill's temperament and, in this, it seems probable he received strong support from the majority of the nation, as well as from the War Cabinet in which all three major parties were represented; indeed the Liberal Party leader, Sir Archibald Sinclair, was Secretary of State for Air and thus directly responsible for the RAF.

An examination of the work of two very different modern critics will illustrate these problems. Max Hastings, a prolific and influential historian, published *Bomber Command* in 1979 and has since frequently commented on the subject in the media. He describes the last months of the war as 'the most futile and the most distasteful phase of the bomber offensive, and it was also that in which the airmen disastrously damaged their place in history'.[40] In his view, the razing of cities could do nothing to hasten the end of the war so the attack on Dresden lacked any strategic meaning. Harris should have been sacked

---

[39] Burleigh, *Moral Combat*, pp. 501–505.
[40] Hastings, *Bomber Command*, pp. 410–424. See especially p. 410.

for his continuing commitment to the area offensive. 'The obliteration of Germany's cities... is a lasting blot on the Allied conduct of the war and on the judgement of senior airmen'.[41] Hastings allowed that what the German people have suffered from the bombing would make them unwilling to embark upon another such national adventure, a very important consideration in the light of the 'stab in the back' myth, after 1918. But he still concluded that 'the cost of the bomber offensive in life, treasure and moral superiority over the enemy tragically outstripped the results that it achieved'.[42]

Hastings is of course entitled to his opinion that the Allies should have shown more compassion towards the German civil population, but his sharp comments on Harris and Bomber Command are undermined by three practical considerations. The war was by no means over in mid-February 1945 and how it ended would be of profound importance to the post-war world. Secondly, precision bombing was by no means as easy to implement as Hastings suggests and was certainly not regularly attained by the American bomber forces. Thirdly, Hastings relies too heavily on complex and ambivalent percentage statistics to argue that Harris deliberately chose not to attack select targets such as transportation and oil in the final months. On the contrary recent research shows that he *did* respond positively to prodding from the Air Staff. Hastings' criticisms rely too much on hindsight and their tone is too polemical.

A. C. Grayling is a modern philosopher who grew up after the war and from boyhood was fascinated by aircraft and the bombing, by both sides, of cities and their populations in the Second World War. In his book *Among the Dead Cities* (2006) he sketches the background to Bomber Command's operations, praising the skill and courage of the air crews and stressing that he is not equating Allied bombing with Nazi barbarism. He knows that strategic bombing was not a war crime in international law until after 1945, but argues that in his opinion it was a war crime nonetheless.

It seems strange that a philosopher who is not a historian would be examining this subject from a moral standpoint over sixty years after the event without placing it within the wider context of the war. In his concluding chapter entitled 'Judgement' he finds that the bombing of Hamburg was an 'area bombing atrocity' because it clearly targeted the civilian population of a large city that was carpet-bombed

[41] Ibid., p. 421.   [42] Ibid., p. 424.

at night essentially to fulfil Harris' aim of 'killing boche'. If this operation was '*unnecessary* and *disproportionate*, to use the language of just war theory, then how much more so were the attacks on Dresden, Hiroshima and Nagasaki?', and the indiscriminate bombing of other German towns in the last months of the war for no better reason than they had not been bombed before.[43] He argues that attempting to bomb specific targets was permissible, but that area bombings were as a whole morally criminal.

He then poses the stark questions: Was the Allied bombing necessary and was it proportionate? He answers both with emphatic negatives and raises further questions about the Allied flouting of humanitarian principles that people have been striving to enunciate as a way of controlling and limiting war. He answers his own question clearly. Was area bombing wrong? Yes, very wrong. He believes that the same moral judgement can be applied to Hamburg, Hiroshima and the World Trade Center ('9/11'). All were atrocities, consisting in deliberate mass murder of civilians to hurt and coerce the society they belonged to.

From a historian's viewpoint there seems to be little worth in passing these harsh moral judgements in distant hindsight and in a historical vacuum from the events that conditioned them. Britain had sought to avoid war and was not equipped to carry out strategic air operations before 1942. After years of failure in land operations and a desperate struggle to survive at sea, Britain and the United States at last gained dominance in the air over Germany in late 1944. Should they then have scaled down their attacks and confined them to targets where civilian losses would be light? Grayling's invocation of the just war concept of proportion is absurd in these circumstances. While it is true that Bomber Command dropped five or six times the tonnage of bombs on Germany than the latter did on Britain this was not due to restraint or moderation on the Nazis' part, but rather to the fact that they were forced to give priority to their Eastern Front and to home defence.[44]

---

[43] A. C. Grayling, *Among Dead Cities* (Bloomsbury, 2006), pp. 272–280; emphasis in the original.

[44] Grayling, *Among Dead Cities*, see especially pp. 272–280. Since I have criticised Max Hastings above it is only fair to note that he was 'irked by a philosopher's high-handed moral condemnation of wartime bombings' in reviewing Grayling's book in *Military History* 12 February 2006.

On a wider view, regrettable though later moralists may find it, Britain's decision to welcome the Soviet Union as an ally in June 1941, a helpful partner of Nazi Germany until brutally attacked, demonstrates that survival was given absolute priority over moral considerations. When, to the surprise of many Allied strategists, the Soviet Union survived the Nazi onslaughts of 1941 and 1942 and was eventually able to go over to the offensive, then it became a vital matter to force Germany to surrender as quickly as possible in the expectation of a long and terrible struggle to defeat Japan. If Germany had won the war then Grayling's strictures against area bombing might have led to war crimes charges against Churchill, Harris and other 'Bomber barons', but there would have been other far more serious consequences. Victory soon created enormous problems with the Soviet Union, but was infinitely better than defeat.

Bomber Command paid a high price for its offensive. From an all-volunteer force of 120,000 fliers, 55,575 were killed in action, nearly 10,000 were shot down and captured alive and another 8,000 seriously wounded.[45] The Command's reputation also suffered lasting damage for its original inflated claim that it could defeat Germany single-handed. Also in its concentration on the offensive against Germany, Bomber Command was sometimes insensitive to the needs of the other Services, giving the impression that these roles were tiresome diversions from its main objective. Even his strongest supporters allow that Harris could be inflexible and obstinate.

Nevertheless Bomber Command made an immense contribution to eventual victory in a number of ways. There was considerable hatred towards the enemy during the war and a demand for retaliation that Bomber Command was able to fulfil, particularly as Britain suffered a series of humiliating defeats with no prospect of victory in sight. Although these emotions were encouraged by propaganda, the reality of Nazi barbarism turned out to be far worse even than 'black propaganda' experts could imagine. Total wars for survival are not fought in an atmosphere of calm and objectivity, and non-militarist nations have to be encouraged to fight – and win. Most war-time hatreds quickly evaporate and are consequently hard to recapture by later historians.

Even Bomber Command's early ineffectual attacks had the significant advantage of showing German citizens that the Nazis could not

45 Burleigh, *Moral Combat*, p. 482.

protect them. Bombing could not break morale under such a repressive regime but it could gradually erode belief in victory.

When it became established after the war that, under Speer's management, German war production had, in some respects, actually increased from early 1943, this seemed to some critics further evidence of the failure of strategic bombing. But, as Adam Tooze has shown, the intensive bombing of the Ruhr between March and July 1943 effectively shattered Speer's plans, particularly in terms of quality. Moreover, bombing denied Germany the freedom to plan war production without interruption, causing such damage and delays that many factories had to be moved underground into disused mines and caves. By 1944 some two million soldiers and civilians were engaged in anti-aircraft defences – more than the total employed in the aircraft industry. By that stage in the war as much as 30 per cent of gun output and 20 per cent of heavy ammunition were diverted to anti-aircraft defences, and although Germany's aircraft production reached a peak in 1944, it still fell far short of the targets set. Richard Overy's remarkable conclusion is that bombing was 'much more effective than the Allies believed'.[46] In terms of the overall strategy agreed by the Allies, bombing did all that was asked of it. The *Luftwaffe* was driven on to the defensive; the enemy's transport system was disrupted; warships, submarines, the V-weapons research centre at Peenemünde were all successfully attacked from the air and the economy eroded to the point where the struggle could not be continued. In particular, both air and ground operations were crippled by lack of fuel.[47]

In conclusion, Germany lost the strategic initiative when forced to devote its main air effort and its great aircraft industry to producing day and night fighters for the defensive role over its cities. This success may be deemed the equivalent of a Second Front.[48] After the heroic defensive achievements of the 'finest hours' in 1940 and 1941, strategic bombing was Britain's most significant offensive contribution to victory over Germany.

[46] Richard Overy, *The Air War 1939–1945* (Europa, 1980), pp. 122–123.
[47] Ibid., p. 118.   [48] Carrington, *Soldier at Bomber Command*, p. 133.

7 THE TRANSFORMATION OF WAR ON THE WESTERN FRONT, 1914-1918

The nature of warfare on the Western Front experienced a remarkable transformation between 1914 and 1918. A largely static siege war, unanticipated by all but a few maverick thinkers, quickly set in, absorbing millions of soldiers whose daily needs were equivalent to those of great cities. Completely new, or relatively untried weapons – aircraft, submarines, tanks, poison gas – were introduced and had to be integrated into traditional arms and institutions. Communications of all kinds in the battle theatre witnessed impressive developments.

All these innovations had to be combined into weapons systems: in land operations entailing not only the co-operation of artillery, cavalry and tanks but also with the revolutionary new potential of aircraft. Some recent analysts have hailed these developments by the end of the war as the advent of 'modern', twentieth-century warfare. War on the Western Front changed almost beyond recognition between 1914 and 1918.

These revolutionary changes have been broadly acknowledged by military historians for at least a generation; their debates have moved on to more complex issues such as the speed at which innovations occurred.[1] In the case of Britain, however, there is still a great gulf between a small number of military historians and their followers, and the general public in understanding and accepting this transformation.

---

[1] See for example Robin Prior and Trevor Wilson, *Command on the Western Front* (Blackwell, 1992), Gary Sheffield, *Forgotten Victory. The First World War: Myths and Realities* (Headline, 2001) and Paddy Griffith, *Battle Tactics on the Western Front* (Yale University Press, 1994).

When these developments are more widely grasped it will probably not end criticism of such emotive topics as generalship, attrition and heavy losses, but it should cause them to be reviewed in a new light. How was it, for example, that the British 'donkeys' were able to win a decisive victory in 1918?

It is not difficult to understand why, in Britain, the Western Front is popularly viewed as an essentially unchanging, static war of attrition in 'the trenches', in which incompetent senior officers (notably the Commander-in-Chief, Sir Douglas Haig) failed to learn lessons from their futile offensives and continued, callously, to sacrifice their soldiers' lives in a long struggle that eventually petered out in a pyrrhic victory.

This negative interpretation owes much to the outpouring of war literature in the late 1920s and early 1930s. The most influential memoir writers and poets, such as Graves, Blunden and Sassoon, were not themselves deeply interested in technical and tactical innovations and their aim was essentially to convey the drama, hardships and suffering that they, and their fellow-soldiers, had experienced. This they achieved brilliantly, in works that have deservedly become classics. They are not at all to blame for not grappling with aspects of the war best left to the military professionals and historians.

More recently, however, popular historians and journalists, such as John Laffin, A. J. P. Taylor and Alan Clark, have reinforced earlier myths of 'butchers and bunglers', and of 'lions led by donkeys', without giving sympathetic attention to the problems that all the belligerents faced and their varying degrees of success in overcoming them. Other influential writers, approaching the war from the viewpoints of literature and culture, have gone further in contending that the war lies outside history altogether and has no historical meaning. Samuel Hynes actually presents this view in *A War Imagined* (1990), while the late Paul Fussell's very influential study, *The Great War and Modern Memory* (1975), stresses the futility of the conflict without examining any of the huge historical issues of its origins, conduct and outcome.[2]

The stage entertainment and later the film of *Oh! What a Lovely War* have been enormously popular since their first appearance in the 1960s. When every allowance is made for the facts that both were tragi-comic entertainments and overtly polemical in lauding the

---

[2] Samuel Hynes, *A War Imagined: The First World War and English Culture* (The Bodley Head, 1990), p. 455. Fussell's influence and limitations are discussed by Sheffield, *Forgotten Victory*, pp. 15–16.

'Tommies' as heroes while deriding the officer class as incompetent and callous snobs, they are still to be deplored from a historical viewpoint in conveying very little sense of chronological development and evading the rather important matter of the Entente's eventual victory. These stereotypes and clichés, reinforcing earlier myths for a new generation, were brilliantly underpinned by the television farce *Blackadder*. Private Baldrick and his pals are endlessly messed about by asinine commanders and cowardly staff officers until eventually sent 'Over the top' and into oblivion.

This is surely the key phrase for reinforcing the popular view of the essential nature of the war on the Western Front. The film clip, purportedly showing infantry going 'Over the top' on the British Army's worst day, 1 July 1916, was actually shot in re-enactment after the event, but it has become the iconic image encapsulating the essential horror of the war in the trenches. Like all such images it has a base in reality: tens of thousands of soldiers did advance into battle like this, but it is misleading in freezing a catastrophic moment for eternity. It obscures the fact that from a very unimpressive start in 1914 and slow progress over the next two years, the British Expeditionary Force did learn and implement 'lessons' at many levels and these had converted it into a very effective, 'modern' Army by the last year of the war, during which it played a leading role in securing victory.

Though well trained and with a phenomenal rate of infantry fire, the BEF at the outset of the war was small (six divisions) and underequipped for the mass operations of huge conscript armies. The outbreak of war also found the Army in a transitional stage between a colonial defence force and one capable of taking on a first-class European enemy. Each of the major arms still tended to behave like independent organisations with proprietary claims to certain weapons and styles of combat. Worse still, since a short, limited war was expected there were no plans for raising a conscript army or to provide munitions, weapons and equipment for a long war. In its early encounters with the enemy, for example, the BEF's artillery was seriously handicapped due to lack of telephones and more advanced observers. It was also short of ammunition of all calibres, and only the four sixty-pounders in each division could reach the enemy's 150-mm howitzers.[3] After the

---

[3] Shelford Bidwell and Dominick Graham, *Fire-Power: British Army Weapons and Theories of War 1914–1945* (Allen & Unwin, 1982), pp. 40, 62, 68 and Sheffield, *Forgotten Victory*, pp. 99–100.

march from the Aisne to the Channel coast and the heroic defence of Ypres at the end of 1914, the original BEF had virtually ceased to exist. The early battles of 1915 demonstrated that the Germans enjoyed a decisive advantage by being on the defensive in well-prepared positions. The BEF's early battles, Neuve Chapelle in March, followed by Aubers Ridge and Festubert in May, all began promisingly but showed the difficulty of converting a break-in to the enemy's defences into a breakthrough. Repeated attacks on unbroken defences resulted only in heavy casualties and a hardening of the trench stalemate. When the Germans went over to the offensive, using gas for the first time at Ypres in April 1915, they too failed to exploit their initial success.

The battle of Loos in late September 1915, the largest the BEF had fought to date, was a disaster, though in mitigation it must be noted that it was undertaken to support French offensives at Vimy and further south in Champagne. There was scant prospect of a breakthrough amid the coal mines and slag heaps north of Loos where German defences were strong. The four-day preparatory bombardment was ineffectual; there were still too few heavy howitzers and field guns, and dud shells littered the battlefield. Under Sir John French's incompetent command, Haig hoped to achieve surprise with the British first use of gas, released in clouds from cylinders, but this proved to be a fickle ally. Initial failure was exacerbated by the tragic sacrifice of two New Army divisions (21st and 24th), which were delayed in an exhausting approach march and then thrown into battle tired and unfed. Unready for battle and confused about the situation or what was expected of them, they were routed. Sir John French was held responsible and shortly afterwards was replaced by Haig as Commander-in-Chief. The battle, which continued into October, cost the BEF 50,000 casualties. Some 15,000 troops were killed or never heard of again – Rudyard Kipling's son John being among the missing.[4]

As Gary Sheffield remarks, the British experience in the year 1915 comes close to resembling the caricature sketched in *Oh! What a Lovely War*. The infantry was struggling to adapt to new conditions, under newly promoted officers still learning their roles, and inadequately supported by artillery that was desperately short of shells. The high command was reluctant to accept that the main lesson of the 1915

4 Bidwell and Graham, *Fire-Power*, pp. 77–79. Sheffield, *Forgotten Victory*, pp. 107–110.

battles was that the best hope of success lay in very brief 'hurricane' bombardments followed immediately by attacks to secure limited objectives. Nevertheless, the small-scale battles of 1915 witnessed the first steps, including the application of scientific methods to gunnery and the incorporation of aircraft into the land battle, which would produce a new style of modern warfare in 1917–1918.

The Somme campaign extended from 1 July into mid-November 1916, but in recent decades, particularly since the publication of Martin Middlebrook's *The First Day on the Somme* (Allen Lane, 1971), as discussed above, it is the first disastrous day that has become an obsessive landmark, used by the press and the media generally to excoriate the high command and the futile sacrifice of trench warfare. Much had been expected from the 'Big Push' to end the war, so disappointment at home was understandable. Nonetheless, modern obsession with this one disastrous day remains puzzling.

There is broad agreement about the reasons for failure on 1 July 1916. The long and intensive bombardment alerted the defenders and chewed up the ground but did not destroy their barbed wire and machine guns or smash their deep dug-outs. The infantry attacked in daylight, largely unprotected by smoke or covering fire, and were mown down, in some tragic cases before they had even crossed their own start line. In those few places where the enemy's front-line defences were breached, as by the 36th (Ulster) Division at Thiepval, reinforcements could not be brought up in time to hold the ground gained.

Contrary to popular belief, however, 1 July was not an unmitigated disaster. On the southern flank XV and XIII Corps took all their objectives. The German defences in this area were less formidable and the attackers were greatly aided by the outstanding success of the French Sixth Army on their right flank. Some of the successful British divisions (notably 18th and 30th) also employed an early version of the 'creeping barrage' that involved a curtain of shells moving ahead of the infantry at a pre-arranged rate of about 100 yards every three to five minutes.[5]

It was a tragedy that the high command, and Henry Rawlinson, Commander of the Fourth Army in particular, failed to exploit this

---

[5] Sheffield, *Forgotten Victory*, pp. 138–139. For the importance of the French contribution see William Philpott, *Bloody Victory: The Sacrifice on the Somme and the Making of the Twentieth Century* (Little, Brown, 2009), Chapter 5.

opportunity but instead persisted with costly attacks at Thiepval, Serre and other sectors where the defences remained largely intact.

The scale of disaster on 1 July was never repeated, but in the succeeding days (between 3 and 13 July) minor assaults resulted in a further 25,000 casualties. The next major offensive, however, on 14 July, showed that some lessons were being learnt: there was more careful planning for specific objectives, the approach march was undertaken by night, the bombardment lasted only a few minutes and the dawn attack achieved surprise. As Liddell Hart recalled 'This time grey-clad corpses outnumbered khaki ones on the battlefield'.[6] Unfortunately there was no consistent improvement or steady 'learning curve': for the remainder of the campaign too many attacks were hastily arranged, small-scale and poorly supported by artillery. Perhaps the most serious failing was that offensives, as at Mametz Wood and High Wood in July and August, were not co-ordinated with corps on either flank.[7]

Critics of the British high command, and the national war effort, should acknowledge that the conception, development and deployment of 'the tank' was an impressive innovation. Haig, who put considerable faith in this new weapon, had fifty at his disposal for their debut on 15 September 1916. It has been argued that Haig should have waited until he had many more, and more thoroughly tested, tanks available so as to achieve a greater shock effect. But it is clear in retrospect that he had no option: tanks might still contribute to an impressive advance in the September offensives, and, more importantly, only by demonstrating their value could he secure political commitment to future large-scale production and improvements.

Some rather hysterical reports greeted the debut of these fearsome monsters but, in truth, tanks were far from being a battle-winner in 1916. They were an infantry-support weapon whose role would be to crush wire, cross trenches, knock out machine-gun posts and protect the infantry from counter-attack. On their debut the few available tanks were spread across the attack sector in batches of three or four and given specific strongpoints as their targets. These cumbersome leviathans were slow (slower than infantry on the battlefield), very apt

---

[6] Sheffield, *Forgotten Victory*, p. 141. Basil Liddell Hart, *Memoirs*, Vol. I (Cassell, 1965), p. 24.
[7] Sheffield, *Forgotten Victory*, p. 141.

to get stuck or break down, nerve-wracking and exhausting for their crews, and vulnerable to enemy gunfire.[8]

In some sectors on 15 September, such as the Ginchy area east of Delville Wood, tanks either failed to make any impact, or even disrupted deployment. However, the four tanks assigned to the Flers area enjoyed a conspicuous and much publicised success. One tank, especially, became famous for crawling along the straggling village street accompanied by cheering infantry.

In reality, success owed at least as much to improved gunnery as to the tanks. Fourth Army's artillery had many more heavy guns and an ample supply of shells compared to 1 July. More than 1,500 guns supported the advance with much improved techniques: high explosive shells were used to smash the enemy's wire; gas shells were first used to neutralise his gunners and a creeping shrapnel barrage covered the infantry's advance. On the debit side this offensive had over-ambitious objectives and there was poor co-operation between infantry, artillery and tanks.

The winter of 1916–1917 witnessed remarkable progress in the British Army's willingness to learn lessons from the Somme campaign. Among the many manuals issued one of the most important was SS135 *Instructions for the Training of Divisions for Offensive Action*. This confirmed the key role of the creeping barrage, which must be followed closely by the assault troops. Further support in developing the offensive would be supplied by snipers, Lewis guns, Stokes mortars and smoke barrages. This was an important step towards co-ordinating the performance of all weapons, including tanks, on the battlefield. The basic infantry unit, the platoon, was also re-organised with the Lewis gun providing firepower and the pivot for its movement. By the beginning of 1917 the future shape of infantry tactics had been settled, and the artillery was undergoing technical reforms that would give it superiority over the Germans for the rest of the war.[9]

Haig and his senior commanders, Rawlinson and Gough, were open to serious criticisms for their conduct of the battle of the Somme. Haig continued to press for a breakthrough into open country, which was simply not an option given the depth of the German defences and

[8] Philpott, *Bloody Victory*, pp. 362–369. J. P. Harris, 'Haig and the Tank', in Bond and Cave (eds.) *Haig*.
[9] Griffith, *Battle Tactics*, pp. 76–788, 193. Bidwell and Graham, *Fire-Power*, pp. 111–115.

the logistical problems caused by even short advances. Nor, as Cambrai would show in 1917, did cavalry or tanks have the mobility and staying power to support an opening on a strategic level.

Nonetheless, much as it may pain the many critics of Haig and the Entente armies, military historians now tend to see the Somme campaign as a vital step in the attritional process that led inexorably to the defeat of Germany on the Western Front. One recent historian, Gary Sheffield, has termed the campaign 'a strategic success'; while another, taking full account of the important French contribution, has called it a 'Bloody Victory'.[10] By the end of 1916, taking into account their monumental failure at Verdun, Germany's military leaders had decided that their troops could not endure another such defensive battle on the Somme front. Accordingly in February and March 1917 they abandoned their positions and retreated to the newly fortified Hindenburg Line, perpetrating a barbaric scorched-earth policy in doing so.

The year 1917 can easily be depicted as an unimaginative continuation by Haig and his commanders of an attrition strategy that achieved little at a prohibitive cost. This impression is strengthened by focusing on the Third Battle of Ypres, which is almost invariably referred to in the media as 'Passchendaele', the final and most hellish phase of a campaign that ran from 31 July until early November. Even this notoriously wet and muddy campaign had a dry, hot spell in September when impressive progress was made, and the year as a whole witnessed developments in weapons and tactics that had been evident in embryo at the end of 1916.

The great Entente offensive at Arras in April and May 1917 has received remarkably little attention from historians or in the media, yet its opening showed great improvements compared with the first day of the Somme. After a five-day bombardment fourteen British divisions attacked on a front slightly shorter than that on the Somme. Employing a greater density of heavy guns with more reliable shells and a more sophisticated form of creeping barrage, Allenby's Third Army succeeded in neutralising the bulk of the German artillery. Another impressive feature was the expansion of ancient caves and tunnels under the city of Arras that afforded shelter to some 25,000 troops

---

[10] Sheffield, *Forgotten Victory*, p. 156. Philpott, *Bloody Victory*, p. 428: 'The war was far from over, but after the Somme there could only be one ultimate victor'.

and enabled them to move in security and secrecy close to the front line. In addition, for their brilliantly successful attack on Vimy Ridge, the Canadian Corps constructed twelve tunnels, the longest of over a mile, to bring their troops close to their jumping-off point for a surprise assault. A section of the tunnels at Vimy and part of the vast complex beneath Arras are open to the public – an enduring testament to the impressive mining and engineering skills used to offset the great advantage enjoyed by the German defenders.

As any visitor will appreciate immediately, the capture of Vimy Ridge was strategically important in giving the Allies a strong defensive position and extensive observation over the Douai Plain. This achievement, celebrated by Canadians ever since, has tended to overshadow the less dramatic successes of Third Army further south where, for example, XVII Corps advanced three and a half miles. On the first day alone Third Army and the Canadians took 9,000 prisoners. The British official historian would later describe 9 April 1917 as 'one of the great days of the War', yet very few people remember it now.

Unfortunately the BEF proved unable to exploit this successful opening by converting its break-in into a breakthrough. Dreadful weather, including heavy snow, hampered air reconnaissance, and the extent of the advance over churned up ground meant that the artillery could not be moved forward to prepare for the next attack before a new defence line was improvised.

The second phase of the battle beginning on 23 April was much less successful. Haig persisted in the battle until mid-May, mainly in an attempt to pin down German forces that would otherwise have been available to oppose Nivelle's over-publicised offensive on the Chemin des Dames. There were some striking tactical successes, such as the Royal Naval Division's capture of Gavrelle, but also disasters, such as 67 per cent losses in the battalion attacking Roeux without artillery cover, and the two battles at Bullecourt where Gough's errors in mishandling tanks and guns did much to sour Anglo-Australian relations. Arras demonstrated that there had been considerable improvements in British offensive skills, particularly in artillery, since the Somme, but there was still much to learn about the new tactical problems posed by more open warfare.[11]

---

[11] Sheffield, *Forgotten Victory*, pp. 162–166. For details of the improvements in gunnery see Griffith, *Battle Tactics*, pp. 85–86.

The capture of the Messines Ridge on 7 June 1917 by Plumer's Second Army was an outstanding set-piece victory with a limited objective. It opened up the southern flank of the enemy's formidable defences in the Ypres salient, but the major offensive was fatally delayed until 31 July, mainly for logistical reasons. Consequently this brilliant one-day victory has been largely eclipsed in the public memory by the dreadful conditions and disappointing outcome of the Third Ypres offensive.

General Plumer and his Chief of Staff 'Tim' Harington were justly renowned for the meticulous training and rehearsals they practised before their battles. Anthony Eden, the youngest brigade major on the Western Front, witnessed these preparations, including the construction of light railways to bring up ammunition for Second Army's 2,266 guns, and the digging of twenty-four tunnels under the enemy positions containing huge mines, nineteen of which were successfully detonated at 3.10 am on the morning of the attack. Eden took part in several studies and exercises before the battle in which Plumer invited questions, which he answered or noted, even from junior officers and other ranks.

Although the Germans had constructed sophisticated defences on the Messines Ridge these were largely destroyed by an eleven-day barrage pumping three and a half million shells into their positions. For once the cliché of an attack going 'like clockwork' was justified: aided by the devastating effects of the nineteen exploded mines, nine divisions swept through the defences and captured all the objectives within a few hours. The successful combination of artillery, infantry, tanks and mines was enhanced by the efforts of the Royal Flying Corps, which regained control over the battlefield after the recent dominance of Von Richthofen's 'Flying Circus'.[12]

The victory at Messines demonstrated the skill of Plumer's staff in overcoming deep enemy defences for a 'bite and hold' attack on a specific objective.

The much more ambitious Third Ypres campaign did not completely negate the progress made by the BEF in the past year, but it did demonstrate in terms of slow progress at enormous cost how much remained to be done to penetrate deep defences to secure distant objectives – in this case the crucial rail junction at Roulers.

---

[12] Sheffield, *Forgotten Victory*, pp. 167–171. For Eden's personal account of the meticulous preparations for the battle of Messines see Bond, *Survivors of a Kind*, pp. 151–153 and also Eden's memoirs *Another World 1897–1917* (Allen Lane, 1976).

It cannot be argued that the BEF's learning process was much developed during the Third Ypres campaign, but an objective survey suggests that progress made in co-operation between infantry, artillery, engineers and air forces was not forgotten. At the heart of the problem was the fact that the Ypres salient was most unsuitable terrain for a major offensive. The enemy had had three years to construct formidable defences on the low ground east of Ypres, and his artillery held a dominant position along the modest heights of the Passchendaele Ridge. The prospects of a breakthrough to reach open country suffered an early setback when a German spoiling attack in mid-July caused the long-planned amphibious assault on the Belgian coast to be abandoned. Three weeks of artillery bombardment subdued the enemy's guns behind the Ridge, but also shattered the fragile drainage system on the low-lying left flank where Gough's Fifth Army was ordered to make an ambitious advance on the first day. Haig probably erred in giving this task to the dashing Gough rather than the more methodical Plumer, but the former was unfortunate to encounter exceptionally wet weather from the outset and through the first half of August. Slow progress and heavy losses caused Haig to transfer the principal attacking role to Plumer's Second Army towards the end of August.

Plumer was doubly fortunate to be allowed three weeks to prepare the next battle and to do so in dry, sunny weather, but his main advantage over Gough lay in careful planning and employing 'bite and hold' tactics for limited objectives. On 20 September, protected by a tremendous barrage 1,000 yards deep, a spearhead of four divisions with a further seven in support, secured all their objectives in the battle of the Menin Road.

Plumer followed up this success with further limited advances in the battle of Polygon Wood (26 September), and Broodseinde (4 October), but then the very wet weather returned with the result that the final weeks of the campaign degenerated into an appalling muddy struggle. After costly attacks in late October and early November the Canadian Corps' heroic efforts succeeded in capturing the whole Passchendaele Ridge. Haig then halted the battle, several weeks too late to prevent the bitter controversy that has haunted the campaign ever since.[13]

[13] Griffith, *Battle Tactics*, pp. 86–89. For a comprehensive survey see Peter H. Liddle (ed.), *Passchendaele in Perspective: The Third Battle of Ypres* (Leo Cooper, 1997).

The BEF's tactical skills were again evident in the artillery's ability to subdue the enemy guns and the infantry's skill in defeating his counter-attacks, but tanks had been largely confined to the roads and made little impact. The outcome of so much effort was an anti-climax. The strategic objectives had not been achieved and no further advance was attempted. On the contrary, when the German offensive began on 21 March 1918 most of the ground won at such cost was abandoned.

The year ended more encouragingly with the outstanding success of Byng's Third Army on 20 November in dry, open country south of Cambrai. The battle, which also ended in anti-climax ten days later, is now chiefly remembered for the dramatic debut of tanks on a large scale, but arguably the artillery's role was even more important. Thanks to meticulous surveying, accurate maps, air photography and scientific location of hostile batteries, British guns could use 'predicted fire'. This signalled a momentous change in preparing for battle. It was no longer necessary to forfeit surprise by preliminary registration of targets; the bombardment could now open up as the infantry attack began. In this case surprise was also achieved by moving up the huge body of nearly 500 tanks by night and concealing them in dense woodland. With a huge advantage in artillery, approximately 1,000 against 150, the enemy batteries were silenced while the tanks, crawling forward along specifically prepared lanes, smashed the wire and crossed the trenches. An unprecedented advance of five or six miles was made, but by the end of the first day momentum was already waning. By nightfall only 297 tanks were still operational and their crews were exhausted. Numerous tanks had been destroyed by field guns firing at short range, notably at the strongly defended village Flesquières, which in effect delayed the advance towards the critical feature of the Bourlon Ridge. This dominating ground was never fully captured. There appeared to be a fleeting opportunity for a break-out towards Cambrai, but tanks lacked the mobility and endurance for this task. The concentration of cavalry was held too far back and some heroic efforts, such as that of the Fort Garry Horse, which penetrated to Rumilly well beyond the St Quentin Canal, failed for lack of support.

The British advance on the first day could be seen as a further development of the 'bite and hold' tactics that had worked so well at Messines. Unfortunately the attackers lost the initiative in the attrition of the following days, particularly around the village of

Bourlon and its wooded ridge, while the rear areas were poorly pre-pared against counter-attack. Not for the first time the Germans quickly recovered from the shock and the loss of their forward defences, rushed forward reserves and recovered most of the ground lost ten days earlier.[14]

The British government had ordered the ringing of church bells to celebrate the victory on 20 November but the rejoicing had been pre-mature. The battle of Cambrai suggested that there had been encourag-ing improvements after the terrible attrition at Ypres, but reserves had been used up and the solution had still not been found to maintaining the momentum once the initial assault slowed down. Fortunately for the Entente, the Germans failed even more dramatically in this respect in 1918.

By the end of 1917 most of the components of modern warfare, or 'deep battle', were in place, with the combination of air power and artillery the most important facet. It is not necessary to claim that Britain led the way in all these developments; given her very small Army and lack of heavy guns in 1914 it is not surprising that she lagged behind the French, for example, in artillery tactics and behind the Germans in the use of stormtroopers and sophisticated defensive methods. Nevertheless the BEF had made strenuous efforts to learn from its mistakes in battle and to profit from expert scientific and engineering help. Although there were dips in the 'learning curve' in 1917 and 1918, by the final year of the war the BEF had reached a plateau of professional achievement in the combination of air and ground forces that would enable it to play a leading role in winning victory on the Western Front.[15]

The role of the Royal Flying Corps (re-named the Royal Air Force on 1 April 1918) had made amazing progress in both size and operational duties since 1914. Its observation role, always of prime importance, had been technically primitive even as late as the battle of the Somme, when pilots had either to land to report on enemy posi-tions, or drop containers onto marked squares. Yet by June 1917 at Messines, Plumer's headquarters deployed no fewer than 280 ground

[14] Sheffield, *Forgotten Victory*, pp. 181–184. Bidwell and Graham, *Fire-Power*, pp. 9–3, 129–135.

[15] Griffith, *Battle Tactics*, pp. 153–155. Jonathan Bailey, 'The First World War and the Birth of Modern Warfare', in MacGregor Knox and Williamson Murray (eds.), *The Dynamics of Military Revolution* (Cambridge University Press, 2001).

wireless stations to receive counter-battery information from aircraft, and it was also able to co-ordinate low-level air attacks against enemy infantry. Another important role was to disrupt enemy transport behind the battle area. In broad, strategic terms it was abundantly clear by the last year of the war that air dominance – if not complete command – over the battle area was vital to the success of the ground forces. Germany had enjoyed brief periods of air superiority in 1916 and 1917 but Britain and her allies had a clear advantage in 1918.[16]

The growing technical complexity of the war is evident in the enormous growth of the specialist organisations. For example, the Royal Engineers grew from 24,000 to 357,000; the Ordnance Corps from 2,500 to 39,000; the Machine Gun Corps from 50,000 (when formed in 1915) to 124,000. The Tank Corps from its inception to 28,000; and the Royal Flying Corps (and RAF) from 1,200 to 144,000. Most significant of all the Royal Artillery grew from 94,000 in 1914 to 549,000 in 1918; that is it more than doubled the size of the whole BEF in the first months of the war.[17]

These remarkable developments did not mean that combat had become easier or casualties lighter. Three vital considerations continued to militate against a clear solution to the semi-siege conditions on the Western Front. First, the communication of orders and information up and down the lengthy chain of command remained slow and ponderous due, above all, to the vulnerability of signal cables in the battle area. Secondly, movement of supplies, ammunition and artillery beyond the railhead was still heavily dependent on horses and mules. Consequently, even in the German breakthrough in March 1918 and the Allied advance to victory between August and November, artillery could only support the vanguard of infantry, tanks and cavalry by the slow restoration of communications and accumulation of ammunition. Lastly, to the very end, the key element at the front remained the 'poor, bloody infantry', leaving the relative security of the trenches to face the hazards of grenades, poison gas, machine guns, shells and even the new menace of direct attack from the air. Advancing in itself was not a panacea. Britain and her allies suffered a rate of casualties in the

[16] Griffith, *Battle Tactics*, pp. 155–157. Bidwell and Graham, *Fire-Power*, pp. 143–145.
[17] Mike Senior, 'Learning Curves and Opportunity Curves on the Western Front', *Stand To!*, 93 (January 2012), pp. 11–14.

victorious advance of 1918 comparable to the notorious losses during the Third Ypres campaign in the previous year.[18]

The transient success of what proved to be the final German offensives in the West in March, April and May and the shock waves they caused in Paris and London should not be underestimated. The Entente was briefly in extreme danger. But the eventual outcome, clear by 18 July when the French Tenth Army successfully counter-attacked on the Marne, was that irreplaceable casualties, a slump in morale and Ludendorff's loss of nerve meant that Germany was now doomed to eventual defeat. On the Entente side the political leaders were mostly slow to realise that the tide had turned. Marshal Foch's appointment, to co-ordinate the Allied armies, though initially seen primarily as a propaganda boost for Allied unity, proved to be of great significance in permitting a flexible strategy of alternating attacks across the whole Western Front. Furthermore, the British Army and Air Forces, with Dominions' divisions and corps playing a prominent role, began to demonstrate the value of the long and uneven learning process. These improvements included the selection of highly competent commanders and staffs, greater uniformity in training and doctrine, and the operational skills to gain battlefield superiority by means of close air–ground co-operation.

On 4 July 4th Australian Division captured the village of Hamel, just south of the Somme, and the well-defended higher ground above in just over an hour. This operation resembled Messines on a smaller scale: a carefully planned attack with a limited objective that succeeded brilliantly. The date (American Independence Day) was also significant in that, overriding Pershing's reluctance to allow American units to be subordinated to Allied commanders, four infantry companies of US 33rd Division took part. A thorough post-battle study, disseminated throughout the BEF, stressed that success was due to careful planning, secrecy and the fine performance of all the arms involved, including tanks and British and Australian gunners. The report also stressed the close cohesion between machine guns, artillery, tanks and the RAF. For this relatively modest operation the Australian Corps could call on more than 300 field guns and howitzers that fired a massive bombardment precisely at the time the assault began. Not all subsequent attacks followed this pattern and not all went so smoothly,

---

[18] Bidwell and Graham, *Fire-Power*, p. 132.

the objectives all quickly overrun with fewer than a thousand casualties. But Hamel did demonstrate the value of the all-arms system now available.[19]

On 8 August on the flat, open country east of Amiens there began a series of skilfully orchestrated battles that heralded Germany's defeat on the Western Front. Ludendorff suffered a nervous collapse and recorded the defeat as 'the black day of the German Army in the history of the war'.[20] Haig correspondingly realised, particularly in view of the unusually heavy haul of prisoners, that the war could be won that autumn. In this he was remarkably prescient. The battle of Amiens witnessed a striking turnaround in Allied fortunes. The German defences were unusually weak, and lightly held by only about 37,000 troops against 100,000 Allies. Fourth Army's attack was led by the Australian and Canadian Corps, but British and French infantry were also heavily involved on the flanks. As on the eve of the Cambrai battle, about 550 tanks were brought up in secrecy for a dawn attack, and almost complete surprise was achieved. A clever signals deception plan enabled the Canadian Corps to move to the Amiens area while the enemy believed it was still near Ypres. Nearly all the German guns had been precisely identified in advance and the majority were destroyed within a few hours. The attackers advanced up to eight miles on the first day, knocked out 450 enemy guns and inflicted about 27,000 casualties.[21]

Impressive though the victory on 8 August and successive days had been it did not lead to a complete breakthrough. German resistance was quickly reorganised and their anti-tank fire was remarkably effective. Quite apart from the exhaustion of their crews and mechanical failures tank strength declined rapidly: only 145 were in action on the second day, 85 on the third, 38 on the fourth and 6 on the fifth. The advance was wisely halted for rest and reorganisation while the enemy was pushed back on other sectors of the front.[22]

[19] For the German offensives in March and April 1918 and the brilliant Allied victory at Hamel on 4 July see Sheffield, *Forgotten Victory*, pp. 188–198.

[20] Philpott, *Bloody Victory*, pp. 517–536. See in particular 'The Black Day of the German Army', p. 519.

[21] Sheffield, *Forgotten Victory*, pp. 198–205. Philpott, *Bloody Victory*, p. 524: 'In four days his (Foch's) Anglo-French forces had retaken more ground than they had managed in four and a half months of 1916'.

[22] Bidwell and Graham, *Fire-Power*, p. 137.

Command of the air had been a vital factor in the victory at Amiens. On the first day thick cloud hampered liaison between aircraft and tanks, but on successive days the attack fighters played a vital role in destroying anti-tank guns. Aircraft spotting for the artillery reported to a wireless centre at corps headquarters that co-ordinated low-level air operations as well as artillery support. Apart from the lack of wireless telephony sets in the tanks to communicate with aircraft, guns, tanks and artillery could all be linked by wireless. This was an outstanding example of technical progress that was surprisingly neglected after 1918.[23]

In the remainder of August and through September a series of well-orchestrated advances kept the enemy off balance and recovered nearly all the ground lost in the German spring offensive. The formidable Hindenburg Line defences were breached at the end of September more easily and with fewer casualties than had been expected.

These operations, during the final 100 days, demonstrate remarkable improvements in Allied command and staff organisation, which had not been achieved earlier. Some of the key aspects were: the refusal to reinforce failure and the ability to maintain operational tempo by switching the fronts of attacks, which required staff work and logistics of a high order. Not least impressive was the devolution of decision-making to the level where commanders could react promptly to tactical opportunities. At corps level, for example, compare Sir Walter Braithwaite's handling of IX Corps with standard procedures in 1916. Braithwaite told his divisional commanders what he wanted them to do, left them to work out how to do it, and then provided everything they needed to put their plans into practice. This did not of course guarantee success, given the unavoidable friction of battle, but it was a huge improvement.

The final weeks of war witnessed steady Allied progress in open country, but this term is deceptive. The old battlefields proved difficult to cross and small pockets of the enemy stubbornly defended rivers, canals and other strongpoints. A dramatic breakthrough never occurred; indeed over the last three months the Allies' advance averaged only one mile per day. Tanks were too slow and unreliable to press the retreating enemy, and heavy artillery was unsuited to the pursuit.

[23] Ibid., pp. 144–145.

The much derided cavalry played an important part in reconnaissance and harrying the rearguards, but Haig now had only a reduced Cavalry Corps of some 14,000 troopers. In these fluid conditions heavy bombardments were seldom necessary; the main duties in the dogged pursuit, often in poor weather, fell to infantry, field artillery and aircraft.

Critics have suggested that most of the credit for British victories in the final phase really belongs to the elite infantry of the Canadian and Australian Corps. Certainly both corps were excellent: their soldiers were all volunteers who were relatively fresh and whose morale was high, as was to be expected of homogeneous organisations proudly representing their emergent nations. They were also led by first-class commanders in Sir Arthur Currie and Sir John Monash respectively. They were certainly responsible for outstanding military feats such as the Australian 2nd Division's capture of Mont St Quentin on 1 September 1918. But the best ten British divisions, in Peter Simkins' authoritative judgement, performed at least as well, if not better, than these Dominions' divisions in the final 100 days.[24]

That the whole BEF had by 1918 attained a high level of professionalism is borne out by the remarkable achievement of 46th (North Midland) Division in forcing a crossing of the St Quentin Canal on 29 September. The canal, about 35 feet wide, 50 feet deep and with very steep banks, was impassable for tanks and a daunting obstacle for infantry. An Australian–American assault on the canal near Bellicourt was checked with heavy losses, mainly because a gap had developed between the creeping barrage and the infantry. At Bellenglise British IX Corps relied on a surprise bombardment by an enormous concentration of heavy guns, followed by a direct assault by 46th Division's infantry.

A spectacular success was achieved due to accurate intelligence, heavy shelling and the dash of the infantry in seizing the bridge at Riqueval. This division had performed badly at Gommecourt on 1 July 1916 and was in no way rated as elite, yet it had proved more than a match for the determined defenders in an almost impregnable position.[25]

---

[24] John Bourne suggests that British and Australian generals had more in common by 1918 than Dominion stereotypes have allowed – see his essay 'The BEF's Generals'. In the final phase of the war Peter Simkins argues that the ten best British divisions were at least as good as the leading Dominions' divisions – see his contribution to Paddy Griffith (ed.), *British Fighting Methods in the Great War* (Frank Cass, 1996), pp. 50–69.

[25] Sheffield, *Forgotten Victory*, pp. 209–210.

In his study the *First World War* (1998) the late Sir John Keegan was dismissive of some younger historians who, he thought, were wasting their energy in trying to show that the BEF's early failures had resulted in a learning process that had borne fruit in the eventual victory.[26] Sir John was right of course to argue that there was no complete solution to the material and tactical conditions that had resulted in such heavy casualties. But he was surely wrong to underrate the remarkable advances achieved by the British forces and to denigrate the efforts of younger scholars to chart this progress. From the small and under-equipped BEF of 1914, Haig's armies had expanded to sixty divisions and more than two million troops. There were spectacular developments in all the traditional arms (especially artillery) and the completely new one of tanks. Beyond all specific developments the BEF developed an all-arms weapons system that, allied to close collaboration with the air forces, surpassed any equivalent achievement by either its allies or its enemies. It must be stressed that the learning process was far from simple or consistent: different arms developed at varying speeds; frictions were not easily overcome; and limitations were still evident in 1918.[27] There was also an element of luck insofar as the British and Dominions forces reached a peak of offensive power just after the final German offensive had exhausted her reserves and sapped her troops' morale.

Statistics can never provide the complete answer, but they do show that British forces played the leading role in the final months of the war. Between mid-July and the Armistice the French, Americans and Belgians together took 196,000 prisoners and 3,775 guns, whereas, with smaller forces, Haig's armies captured 188,700 prisoners and 2,840 guns. As Professor Gary Sheffield concludes, it was 'by far the greatest military victory in British history', but one that a substantial section of the public has either forgotten or has never heard of.[28]

---

[26] John Keegan, *First World War* (Pimlico, 1999), p. 315.

[27] Jonathan Boff, *Winning and Losing on the Western Front* (Cambridge University Press, 2012).

[28] Sheffield, *Forgotten Victory*, pp. 220, 234. John Bourne reaches an even sharper conclusion regarding Haig's reputation – 'The scale of his victories was the greatest in British military history. His countrymen have never forgiven him', *Britain and the Great War*, p. 174.

8 THE BRITISH ARMY'S LEARNING PROCESS IN THE SECOND WORLD WAR

In some respects the British's Army's trajectory, in the sense of developing operational skills, was similar in the two world wars. It entered both major European conflicts at their outset and, in comparison with both allies and enemies, was small and under-equipped. It suffered a series of reverses, retreats and outright defeats, worse in the later war, but also learnt from these experiences to become more effective and more professional in the second half of both wars. But there was also a huge contrast, which makes comparison of the learning processes difficult. In the second war the Army confronted the main enemy (Germany) in the principal theatre, North-West Europe, only briefly in 1940 and at greater length in 1944–1945 when it became the junior partner to the United States. Moreover though still stubborn and skilful in defence, the *Wehrmacht* was suffering devastating losses in the vastly larger struggle on the Eastern Front. Consequently, in sharp contrast to 1914–1918, the British Army never became the principal Service between 1939 and 1945 and played a far less dominant role in the outcome. Moreover, although the Army fought in numerous and varied theatres in both wars, there was no doubt, particularly after 1915, that it was on the Western Front that the war would be decided and that Britain must make her main effort there, no matter how high the cost. For the strategic reasons mentioned above this did not turn out to be the case after May 1940, so the Army had to adjust to remarkably differing conditions in the Middle East (especially North Africa), Italy and North-West Europe. This latter consideration, and the comparatively small scale of Britain's land forces, made it harder to evolve in the spectacular ways witnessed in 1916–1918, but this also helps to explain why there has been far less criticism of the slow pace of adaptation and development in professional skills, particularly all-arms co-operation in battle, between 1939 and 1945.

The ill-fated campaign in France in 1939–1940 revealed that many lessons of the First World War had been neglected or experience not built upon. This was mainly due to political decisions such as ruling out the possibility of commitment to a Continental War during the prevalence of the 'Ten Year Rule' until 1933, which ensured that the Army's principal role would revert to imperial policing and imperial defence. But even more influential than strategic priorities was the profound political belief that the British people must never again be subjected to a Continental blood-letting like that of 1914–1918.

The Army's leadership in the 1930s may be criticised for not doing more to challenge inadequate budgets, slow progress in weapons development (especially as regards tanks and mechanical vehicles) and the almost total absence of large-scale manoeuvres or service training with higher formations. This lack of experience or recent training was a serious handicap for officers who suddenly found themselves commanding divisions and corps on the outbreak of war.

In the autumn of 1939 the five regular divisions of the Home Army, now styled the Field Force, were transferred to France smoothly and without enemy interference, in the months before May 1940, were followed by five territorial divisions and three labour divisions, not regarded as suitable for combat. As by far the senior partner in numbers of divisions, and because it was defending its own homeland, France largely determined Allied strategy. Sheltering behind the Maginot Line, in an almost entirely defensive position, the Allies would slowly build up their forces for an eventual controlled, methodical advance. During this first phase the Field Force would prepare static defences along a vulnerable sector of the Franco-Belgian frontier on the assumption that Germany would soon launch an offensive. To many British veterans, who had experienced these unappealing lowlands before, the early months of the conflict seemed uncannily reminiscent of the First World War show, though this time the German offensive was surprisingly delayed.

This unimaginative Allied strategy, which assumed that time was on their side, neglected ample opportunities to learn lessons from the new style of combat demonstrated by the *Wehrmacht* in Poland.

Reports stressed that victory had been won by the bold, deep thrusts of the Panzer spearhead; the close support of the *Luftwaffe* and its success in destroying the enemy's command and control system; and, most importantly, the rapid tempo of German operations both in the air and on the ground.

The unexpected breathing space afforded by the months of 'phoney war' was not well used by the Allies. In an atmosphere of complacency and deepening boredom there was little realistic training or all-arms practice: many British soldiers later recalled that they had not seen a single tank in this period. An unusually severe winter from January 1940 onwards, punctuated by frequent false alarms of imminent enemy attack that entailed manning the forward defences, had a further depressing effect on morale.[1]

The disaster that overtook the Allies in the days after 10 May was mainly due to French political and strategic errors at the highest levels, magnified by the rapid abandonment of the Meuse defences and the disintegration of the command structure. The commanders of the Field Force could later claim that they had been let down by their allies (especially the Belgians), and had not been defeated in a significant battle. This was true up to a point, but it did not take account of numerous British failures. Lord Gort's personal place in the Allied command structure was complicated and ambivalent; it quickly led to bickering through the winter and breakdown when hostilities began. His resort to his right of appeal to the British government in disagreement with French strategy was proved justified by subsequent events, but it exacerbated inter-Allied discord. British and inter-Allied communications were appallingly bad: radios were desperately few and unreliable and there had been very little practice in their use; telephone lines could often not be laid or maintained in combat conditions; and dependence on local post offices proved an egregious mistake. Lord Gort compounded an already acute problem of communications by moving to an advance command post where he was at times out of touch with his own headquarters. Indeed Allied communications were like a disturbed ants' nest in the critical days after 10 May, with officers trying to make personal contact on congested roads packed with refugees, and with no one in overall control.[2]

[1] Brian Bond, *British Military Policy*. David French, *Raising Churchill's Army: The British Army and the War Against Germany 1919–1945* (Oxford University Press, 2000), pp. 165–166, 179–181.
[2] Bond, *Britain, France and Belgium*. Bidwell and Graham, *Fire-Power*, pp. 209–214.

The superior tactical and higher training of the *Wehrmacht* in peace time paid immediate dividends. A key factor in the success of Blitzkrieg was that its relentless drive at high tempo disrupted the Allied command, communications and intelligence networks. In the restricted battle theatre of France and Belgium, given the fragility of those nations' political systems and mutual suspicions, there was neither time nor space to recover from the paralysis, defeatism and quest for scapegoats that rapidly set in.[3]

The effects of the rapid advance of the *Wehrmacht* was magnified by the dominance of the *Luftwaffe* in support of ground operations. The almost complete failure in Britain to develop Army–Air co-operation in the inter-war decades was now brutally exposed. British Air Forces in France, under Gort's control, consisted of an Air Component for the Field Force of only five Lysander recce squadrons, four Blenheim bomber squadrons and six Hurricane fighter squadrons. In addition there was an Advanced Air Striking Force (AASF) of ten squadrons of Battle light bombers, placed under French control. These proved to be virtually useless against German fighters and anti-aircraft guns. In comparison the *Luftwaffe* deployed some 1,000 fighters and 1,700 bombers.

There was widespread bitterness among survivors from Dunkirk that the Field Force had been badly let down by the RAF. This was justified in so far as during the retreat to the coast British soldiers saw the skies dominated by the *Luftwaffe* with scarcely an RAF fighter to be seen. In mitigation it can be pointed out that the RAF suffered horrendous losses in trying to prevent the enemy crossing the Meuse, and in defence of the Dunkirk perimeter and the Channel crossings. Nevertheless the charges must stand to the extent that Bomber Command had no policy for close ground support, preferring to attack targets in the Ruhr; and the system for the co-ordination of fighter attacks at airfields was cumbersome in the extreme. Three hours was rated a good response time between request to attack a specific target and action. Here was a case where Army liaison officers at the AASF headquarters did learn lessons in Army–Air co-operation that would eventually pay dividends in North Africa.[4]

Considering that Britain had first developed tanks in the First World War and led the world in theories of armoured warfare in

---

[3] French, *Raising Churchill's Army*, pp. 174–177.
[4] Bidwell and Graham, *Fire-Power*, pp. 213–214.

the 1920s, she was surprisingly unprepared in this respect in 1939. The soon-to-be-famous 7th Armoured Division was preparing for war against the Italians in Egypt, but 1st Armoured Division at home was far from ready for war in 1939. It began to arrive piecemeal in France only in late May 1940 when it was too late to influence the outcome of the battle. The Field Force's slow-moving infantry support tanks were unsuitable for use in the chaotic retreat to the Channel coast. A small-scale action around the western fringes of Arras on 21 May, later dignified by the term 'counter-attack', gave a hint of what might have been had even one complete armoured division been available. A tiny improvised force composed essentially of two territorial infantry battalions and seventy-four tanks, without air cover, caught Rommel's 7th Panzer Division on the move, ahead of its supporting guns and infantry. The German tanks were scattered as 'Frankforce' made progress round the south-west of the city. By the end of the day the British forces were exhausted and the German order of battle was quickly restored. Psychologically the attack was successful out of all proportion to its scale because the enemy high command, and Hitler himself, were expecting a much larger Allied counter-offensive, which never came.[5]

It must be stressed that despite a confused command system, poor communications and inadequate air cover, the Field Force performed well in its advance to the Dyle Line and its initial resistance to the advance of Army Group B, which had only three Panzer divisions. Later the British part in the improvised defence of the shrinking Dunkirk perimeter was resolute and impressive. Between these episodes, however, the retreat to the coast was, to put it mildly, disorganised. Lacking most of its transport and, in some cases its officers, the battalions and smaller groups made their own way back as best they could in a desperate effort of *sauve qui peut*, which was mercifully eclipsed in the public memory by the heroics of the evacuation.

In the immediate aftermath of Dunkirk there was little leisure or inclination to digest and implement the lessons of the shattering experience at the hands of an enemy markedly superior in most aspects of modern warfare. The Field Force had lost, or been forced to abandon, nearly all its guns, tanks, lorries and heavy equipment. The large number of evacuated troops did not constitute an army capable of holding a line against an invasion that seemed imminent.

[5] See my essay on the Arras operation pp. 61–84 in *Old Battles and New Defences* (Brassey's, 1986).

Even after the immediate danger of invasion had passed, however, there was a marked reluctance to undertake a radical overhaul of doctrine, training and organisation with a view to making the Army more effective in the combined employment of artillery, tanks, motor transport, aircraft and wireless communications. There was admittedly some confusion as to what the main lessons were, and it would not be frivolous to summarise the views of some senior officers like Brooke (a corps commander in 1940) and Pownall (Gort's Chief of Staff) as 'don't risk another Continental war with the Germans without an overwhelming numerical and material superiority'. Churchill, too, would underwrite this pessimistic attitude, founded on the belief that the Germans were superior as individual solders and in their military system. Consequently, some senior officers sought refuge in complacency, and in lessons that did not require an admission of past errors or the need for drastic changes. Thus the defeat was described as due to special circumstances that were unlikely to recur.[6]

Another evasive answer, though based on a good deal of truth, was that Britain had been let down by its allies: France for broad strategic and political failings; and Belgium for suddenly ceasing to fight without due warning on 27 May, thus exposing the Field Force to annihilation. Needless to say, these former allies both made similar accusations against Britain's political and military leaders. A more far-reaching explanation and excuse was that Germany's victory was due largely to a huge superiority in weapons and equipment, notably armoured vehicles and aircraft. British analysts considerably over-estimated Germany's material superiority, for example in tanks, and admitted only much later that overall the Allies enjoyed approximate parity in terms of divisions and the quality of weapons deployed.[7] Material advantages certainly counted, but the fundamental reasons for the Germans' success lay in superiority in doctrine, operational strategy and the close co-ordination of their ground and air forces. These lessons were not fully grasped and certainly not implemented to any degree in 1940, so that the shock of crushing defeats at German hands had to be experienced over again in North Africa in 1941 and 1942.

In the global context of the Second World War the North African theatre now seems peripheral. But between mid-1940 and mid-1943 it was the British Army's principal commitment and one that

---

[6] French, *Raising Churchill's Army*, pp. 194–195.
[7] B. H. Liddell Hart, *History of the Second World War* (Cassell, 1970), pp. 65–86.

dominated media coverage – radio, newspapers and above all newsreels – for a public avid for the latest information about Benghazi, Beda Fomm, Tobruk and El Alamein – but was less well informed about the titanic struggle taking place on the Eastern Front.

The vast distances, extreme climatic conditions and sparse population gave the Desert War a romantic appeal to civilians at home as an almost ideal campaigning area where military skills and courage were at a premium without the moral dilemmas and ideological issues prevalent in urbanised Europe. But, as has been shown in an earlier chapter, combat conditions were far from romantic or 'cushy', imposing terrible strains and hardship on all the belligerents and, in particular, presenting gigantic challenges for supplies of all kinds.

Britain had had initial advantages in its huge base facilities around Cairo and from its military training in Egypt in the 1930s, yet in the broad consensus of historians its multi-national forces fared badly once a small *Wehrmacht* contingent arrived to reinforce the Italians early in 1941. The Germans manoeuvred in concentrated formations so that tanks, guns and motorised infantry could all support each other without the need for redeployment. Isolated British columns were frequently overrun by a whole division. As Lord Carver summed up, the main British weakness was 'the failure to develop tactics for a concentrated attack employing tanks, artillery and infantry in depth on a narrow front'.[8] British tanks repeatedly charged at the enemy on a broad front to be destroyed by his tanks or, more often, anti-tank guns. British commanders did better when operating on a narrow front with a clear objective and infantry as the main arm. 'It was a fluid, open battle in the flat desert that baffled them'.[9]

These weaknesses were not apparent in the initial, brilliantly successful campaign against the Italians. Between 9 December 1940 and 7 February 1941 Lieutenant General Sir Richard O'Connor's forces, though heavily outnumbered by the Italians advanced 500 miles, inflicted 13,000 casualties, took more than 100,000 prisoners and 1,000 guns. O'Connor's force of two divisions was well trained, entirely motorised and possessed superior tanks and guns. Italian doctrine put

---

[8] Bidwell and Graham, *Fire-Power*, pp. 224–226. Lord Carver is quoted on p. 225. The authors' chapter 'The Sand Model' provides an excellent survey of the technical and tactical problems of the Desert War. See also E. K. G. Sixsmith, *British Generalship in the Twentieth Century* (Arms and Armour Press, 1970), Chapter 11.

[9] Ibid., p. 225.

the emphasis on defensive fire rather than movement, and their lack of motor transport placed them at a critical disadvantage. Moreover intercepted radio traffic revealed that the Italians were unable to interfere effectively with the British advance, thus permitting O'Connor to cut across the cord of Cyrenaica and capture the bulk of the enemy's Tenth Army at Beda Fomm.

This dramatic and relatively easy victory had some unfortunate consequences. It convinced many armoured corps officers that dispersal could bring important tactical benefits, because concentrated forces were easily spotted from the air and, more importantly, that battles could be won by manoeuvre alone. It would take more than a year of painful experience for the British to learn how to operate tanks and artillery within an armoured division; for infantry to co-operate more closely with tanks; and for anti-tank guns to be the principal counter to enemy tanks.

Although there was some understanding that risks taken against the defensive-minded Italians would be dangerous against the Germans, the boldness, speed, aggressiveness and sheer operational flair of Rommel's leadership repeatedly surprised and disorganised his opponents. In March and April 1941 the Axis forces drove their enemy back to the Egyptian frontier, investing Tobruk in the process. In May and June two British counter-attacks (codenamed Brevity and Battleaxe) were defeated. On a much greater scale, Operation Crusader in November and December was more successful in revealing the debit side of Rommel's inferior logistics and excessive risk-taking. The Axis forces lost more heavily and Tobruk was relieved. But so remarkable was the enemy's resilience that another counter-offensive was launched in January 1942 that drove the Allies back to the Gazala Line.[10]

It is astonishing that for most of 1941–1942 the German Africa Corps consisted of only three divisions: 15th and 21st Panzer and 90th Light Division. From August 1941 Rommel's command was expanded with the addition of two Italian Corps to form the Panzer Group Africa. In sharp contrast to the greater continuity and combat experience enjoyed by Rommel and his German divisions, the British Western Desert Force (renamed Eighth Army from September 1941), put twenty divisions or their equivalents into action under six different commanders. Only four of these divisions fought in more than two battles.

---

[10] French, *Raising Churchill's Army*, pp. 214–217.

The superiority of the Axis forces was most evident in their combined arms tactics. Anti-tank guns (notably their 50-mm and 88-mm guns) were used well forward with tanks to check or destroy the inadequately supported British armour. When advancing, Panzer divisions moved in compact all-arms battle groups that could provide rapid mutual supporting fire. British failure to achieve such concentration resulted in the repeated overrunning and destruction of isolated brigades. A catastrophic example occurred on 12–13 June 1942 when three armoured brigades under the control of 1st Armoured Division were shattered by Rommel's anti-tank gun screen. These repeated disasters were probably due less to former cavalry regiments' addiction to the charge than to inadequate training in all-arms co-operation, and the tank regiments' belief that they could operate successfully without close infantry and artillery support.

Critics have pointed out that it took a series of defeats before the basic problem of better all-arms co-operation was fully accepted in 1942. Even then adaptation proved difficult. New tactics were needed for British armour to lure the enemy onto vital ground where he could be destroyed by field artillery in the anti-tank role. Another critical area lay in poor communications. Radios were in short supply and often proved ineffectual due both to technical deficiencies and to atmospheric conditions. Breakdown in communications often contributed to the tendency of armoured units to be scattered and therefore to have to fight in isolation.[11]

Perhaps the most important factor in accounting for the poor British performance in the desert in 1941–1942 was in the weakness of air support to land operations. Rommel owed much of his success in his early offensives in 1941 to almost complete dominance in the air. The RAF's shortage in numbers was also made worse by poor serviceability and the diversion of aircraft to Greece early in 1941. While there was certainly a cause for friction in the RAF's determination to keep control of all its aircraft, the greater problem lay in methods by which the soldiers could convey their needs to the Air Staff and to direct air attacks on ground targets in the obscure dust-shrouded conditions of desert warfare. The solution required close liaison between the 'client' ground commanders, rapid communication as to the target, rapid processing of the request and a rapid response. During Battleaxe, for example,

[11] Ibid., pp. 220–227.

the ground force's commander Beresford-Peirse, complained that the headquarters of his supporting air group was sited a hundred miles to the east, consequently quick-response calls for fighter support were impossible. By the time of Crusader, however, the creation of the Desert Air Force was beginning to have beneficial effects; in particular response time was greatly reduced from the three hours it had often taken earlier in the year.[12]

Although the Desert Air Force could not prevent the fall of Tobruk, it had by then obtained superiority over the battle zone and was able to inflict severe losses on the enemy artillery. Its control system was also by now so proficient that it was able to protect Eighth Army very effectively on its long retreat to El Alamein. The Desert Air Force also performed magnificently at Alam el Halfa, but missed a wonderful opportunity to destroy the Axis forces as they retreated at the end of the battle of Alamein. Early on 5 November air reconnaissance reported a solid mass of vehicles packing the road all the way to Mersa Matruh, but the resort to high-level bombing failed to make much impression on this 'sitting target'. Nevertheless the complex liaison system established in 1942 to ensure close and effective air–ground co-operation was a tremendous achievement, worthy of comparison with the most important technical and organisational innovations of the First World War.[13]

Montgomery was fortunate in the timing of his appointment as commander of the Eighth Army in August 1942. Auchinleck had clearly stopped Rommel's advance in the first battle of Alamein, but the Africa Corps still had to be defeated. Montgomery could be confident of receiving a steady flow of tanks, vehicles and fuel whereas Rommel's supply route was being throttled by Allied air and sea interdiction. Montgomery had two further advantages. Churchill had harried Montgomery's predecessors relentlessly to mount offensives before they were ready, but 'Monty' now had the prestige and professional confidence to insist that he must be the judge of when his plan could be successfully implemented. Secondly, following the virtual breakdown in responsibility between the Middle East headquarters in Cairo and the field commander in the Western Desert, Montgomery was fortunate to have

[12] Bidwell and Graham, *Fire-Power*, pp. 250–251. French, *Raising Churchill's Army*, p. 237.
[13] French, *Raising Churchill's Army*, pp. 236–239. Sixsmith, *British Generalship*, pp. 241–242.

the suave and easy-going Alexander as his nominal superior, allowing him to impose his own dominant personality and unique professional style on his multi-national forces in the field. But for the tragic death of 'Strafer' Gott in an air crash, Montgomery would not have been offered this opportunity and the successful pairing with Alexander would not have happened.

Montgomery's spiky character made him many enemies, and his marked failure, even after the war and to the end of his life, to acknowledge Auchinleck's achievement, testified to the harsh, ungenerous side of his nature. Nevertheless his boundless self-belief, ruthless professionalism and ability to enthuse his polyglot soldiers together proved precisely the tonic needed after the hectic advances and retreats of the previous two years.

Montgomery quickly impressed his personal style of command on his senior subordinates. To avoid delays in the tempo of operations written orders were largely discarded in favour of verbal orders in face-to-face meetings or by telephone. The new commander went out of his way to speak directly to his officers and to make sure they made his plans absolutely clear to their men. He also set an example of controlling the battle from a forward headquarters and encouraged his subordinates, down to divisional commanders, to do the same. He also broke with British Army tradition in denying his commanders any latitude in the interpretation of orders. His insistence on exercising 'a firm grip' was essential to ensure that his 'master plan' could not be undermined or watered down by individual commanders in battle. He was less original, but still justified, in stressing that massed artillery was a major factor in winning battles. The relatively short and restricted front at Alamein permitted such a concentration of artillery, and its power was increased by the timely arrival of sufficient six-pounder anti-tank guns. The principle of concentration was also evident in the narrow front of about 7,000 yards at the start of the battle of Alamein, and some later desert battles were started on even more confined boundaries.

Montgomery's method of conducting battles in the desert was well adapted to the strengths and weaknesses of the forces at his disposal: he possessed a clear superiority in weapons and equipment and enjoyed virtually complete command in the air; but had always to be aware of his limited manpower resources. He also inculcated throughout his command that victory must depend on the intimate co-operation of all arms: no one arm by itself could wage war successfully.

Montgomery's theory and practice of battle had their limitations – he was logistically cautious and was reluctant to let fluid operations develop – but he had definitely devised a better standard of all-arms co-operation than had prevailed before 1942.

The reasons for Eighth Army's successful operations from October 1942 should now be clear. Whereas the British and their allies were materially improving and their morale was buoyant, the Axis forces were over-stretched and weary. Rommel himself was ill and had been forced to fly home for treatment before the decisive battle. The varied and potentially discordant national contingents in Eighth Army were now held together by a dominant personality whose careful planning and strictly controlled strategy served to convince the whole Army that it would now advance to victory. Once the break-out from El Alamein was achieved early in November and the Torch landings simultaneously succeeded in Tunisia, it was clear that the black humour of 'going up to Benghazi for Christmas and coming back early in the New Year' would not be repeated. The fate of the Axis forces in North Africa had been sealed when they were forced to retreat over 1,000 miles to the Mareth Line in Tunisia.[14]

The operational skills developed in the North African Desert proved of little relevance in the slow-moving attritional struggle up the Italian peninsula between September 1943 and the end of the war. Several historians have commented that this campaign was the closest undertaken by the Army in the Second World War to the murderous struggle on the Western Front in the earlier war. The tactical problems were different but even more formidable: successive skilfully defended mountain chains had to be stormed, and marshes and broad rivers crossed. In complete contrast to the desert, wide-ranging manoeuvre was rendered impossible by the terrain and logistic hazards. This was fundamentally a conflict of minor tactics in which the infantryman's skills and endurance were paramount. The deployment of guns was severely restricted by the terrain with the Allied forward positions often overlooked by the enemy. Mortars were more useful, but the transport of munitions, usually by mules or porters over rocky terrain, was difficult and exhausting. As General Sir David Fraser comments:

[14] French, *Raising Churchill's Army*, pp. 247–258. For a critical analysis of British shortcomings in the Desert War see Bidwell and Graham, *Fire-Power*, pp. 228–247. For a more personal account, enhanced by knowledge of the generals concerned, see Sir John Smyth VC, *Leadership in War*, Chapter 3.

> The army was not organised for so harsh and primitive a struggle.
> Supported by a mass of road transport, adapted to war in the
> huge spaces of Africa or ready for a campaign supported by a
> sophisticated road system, the British Army was now to fight in
> mountains, over country where most of its support represented
> little but encumbrance.[15]

The Italian campaign showed that no level of military genius and no amount of heavy equipment can overcome determined, well-sited defences in confined areas and in appalling weather. Also, given the poor quality of the roads, even in good weather armoured formations could make little impression. In the Liri Valley there was only one first-class road, elsewhere engineers had to bulldoze farm tracks and even then the infantry often had to carry their own heavy weapons and cumbersome radios.[16]

There was considerable Anglo-American friction among senior commanders in both the Salerno and Anzio landings and numerous operational errors, but the long stalemate before the Gustav Line, whose defences were anchored by Cassino and its dominating mountain, suggested that almost impossible conditions of terrain and weather constituted the main obstacles to the advance on Rome, which was not occupied until 5 June 1944.

When every allowance is made for the *Wehrmacht*'s enormous advantage in being almost entirely on the defensive, the fact remains that enemy resistance was formidable. In Field Marshal Albert Kesselring they had the best commander in the theatre. Most German battalions were badly under-strength and lacking in motor transport, dependent on horse draught for their few guns and scarce supplies, and with very little air support, but they put up a tremendous fight for every defended position. The Allies enjoyed a clear superiority in tanks and artillery supported by a dominant Tactical Air Force. Their remarkable supply lines stretched across the Mediterranean to Tunisia and along the coast as far as Egypt.[17] Given these advantages, the slow progress served to

---

[15] David Fraser, *And We Shall Shock Them: The British Army in the Second World War* (Hodder & Stoughton, 1983), p. 275. French, *Raising Churchill's Army*, pp. 274–275.

[16] Bidwell and Graham, *Tug of War. The Battle for Italy: 1943–5* (Hodder & Stoughton, 1986), pp. 290–291. Sixsmith, *British Generalship*, pp. 243–244.

[17] Bidwell and Graham, *Tug of War*, pp. 398–399.

confirm Churchill's profound conviction that the German soldier was a superior warrior and that every effort had to be made to contain as many enemy divisions as possible, which would otherwise be available to oppose the Allied invasion of France.

In March 1918 the Allies had been obliged to resist the final desperate German offensives in the West before the eventual advance to victory could begin. In 1944 to achieve a foothold in France the Allies had to overcome operational challenges of a far greater magnitude. Had the invasion been attempted in 1943 Churchill's and Brooke's fears of a disaster might well have been realised. Even Operation Overlord, launched on 6 June 1944, might have stalled but for all the advantages built up in the preceding months: virtually complete command of the air; destruction of the enemy's supply lines in France by the Resistance and saturation bombing; a gigantic preparatory bombing of the landing areas from the air and sea; and brilliantly successful deception measures that detained vital German reserves in the Pas de Calais for several weeks.

Recent television programmes, eager to emphasise Allied errors and disasters, have focused attention on the American ordeal at Omaha Beach, but by nightfall it was clear that Overlord had been an outstanding success. On that momentous day more than 130,000 Allied ground troops and 23,000 airborne troops were landed at the cost of some 12,000 casualties. Nearly 200,000 naval personnel in 7,000 vessels had supported the landings, and 14,000 sorties were flown. Subsequent reservations about the Allied performance in the remainder of the fiercely contested attritional struggle must be set against this magnificent feat of arms.[18]

The anxieties long held by Churchill about the operational difficulties posed by the cross-Channel invasion were understandable. The Prime Minister's low estimation of the British Army's fighting ability and the quality of the individual 'Tommy' compared with his German counterpart also had some basis in truth. But he was insensitive to the essentially civilian nature of 'his Army' by this late stage in the war. Nor was he sufficiently appreciative of the marked improvement in battlefield competence since the later months of 1942.

[18] For a concise account of the Normandy campaign see Carlo D'Este, 'The Army and the Challenge of War 1939–1945', in David Chandler and Ian Beckett (eds.), *The Oxford Illustrated History of the British Army* (Oxford University Press, 1994), pp. 296–300. See also Max Hastings, *Overlord. D-Day and the Battle for Normandy 1944* (Pan Books, 1985).

Not only the Prime Minister but also numerous officers suspected that their civilian soldiers were lacking in the willpower and determination routinely displayed by German soldiers, not to speak of the Japanese. This deficiency should not have been surprising given the militaristic and ideological training given to a generation of young Germans, and the arrogance they had developed as a result of conquering most of Europe between 1939 and 1941. It certainly proved true that British soldiers who had fought through Africa and Italy displayed signs of war-weariness in the summer of 1944.[19] Divisions from the Eighth Army transferred to France to form the elite spearhead turned out to be lacking in dash, whereas the divisions that had waited so long in England for this opportunity – and ordeal – were fresh but inexperienced.

The unpleasant reality had to be faced that after the break-out from Normandy and the rapid advance across France to the Belgian frontier, there was no easy progress to be made against the stubborn and skilful defences put up even by the remnants and reserves that the *Wehrmacht* could spare from the Eastern Front. Particularly for the infantry, the final months of the Second World War were as exhausting and 'horrific' as the fighting on the Western Front in 1916–1918. This can be confirmed by comparative casualty figures: in the Third Ypres campaign of 1917 British and Canadian forces suffered 244,000 casualties or 2,121 a day – Normandy cost the Allies more than 200,000 casualties at 2,354 a day – the vast majority inflicted on front-line infantry. In addition to physical injuries, the infantry especially displayed severe psychological symptoms, resembling shellshock in the earlier war, but now termed 'battlefield exhaustion'. Allied psychiatrists warned, during the intensest fighting in Normandy, that this phenomenon was approaching a point of crisis. 'All the infantry divisions in action since D-Day, the 3rd British, 3rd Canadian, 50th Northumbrian and 51st Highland, were in a dreadful condition and were evacuating battle exhaustion casualties by the hundreds'.[20] After a brief lull in the late summer, battle exhaustion again posed acute problems in the fierce fighting for Antwerp and in the approach to the Rhine. 'The only realistic way of reducing battlefield exhaustion was to lower the intensity, cost and duration of combat'.[21]

[19] French, *Raising Churchill's Army*, p. 284. D'Este, 'The Army and the Challenge of War', pp. 296–300.
[20] Terry Copp's essay in Addison and Calder (eds.), *Time to Kill*, pp. 147–158.
[21] Ibid., pp. 150–151.

A vital consideration affecting virtually every aspect of the Army's organisation and approach to battle, from late 1942 onwards, was the looming crisis in suitable military manpower. In mid-1943, for example, the equivalent of four divisions at home were disbanded and, later that year, on the assumption that the European war would end by the autumn of 1944, the Army was allocated an intake of only 150,000 recruits. In preparation for Overlord six divisions in England with low establishments were reduced to cadres. A further desperate remedy in 1944 was to transfer airmen and gunners to the infantry, a gamble that paid off in terms of speedy adaptation to their new units. On 10 June 1944, for example, 2nd Battalion Scots Guards received about 400 very recalcitrant reinforcements from the RAF Regiment wearing their sky-blue uniforms, yet in a few weeks they had been transformed into proud members of their new units. Even so, at the end of the year, Montgomery was obliged to disband two complete divisions. At the peak in July 1944 Montgomery had only thirteen British divisions under his command. Churchill was desperately worried about the effect of this manpower shortage on his ability to influence Allied strategic and political decisions but in reality, in the last year of the war in Europe, 'the process of shrinkage was inexorable'.[22]

Montgomery's professional inclination to fight tightly controlled battles with heavy reliance on firepower and a minimum of risk was reinforced by his awareness of the growing manpower crisis. He accepted that he could afford to be prodigal with munitions and equipment but must husband his human resources very carefully. In the Normandy bridgehead he relied mainly on air bombardment to destroy the city of Caen, and on 18 July he allowed General Dempsey to mount an all-armoured attack with three divisions, Operation Goodwood, in an effort to break out of the bridgehead.

Montgomery's cautious, rigorously controlled approach to battle clearly had its drawbacks. Frontal assaults on narrow fronts could usually be quickly contained. Furthermore logistical support was a prime consideration in all major battles, thus limiting opportunities for rapid advances. In any case fluid operations were contrary to

---

[22] Elliott, *Esprit de Corps*, pp. 104–107 shows how airmen and soldiers from other regiments quickly became proud of their new 'club'. French, *Raising Churchill's Army*, pp. 244–246 stresses Britain's acute shortage of military manpower in the final year of the war.

Montgomery's insistence on careful supervision and firm control from the top.

At the tactical level British combined arms operations continued to reveal shortcomings that reduced the tempo of operations. In a typical attack infantry advanced closely behind heavy barrages and were trained to reach enemy positions within two minutes of the barrage lifting, that is before the enemy was able to counter-attack. Such a thorough artillery preparation cratered the ground so severely that the infantry's advance was delayed. Heavy artillery support also encouraged junior leaders to rely on the gunners to blast a way through for them. The Germans were also adept at rushing up reserves to nullify the attack or slipping away to man the next defensive position. Unfortunately, as has already been shown, inter-arm co-operation frequently broke down due to various causes such as poor reconnaissance, inadequate fire-plans or infantry battalions being thrown prematurely into attacks without armoured support. The most serious cause of failure, however, lay in communications breakdown. At unit level battalions had to provide their own and this remained an acute problem. Infantry had to wait the longest for sufficient radio equipment, the sets they did receive were cumbersome and they operated on frequencies very vulnerable to interference. Consequently, communications between infantry and their supporting tanks remained an unsolved problem to the very end of the war.[23]

Montgomery's uncharacteristically bold attempt to end the war in 1944 by driving into the Ruhr via the bridge at Arnhem proved a costly failure. Although Lieutenant Colonel John Frost's 2nd Parachute Battalion held the north end of the bridge for much longer than expected, the failure of XXX Corps to link up from the southern side proved fatal. The episode exposed serious flaws in British planning in what was from the start a very ambitious and risky project. Firm intelligence that two Panzer divisions were recuperating near Arnhem was ignored at Montgomery's headquarters; the glider landings and parachute drops were much too far from the objective; and, most astonishingly, no arrangements were made for direct air support for the 1st Airborne Division. In the absence of Air Support Signals Units (ASSUs), communications between the Airborne Division and the Tactical

[23] D'Este, 'The Army and the Challenge of War', pp. 298–300. French, *Raising Churchill's Army*, pp. 262–272.

Air Arm in England were completely lacking. The Bomber Group (no. 83), which could have used its Typhoons with tank-busting rockets, was not permitted to intervene until too late. The battle has come down in history as a gallant failure on an epic scale, but it was a failure nonetheless. Of the 10,300 soldiers who had landed near Arnhem, 1,300 had been killed and more than 6,000 captured. 1st Airborne Division was not reconstituted after the battle.[24]

By the final year of the war in North-West Europe, the British Army had achieved a high degree of competence in many aspects of fighting at the tactical and operational levels. Ground–air co-operation and artillery support techniques were in some respects superior to the *Wehrmacht*'s. Dispensing wherever possible with written orders in favour of verbal instructions brought great improvements in flexibility and speed, and there was greater awareness among senior commanders of their freedom to make decisions within a common doctrine. This is not to say that the Army had espoused a system like the *Wehrmacht*'s that allowed, even encouraged, decentralised decision-making to subordinate commanders. British adherence to autocratic control from the top did constrain the initiative of subordinates and gave the Germans a considerable advantage. In the chaos of battle, and particularly when communications broke down a German officer was more likely to use his own initiative in accordance with his understanding of his senior officer's intentions.[25]

In the light of the series of defeats and disasters the British Army suffered between 1940 and 1942 and its less than brilliant performance thereafter, one might expect to find a legacy of public disillusionment and criticism comparable to that directed at Haig and his generals. There have been some very critical histories, such as Correlli Barnett's *The Desert Generals* (1960), but on the whole this has not happened. Five explanations are suggested here but the emergence and persistence of myths is a mysterious phenomenon not easily pin-pointed by historical analysis. In the first place, defeats in the early part of the war, such as Norway, were deliberately played down in comparison with the legendary victory 'against the odds' in the Battle of Britain. Even the debacle culminating at Dunkirk was astonishingly converted into a

---

[24] D'Este, 'The Army and the Challenge of War', pp. 300–302. Bidwell and Graham, *Fire-Power*, pp. 273–275.

[25] French, *Raising Churchill's Army*, pp. 282–285.

national myth of miraculous escape, though Churchill was well aware of the magnitude of the disaster resulting from France's collapse.

Secondly, despite Churchill's attainment of colossal, almost superhuman, status in and after 1940, it was widely understood that he bore a major responsibility for several of the worst disasters including Norway, Greece, Crete and Singapore. British commanders, with the notable exception of General Percival at Singapore, got off lightly compared with the vitriolic attacks on Haig and the Western Front commanders. Moreover, as discussed in an earlier chapter, Churchill brilliantly re-fashioned events to his own advantage in his magisterial account of *The Second World War*, which was so influential in the early post-war years.

Thirdly, war-time reporting and propaganda, mostly in terms of radio, newsreels and newspapers, understandably played down disasters (for example, the sinking of the SS *Lancastria*[26] with the loss of 3,000 troops being evacuated from Western France in 1940 was completely censored), whereas even minor successes, such as the triumph over the *Graf Spee* in December 1939, and the liberation of British captives from the German transport ship *Altmark* in February 1940, were celebrated in heroic terms. The surrender of Tobruk and the disastrous Dieppe Raid in 1942 could not be concealed, but, later that year, El Alamein was hailed as the crucial turning point in the war from the British perspective. Very few British people during the war, it may be safely speculated, could have accurately compared the extent of German losses at Alamein with those suffered at Stalingrad a few months later. As Churchill later remarked with typical exaggeration, 'before Alamein we never won a victory and after it never suffered a defeat'.

The fourth, and by far the most important consideration in 1945, was that casualties had been light compared with those suffered in 1914–1918. The approximate total of 385,000 Service personnel killed and wounded would have been much higher had Britain not fought most of the war between 1940–1944 in peripheral theatres outside North-West Europe. But even so it could be argued in the Army's defence that greater reliance on machines and firepower, accompanied by a much keener sense that heavy casualties were unacceptable, had together secured a notable reduction of losses suffered by the 'poor, bloody infantry'.

---

[26] Basil Karslake, *1940. The Last Act* (Leo Cooper, 1979), p. 206.

Finally, in 1945, there was an overwhelming sense of public relief and euphoria, but also of a pervasive weariness in the realisation that 'We', the British and Commonwealth peoples (the American role was under-emphasised), had won the war after so many years of hardship and struggle. In view of the fervent hopes that after this second great ordeal of 'total' war against Germany a 'brave new world' really would be created, critical discussion of the British Army's performance could safely be left to historians in the distant future.[27]

[27] David French's extensive bibliography suggests that, with a few obvious exceptions, scholars have only recently begun to subject the British Army's performance in the Second World War to critical analysis.

9 AFTER THE WARS: BRITAIN'S GAINS AND LOSSES

In 1918 British and Dominion forces played a crucial role in winning the war on the Western Front. The Royal Navy and the recently created Royal Air Force also ended the war in strong positions vis-à-vis present allies and future rivals. Lloyd George had enhanced his power base at the head of a coalition government by means of the 'Khaki Election' held in December 1918. In the prolonged peace negotiations at Versailles he secured virtually all Britain's war aims both as regards security in Europe and also in the wider world. With the additions of Mandates in the Middle East and Africa the British Empire was enlarged, if not politically enhanced, and reached its greatest extent. Even allowing for the heavy debits of unprecedented casualties, loss of trade and indebtedness to the USA, this was a tremendous achievement, not just for the armed forces and the government, but for the nation as a whole. Yet the outcome of the war was soon to be regarded as, at best, a Pyrrhic victory or at worst as a futile enterprise that had neither put an end to wars nor created a 'land fit for heroes'.

By contrast, in 1945 Britain's war effort was flagging, particularly as regards the Army, which was desperately short of trained manpower. By 1944 Britain had clearly become the junior partner to the USA and this was made painfully evident in a series of political and military decisions. Moreover, between 1941 and 1945 there could be no illusions about the dominant role of the Soviet Union in first absorbing the shock of Nazi invasion and then remorselessly wearing down and defeating the *Wehrmacht*; in the process suffering horrendous losses that dwarfed those in other theatres.

In contrast to Lloyd George, Winston Churchill suffered a humiliating electoral defeat immediately after the end of the war in Europe and was replaced by Attlee, who became Prime Minister on 26 July 1945 and took Churchill's place at the Potsdam Conference. Churchill had failed in a valiant attempt to restore a democratically elected government for an independent Poland and, more widely, to stem the tide of Soviet-backed Communist control of most of Central and Eastern Europe. Furthermore, Britain was left financially and industrially impoverished, and her hold on the Empire had been fatally undermined, most critically by Japan's rapid conquest of Malaya with the humiliating surrender of Singapore and her subsequent drive to the north-east borders of India.

Paradoxically, however, the outcome of the Second World War was generally regarded – and still is – as a greater triumph than that of victory in the First World War. This study has attempted to account for this anomaly by examining the role of hindsight, which has distorted popular interpretation of the two wars.

Recent historians, including A. J. P. Taylor, Margaret Macmillan and David Stevenson, have been generally sympathetic towards the intractable problems confronting the peace-makers who met at Versailles between December 1918 and June 1919; showing why the terms of the settlement were unavoidably based on controversial compromises that failed to produce a Utopian world free from war.[1]

The Versailles Peace Treaty with Germany had numerous defects and problematic loose ends but this was bound to be the case. Fighting did not end neatly on 11 November 1918 but continued in widespread sporadic conflicts in, for example, the former Ottoman Empire, Eastern Europe and in Germany itself. Revolution and civil war engulfed the former Tsarist Empire and threatened to break out in several other countries, notably those which had experienced defeat and others, such as Ireland, which saw their oppressor's grip loosened by the war. Several new countries had already emerged before November 1918 from the break-up of the Hapsburg and Ottoman Empires, defying neat and tidy settlements on the basis of national self-determination or economic viability. The chief European peace-makers, France, Britain and Italy, all had separate and in some respects, irreconcilable, priorities,

---

[1] See especially Margaret Macmillan's *Peacemakers: Six Months that Changed the World* (John Murray, 2002), pp. 203–204, 475–489.

while President Woodrow Wilson introduced disturbing idealistic notions of international security through his championship of a League of Nations that his country would soon prove unwilling to endorse.

The future of Germany lay at the centre of the peace-makers' problems. When the Armistice was signed on 11 November the Kaiser had already fled to Holland and a Republic had been proclaimed. The country was in turmoil with widespread strikes and civil unrest but, apart from a tiny corner of upper Alsace, German troops were still everywhere fighting on foreign soil. Many regiments would soon march home still bearing arms, garlanded and with bands playing. The German Socialist delegates who signed the Armistice knew that their country could not continue the struggle, but wrongly assumed that Wilson's Fourteen Points would form the basis for negotiations in which they would participate. These assumptions proved illusory, thus causing a sense of injustice even before the terms were known. Although the Germans had imposed severe reparations demands on France in 1871, and in 1918 had inflicted a draconian peace settlement on Russia in the Treaty of Brest-Litovsk, and harsh economic terms on Romania in the Treaty of Bucharest, their delegates were bitterly resentful at the terms the Allies obliged them to sign. Reparations presented the most intractable problem. Britain, France and Belgium all expected compensation for war damage and human losses, but could not agree on the total amount, their relative percentages and the schedule for payments. After months of wrangling and delays due in part to British objections, a decision on the total sum to be paid was deferred until 1921 by which time public passions had cooled considerably. Germany was required to pay 132 billion gold marks or £6.5 billion, but it was recognised that her ability to pay would have to be taken into account.

In the longer term what counted far more than the sums involved (and the fact that only a small part of the total was ever extracted) were Articles 231 and 232 of the Treaty. The former assigned responsibility to Germany and her allies for all the damage caused by the war; the latter Article modifying this unlimited liability to specific damages. The former Article, known as the 'war guilt clause', had been insisted upon by Britain and France to establish Germany's legal liability for reparations, but it provoked undying resentment and, with hindsight, was not worth all the trouble it caused.

Resentment against the Treaty was widespread in Germany, but particularly on the part of the military and their conservative sympathisers, who quickly established the 'stab in the back' myth. Why, these groups protested, should Germany lose 13 per cent of her territory and 10 per cent of her population? Why should Germany be forced to disarm unilaterally, and why, above all, should she be obliged to take sole responsibility for causing the war?

In the event Germany paid only about £1.1 billion, which, in relation to national wealth, was rather less than France had repaid Germany after 1871. Unfortunately, for the future of Europe, Germany's statesmen never admitted that they were primarily responsible for the war; reparations were held to be unjust and to be ruining the country. Britain was unwilling to use the sanctions available under the Treaty to enforce payment or prolong the occupation of the Rhineland, while France's occupation of the Ruhr in 1923 only exacerbated German resentment. By the 1930s both Britain and France preferred to appease rather than confront Germany over the latter's determination to challenge the punitive terms of the Versailles Treaty.[2]

German sympathisers in the West who later argued that she had been treated too harshly had missed the point that the Allies had failed to impress the scale of their victory on the enemy nation. The Allied governments, and nearly all their military leaders, including Foch and Haig, were willing to accept the Armistice without pressing on to an invasion of Germany, partly because they wished to prevent further bloodshed and suffering on all sides, but also because they believed the enemy's powers of resistance were still strong and might easily prolong the war into 1919. Only after the Armistice had been accepted did the British War Cabinet learn that revolutionary groups had established soviets in several German cities, bringing the state itself to the brink of complete collapse. As David French has written, 'Had the Entente invaded Germany and imposed harsher armistice terms, the Weimar regime might have been able to democratise the post-war officer corps, and so rob the *Reichswehr* of its ability to organise a militarised Germany which would once again be capable of waging industrialised warfare.'[3]

Did the Allies' failure to press home their military supremacy by accepting a premature armistice, followed by the punitive aspects of the Versailles Treaty, which caused such bitter and lasting resentment, lead

[2] Ibid, pp. 490–491.
[3] French, *The Strategy of the Lloyd George Coalition*, pp. 283–284.

inexorably to the downfall of the Weimar Republic and the outbreak of another and even more terrible world war? Historians should be very wary of using the word 'inevitable', and in this case it seems far from certain that hatred of the Versailles Treaty would lead directly to the advent of Hitler and all that followed up to 1939. The separation of East Prussia from the rest of Germany and the establishment of Danzig as a free city were certainly irritants but not a sufficient cause for war in the West. France was greatly weakened by the war and, deprived of the support from the USA and Britain promised in the peace negotiations, was most unlikely to risk another war with Germany. Indeed the latter became a guarantor of the post-1918 boundaries in Western Europe as a signatory of the Locarno Treaty in 1925. The last British troops were withdrawn from the occupied zone of the Rhineland in 1929, and it was evident by then that Germany could quite soon regain full control of her former western boundaries without war. As Margaret Macmillan concludes, 'with different leadership in the Western democracies, with stronger democracy in Weimar Germany, without the damage done by the Depression, the story might have turned out differently... The Treaty of Versailles is not to blame.'[4]

Britain ended the war in an impressively strong position with the largest army, navy and air force in the world. Already, at the time of the Armistice, she had achieved some of her main war aims: German forces had withdrawn from France and Belgium; much of her High Seas Fleet was in captivity in Scapa Flow; and all her U-boats had been captured. The Versailles Treaty confirmed the loss of all Germany's overseas territories and effectively disarmed her. Germany's Army would be limited to 100,000 men (all regulars), and her Navy to 15,000 career sailors. She would have no air force, tanks, armoured cars or submarines. Only a few factories would be allowed to produce war materials, and all imports that might be used for rearmament were forbidden. Furthermore, public services and private societies were to be strictly supervised to prevent clandestine training of soldiers and air-men. Consequently, until the Nazis came to power Germany remained extremely weak militarily, with defence spending less than 1 per cent of national income. She was thus totally unable to wage offensive oper-ations, and was scarcely able to defend her own borders. It was a cause of bitter resentment that the Allies' rash promise that they too

---

[4] Macmillan, *Peacemakers*, p. 493.

would implement similar drastic disarmament measures were not fully implemented.[5]

In retrospect the collapse of the post-war settlement and the slide towards another world war may seem inevitable, but this was far from clear in the 1920s. Certainly there were ominous signs such as America's withdrawal from Europe, the obvious limitations of the League of Nations, and France's vulnerability in relation to an economically resurgent Germany. Nevertheless a recent scholarly survey has concluded that 'the treaty could have stopped another bloodbath if it had been upheld'.[6]

Britain's outstanding success in achieving her main war aims regarding the Continent and the protection of her Empire were purchased at a tremendous cost to her domestic industry and finance. About 40 per cent of the merchant fleet had been sunk, the railways overworked and the best coal seams ruthlessly exploited. Concentration on military transport had not created a basis for the mass production of automobiles. Financial losses were also extremely serious. Britain had lost about £1,825 million to her allies and borrowed a further £1,340 million. The government owed about £850 million to the United States and was, in turn, owed more than twice that sum by former allies, principally Russia. Although inter-Allied debts soured international relations for many years, in A. J. P. Taylor's opinion, Britain's global financial position was not seriously damaged in the 1920s. A much more alarming situation was caused by the huge increase in the National Debt, which was fourteen times greater at the end of the war than in 1914. Servicing it took nearly half of the yield from taxation, which, post-war governments decided, must entail economy in every sphere of public expenditure. This did much to undermine electoral promises of a new and better country for returning servicemen. Clearly these drastic measures contributed to the rapid growth of disappointment in the 1920s with the anticipated benefits of military victory.[7]

Nevertheless domestic hardships did not immediately eclipse public appreciation of the nation's great achievements in the war. The Army's reputation had never been higher. Though later to be vilified,

[5] French, *The Strategy of the Lloyd George Coalition*, pp. 283–284. Stevenson, *With Our Backs to the Wall*, pp. 522–524.

[6] David Stevenson, *1914–1918: The History of the First World War* (Allen Lane, 2004), p. 529.

[7] A. J. P. Taylor, *English History 1914–1945*, pp. 120–136.

Earl Haig was regarded as a national hero and when he died prematurely in 1928, mainly as a result of over-working for the better treatment of ex-servicemen, his lying-in-state and funeral attracted huge, reverent crowds in both London and Edinburgh.

Beyond all the tangible achievements, as embodied in the peace settlements, lay the intangible benefit of national prestige. 'The willingness of British policy-makers to sacrifice almost three-quarters of a million men to defeat the Central Powers made a profound impression on the minds of its former enemies.'[8] This should have remained a powerful instrument in Britain's diplomatic armoury because other powers held it in such great respect. Tragically, policy-makers in the 1920s and 1930s, perhaps unduly influenced by the growing national concern with loss and mourning, behaved increasingly as though Britain had lost the war. This neglect of the priceless asset of national prestige found political expression in the policy of appeasement towards Nazi Germany, and culminated in Neville Chamberlain's naïve and spineless behaviour during the Munich crisis, causing Hitler to describe him and his colleagues as 'little worms'.[9] The generation of men and women who had won the war and achieved a triumphant peace settlement should not be held responsible for the abysmal performance of Chamberlain and his principal colleagues, few of whom had seen active service.

In reality Chamberlain had quite a good hand at the time of Munich: Britain was still a world power with the most powerful navy, a global empire and access to vital overseas commodities. By contrast Germany's forces, and especially her navy, were far from ready for a major war, and Hitler knew it. But Chamberlain played his hand badly because he assumed that behind his arrogant, bullying façade Hitler basically, like himself, wanted peace after the settlement of specific demands, and therefore could be appeased.

Less than a year later Britain would go to war with Germany in fulfilment of her guarantee to Poland – an even more distant country than Czechoslovakia for whom no immediate aid was available. This left Britain in an ambivalent position; formally at war but reluctant to hot up land and air operations and still hoping that a negotiated peace was achievable.

[8] French, *The Strategy of the Lloyd George Coalition*, pp. 296–297.
[9] Ibid., pp. 296–297.

When Churchill became Prime Minister in May 1940 his position was much weaker, and would soon become desperate. He was not popular with the Conservative Party, whose leader Chamberlain remained for the next few months, and he himself was largely responsible for the debacle in Norway that, ironically, had given him his chance to lead the country. The Nazis had overrun Denmark and Norway and would shortly defeat the Low Countries and France. Germany and the Soviet Union were still committed to a mutually beneficial pact, and the United States showed little sign of willingness to enter the war on Britain's behalf.

In these dire circumstances John Charmley's contention that Churchill's appeasement of Roosevelt and, after June 1941, Stalin was analogous to Chamberlain's appeasement of Hitler and so contributed to 'the end of glory' for Britain and the Empire is not convincing because Churchill had little room to manoeuvre. Half-American himself, Churchill did indeed place excessive faith in his friendship with President Roosevelt, and belief in a special relationship between the two very different peoples, but it is difficult to see an alternative.[10] Similarly, though holding few illusions about the repressive Soviet system, Churchill felt obliged to trust in Stalin's ultimate integrity and good faith because he judged, correctly, that only the Red Army could hold up and eventually destroy the majority of the *Wehrmacht*'s divisions. Stalin's undertaking not to impose a Communist regime in Greece gave Churchill hope for broader co-operation after the defeat of Germany, but the latter's efforts to secure free elections and a genuine measure of independence for a reconstituted Poland were to be cruelly disappointed.

The tough bargaining position of the United States was made clear as early as the summer of 1940. Britain desperately needed destroyers to protect the Atlantic convoys and was offered fifty American ships of First World War vintage in return for the 'free gift' of facilities in Newfoundland and Bermuda and ninety-nine-year leases on bases in the Caribbean and British Guiana. The War Cabinet felt obliged to accept these harsh conditions.

Even more ominous for Britain's commercial and financial future was the 'lend-lease' agreement of March 1941, which was far

[10] John Charmley, *Churchill: The End of Glory: A Political Biography* (Hodder & Stoughton, 1993), pp. 514–579.

from being an act of disinterested American generosity as later propaganda suggested. Britain had already committed herself to a huge
purchasing programme of war materials in the United States and her
stock of gold and dollar reserves was near exhaustion. It was clearly
to America's advantage to remain neutral while British and Imperial
forces carried her weapons and material into battle. Although likely
that America would eventually be drawn into the European conflict to
protect her own lives and interests, it took Hitler's quixotic declaration
of war on her after Pearl Harbor to bring this about in December 1941.
By then Britain had been at war, much of the time in great peril, for
twenty-seven months.[11]

In his study *The Collapse of British Power* (1972), Correlli Barnett is very critical of Churchill for waging all-out war in the pursuit of
'victory', virtually as an end in itself and without due consideration of
the nation's longer-term economic interests. Under his leadership the
entire nation and its resources were mobilised for war. Barnett's alternative strategy was to postpone the collapse of the economic foundations of British power for as long as possible by waging war on a scale
commensurate with her reserves of gold and dollars. In practice this
would entail hanging on, effectively on the defensive, in the hope that
more powerful allies might eventually be drawn in. In hindsight there
is much to be said for such a Fabian strategy, and to be fair it was
this optimistic vision that underlay Churchill's courageous rhetoric in
1940. It is far from clear, however, that the United States would have
intervened in the European conflict without clear evidence that Britain
would stay in the war, fight offensively, and provide a secure base for
American forces.[12]

Churchill's bellicosity and propensity for risk-taking did indeed
contribute to a series of disasters, including Norway, Greece and Crete,
the loss of Prince of Wales and Repulse, Singapore, Dieppe and Tobruk,
but this was the debit side of Churchill's leadership, which had to be
accepted as the price for his dynamism, offensive spirit and faith in
eventual victory, even in the darkest days of 1940 and 1941. It may also
be doubted that the public's morale and willingness to fight on would
have been maintained without Churchill's courageous rhetoric and his

[11] Max Hastings, *Finest Years. Churchill as Warlord 1940–45* (Harper Press
paperback, 2010), pp. 173–174, 183–184, 189, 548. David Reynolds, *In Command
of History*, pp. 200–202.
[12] Barnett, *The Collapse of British Power* (Methuen, 1972), pp. 589–592.

aggressive strategy with the promise of eventual victory. Furthermore, the very fact of the British forces' mediocre performance in offensive operations before El Alamein in October 1942 made it imperative for the nation to be seen to attempt to 'punch above its weight' in order to maintain its influence on its much stronger allies as the tide turned towards eventual victory.

Churchill and his strategic advisers (the Chiefs of Staff) achieved a remarkable success in persuading the United States to make its initial intervention in the European war in the peripheral North African theatre in November 1942; followed by an even more impressive negotiating feat at the Casablanca Conference in January 1943 by getting an agreement to follow up victory in North Africa by a joint invasion of Sicily. However, by this time the Western Allies knew that Germany was deploying more than 200 divisions on the Eastern Front as against twenty-five in the whole Mediterranean theatre.[13] Clearly, American insistence on an Allied invasion of North-West Europe could not be put off indefinitely. At the Teheran Conference in November 1943 Churchill was made acutely aware of his waning influence in relation to both the United States and the Soviet Union.

The last occasion on which Britain could claim to be the senior partner in relations with America was Operation Overlord in June 1944 when Montgomery was in overall command of the Normandy landings. In July Churchill could still insist that the British Empire had more divisions than the United States 'in fighting contact with the enemy', but the balance would soon swing to three to one in the latter's favour. The unpalatable truth for Britain was that as a great surge occurred in the arrival of new American divisions in Europe the former was running out of combat troops, especially infantry replacements. The changing nature of the relationship was symbolised by Montgomery's subordination to Eisenhower's overall command on 1 September 1944, which placed him on an equal footing with the American Army commanders, Bradley and Patton.

After the failure of the Arnhem operation in September it became clear that the European war would drag on into 1945 with the relative decline in British military manpower and war production

---

[13] French, *Raising Churchill's Army*, p. 274. In mid-1944 the German Army numbered 237 divisions, more than two-thirds of them on the Eastern Front. The Russians had 480 divisions.

causing the United States' predominance to become ever stronger. Neither at the Yalta nor the Potsdam Conferences could the British leaders speak as equals: hence the failure of the British aim for the Western Allies to reach Berlin and Prague before the Russians, and Truman's insistence, at Potsdam, that Anglo-American forces must withdraw to the agreed occupation zones so as not to harm Soviet–American relations.

At Yalta Churchill strove in vain to secure agreement on a strong, free and independent Poland. 'He stressed Britain's debt of honour to the Poles, whose independence they had ineffectually guaranteed in 1939.'[14] He received very little support from the ailing Roosevelt, who made the shocking declaration at the first plenary session that American forces would be withdrawn from Europe within two years. Given the Red Army's presence in Poland, Churchill could only extract a bland reassurance from Molotov that the existing pro-Soviet Polish government would be widened and that eventually 'free and unfettered elections' would be held 'on the basis of universal suffrage and a secret ballot'. On returning from Yalta, Churchill told the House of Commons 'he was sure that Stalin and the Soviet leaders wished to live in honourable friendship and equality with the Western democracies'. He believed that 'their word is their bond'. The ensuing debate aroused intense passions with twenty-five MPs daring to vote against the government for what they regarded as a shameful sell-out of the Polish government in exile and its forces gallantly fighting for the Allied cause.[15] Churchill was bitterly disappointed when his hopes were soon shown to be delusory but, in retrospect, felt that he had had no alternative but to trust Stalin's assurances, given that the European war was far from over and Soviet forces were expected to play a vital role in the defeat of Japan.

So obsessed was Churchill with the fate of Poland that he briefly appeared willing to start a third world war by attacking the Soviet Union. In mid-May 1945 he secretly instructed his military planners to draft a paper on 'Operation Unthinkable': namely how to impose upon Russia the will of the United States and the British Empire in order to get a fair deal for Poland. Hostilities were scheduled to start on 1 July 1945. An extraordinary additional note to the planners was

[14] Reynolds, *In Command of History*, p. 467. [15] Ibid., p. 469.

that they could count on the use of German military manpower and what remained of the enemy's industrial capacity. Later, in 1954, there was an impassioned but unresolved public dispute as to whether or not Churchill had told Montgomery in 1945 to stockpile captured German weapons so that they could be quickly issued to German soldiers for use against the Russians. Documentary proof was lacking but it seems quite possible that Churchill did flirt with this astonishing idea. The resulting draft plan proposed a huge Allied offensive in the Dresden area, but warned that this would not secure a lasting result. The Allies would have to wage a total war, and would have to penetrate far more deeply into the Soviet Union than the *Wehrmacht* had managed. Would the Americans even have contemplated the venture, bearing in mind that Japan was still undefeated? In his diary entry for 24 May, Brooke dismissed the scheme as fantastic and added that from now on Russia would be all-powerful in Europe.[16]

At the start of the Potsdam Conference on 17 July 1945, and shortly before Churchill heard that he had lost the general election, he made a last, vain attempt to persuade Truman to stand firm with him to secure an acceptable settlement for Eastern Europe with the Russians. Unfortunately Britain's desperate financial position entailed that she was utterly dependent on American goodwill. Churchill pointed out that Britain had spent more than half her foreign investments for the common cause and was now ending the war with a huge external debt. Truman said he would do his utmost to help, but a month later he abruptly terminated lend-lease to propitiate Congress.[17]

Britain's great achievement in the Second World War was, at first, to avoid defeat and then by her stubborn resistance tempt Hitler into risking a two-front war. Then, with her own war capacity diminishing, she secured more powerful allies whose gigantic war-making powers more than outmatched those of Germany and Japan. Consequently it is an exaggeration to claim that Britain 'won the war'; rather she played a significant role throughout and deservedly finished on the winning side.

Victory left Britain triumphant, relieved and impoverished. With lend-lease due to end on VJ Day, the financial and economic

---

[16] Reynolds, *In Command of History*, pp. 476–477. Hastings, *Finest Years*, pp. 571–575.

[17] Reynolds, *In Command of History*, p. 480.

burden created by the war seemed (in A. J. P. Taylor's phrase) 'almost beyond bearing'. Her external debt amounted to more than £4,198 million. She had drawn heavily on overseas investments and other capital assets. Her 'invisible income' from international financial transactions had been halved. The mercantile marine had been reduced by a third, and exports were little more than 40 per cent of the pre-war figures. Britain would have to export far more than she had done before the war, but in the immediate future this seemed impossible. In these dire circumstances the war-weary public still expected their war-time sacrifices to be rewarded with better living standards in a 'brave new world'.[18]

Within a very short time, months rather than years, Churchill's foreboding about the future of Central and Eastern Europe was completely justified. Allied victory over Germany had, in effect, replaced one appalling tyranny by another. Indeed in one important respect Soviet Communism appeared even more sinister and dangerous than Nazism: namely that its ideology exerted a profound, seductive influence on a significant number of Western intellectuals and politicians; an influence that remained remarkably persistent until the eventual demise of the Soviet Union.

Despite Churchill's many shortcomings as a war leader and his post-war achievement in exaggerating his own and Britain's importance in relation to allies, Max Hastings is surely right to conclude that 'No honourable course of action existed which could have averted his nation's bankruptcy and exhaustion in 1945, nor its eclipse from world power amid the new primacy of the United States and Russia'.[19]

[18] Taylor, *English History*, p. 599. Hastings, *Finest Years*, pp. 589, 591.
[19] Hastings, *Finest Years*, p. 594.

APPENDIX

A selection of provocative remarks about the First World War that prompted me to write this book.

'And that's why we lost the First World War.' Lady novelist in a radio discussion on the harmful influence of the public schools in *Stop the Week*, 21 February 1987. None of the panellists queried this opinion.

'Watching Field Marshal Haig up a ladder, steering more Tommies towards senseless slaughter, you're inclined to laugh in disbelief.' Review of *Oh! What a Lovely War* in Newcastle. *Daily Telegraph*, 24 March 2010.

'We are still defined by that pointless war.' Simon Heffer, *Sunday Telegraph*, 2 August 2009.

'The worst war that ever happened.' Review of television presentation of *Birdsong*, *Daily Telegraph*, 23 January 2012.

'Arsenal imploded at Newcastle, while Field Marshal Haig also failed to produce a Plan B.' Caption to photograph in a report by Brian Moore, *Sunday Telegraph*, 10 February 2011.

'It was suicide warfare by 19th century armies equipped with 20th century weapons. If it weren't for the Americans plunging in the war would have been won by Germany. Yet all leaders – Wilson, Lloyd George, Clemenceau...not to mention that arch-criminal Haig – should have been shot in the back as cowards who had sent young men to die for *Dolce et Decorum Est*.' Taki in *The Spectator*, 28 January 2012.

'Butchers and Bunglers of the Western Front.' Title of book by John Laffin.

'Laurels and Donkeys.' Title of an anthology compiled by Andrew Motion.

'To me, these soldiers in the First World War were sent off like cattle... it was senseless. This wasn't a "Hitler War", it wasn't about Britain's survival... It's always old men sending young men to war.' Michael Morpurgo author of *War Horse*. Interview reported in the *Daily Telegraph*, 9 October 2012.

'Gargantuan Imbecility.' Interview with the cast of *Blackadder* in which Rowan Atkinson is quoted as saying 'It is very difficult to exaggerate the absurdity and horror of the First World War. It may sound ridiculous for someone to face a court martial for shooting a pigeon but madder things happened in reality. Towards the end of the war 30 soldiers were court-martialled and shot in France by our own side for not wearing a hat in the trenches.' *Daily Telegraph* television review, 6 October 2012.

These and numerous similar comments suggest that many prominent individuals are willing to make public pronouncements on distant historical events about which they have strong feelings but limited knowledge. This is confirmed by a recent poll for *British Future*, a non-partisan body dedicated to exploring issues of national identity. Fewer than half of those polled between the ages of 16 to 24 knew that the First World War began in 1914 and ended in 1918. Around 60 per cent of those interviewed were unaware that Australia, Canada and India had sent men to fight on Britain's side. The survey revealed that not just children but their parents too were ignorant of some of the most basic facts about the war. Report in the *Sunday Telegraph*, 4 November 2012.

SELECT BIBLIOGRAPHY

Addison, Paul and Calder, Angus (eds.), *Time to Kill: The Soldier's Experience of War in the West 1939–1945*, Pimlico, 1997 (essays by Paul Addison, Jeremy A. Crang, John Ellis, Richard Overy, Gary Sheffield and Terry Copp)

Addison, Paul and Crang, Jeremy (eds.), *Firestorm: The Bombing of Dresden, 1945*, Pimlico paperback, 2006 (essays by the editors, Hew Strachan, Sebastian Cox and Richard Overy)

Ashworth, Tony, *Trench Warfare 1914–1918: The Live and Let Live System*, Macmillan, 1980

Barnett, Correlli, *The Collapse of British Power*, Eyre Methuen, 1972

Beckett, Ian F. W., *The Great War 1914–1918*, Longman, 2001

Bell, Philip, *John Bull and the Bear: British Public Opinion, Foreign Policy and the Soviet Union 1941–1945*, Arnold, 1990

Bidwell, Shelford and Graham, Dominick, *Fire-Power: British Army Weapons and Theories of War 1904–1945*, Allen and Unwin, 1982

Bidwell, Shelford and Graham, Dominick, *Tug of War: The Battle for Italy: 1943–5*, Hodder and Stoughton, 1986

Boff, Jonathan, *Winning and Losing on the Western Front*, Cambridge University Press, 2012

Bond, Brian (ed.), *The First World War and British Military History*, The Clarendon Press, 1991

Bond, Brian, *Survivors of a Kind: Memoirs of the Western Front*, Continuum, 2008

Bond, Brian, *The Unquiet Western Front: Britain's Role in Literature and History*, Cambridge University Press, 2002

Bond, Brian et al., *Look to Your Front: Studies in the First World War*, Spellmount, 1999

Bourne, John, *Britain and the Great War 1914–1918*, Arnold, 1989

Burleigh, Michael, *Moral Combat: A History of World War II*, Harper Press, 2010

Carrington, Charles, *Soldier at Bomber Command*, Leo Cooper, Pen and Sword, 1987

Carver, Michael, *Out of Step: The Memoirs of Field Marshal Lord Carver*, Hutchinson, 1989

Cecil, Hugh and Liddle, Peter (eds.), *Facing Armageddon: The First World War Experienced*, Leo Cooper, Pen and Sword, 1996 (essays by Gary Sheffield, Peter Loewenberg and Alyson Jackson)

Charmley, John, *Churchill. The End of Glory: A Political Biography*, Hodder and Stoughton, 1993

Churchill, Winston, *The Second World War* (6 vols.), Penguin, 2005

Clark, Alan, *The Donkeys*, Hutchinson, 1961

Dennis, Peter and Grey, Jeffrey (eds.), *Defining Victory 1918*, Department of Defence, Canberra, 1999 (essays by Robin Prior, Trevor Wilson, Gary Sheffield and John Bourne)

Douglas, Keith, *Alamein to Zem Zem*, Penguin Books, 1969

Elliott, W. A., *Esprit de Corps: A Scots Guards Officer on Active Service 1943–1945*, Michael Russell, 1996

Ellis, John, *The Sharp End of War: The Fighting Man in World War II*, David and Charles, 1980

Fraser, David, *Alanbrooke*, Collins, 1982

Fraser, David, *And We Shall Shock Them: The British Army in the Second World War*, Hodder and Stoughton, 1983

French, David, *Raising Churchill's Army: The British Army and the War Against Germany 1919–1945*, Oxford University Press, 2000

French, David, *The Strategy of the Lloyd George Coalition, 1916–1918*, The Clarendon Press, 1995

Grayling, A. C., *Among the Dead Cities*, Bloomsbury, 2006

Griffith, Paddy, *Battle Tactics of the Western Front: The British Army's Art of Attack 1916–1918*, Yale University Press, 1994

Hastings, Max, *Bomber Command*, Pan Books, 1981

Hastings, Max, *Finest Years: Churchill as Warlord 1940–45*, Harper Press paperback, 2010

Hastings, Max, *Overlord: D-Day and the Battle for Normandy 1944*, Pan Books, 1984

Hawkins, Nigel, *The Starvation Blockades: Naval Blockades of World War I*, Leo Cooper, Pen and Sword, 2002

Howard, Michael, *Captain Professor: A Life in War and Peace*, Continuum, 2006

Joly, Cyril, *Take These Men*, Constable, 1955

Kennedy, Paul, *The Rise and Fall of British Naval Mastery*, Allen Lane, 1976

Laffin, John, *British Butchers and Bunglers of World War I*, Sutton, 1988

Liddell Hart, B. H., *A History of the World War 1914–1918*, Faber and Faber, 1934

Liddle, Peter, Bourne, John and Whitehead, Ian (eds.), *The Great War 1914–1945*, Vol I, Harper Collins, 2000 (introduction and essay by John Bourne)

Lindsay, Martin, *So Few Got Through*, Collins, 1946

Macmillan, Margaret, *Peacemakers: Six Months that Changed the World*, John Murray paperback, 2002

Majdalany, Fred, *Cassino: Portrait of Battle*, Corgi paperback, 1959

Newton, Douglas, *British Policy and the Weimar Republic 1918–1919*, The Clarendon Press, 1997

Offer, Avner, *The First World War: An Agrarian Interpretation*, Oxford University Press, 1991

Overy, R. J., *The Air War 1939–1945*, Europa, 1980

Overy, R. J., *War and Economy in the Third Reich*, The Clarendon Press, 1994

Parker, Peter, *The Last Veteran: Harry Patch and the Legacy of War*, Fourth Estate, 2009

Philpott, William, *Bloody Victory: The Sacrifice on the Somme and the Making of the Twentieth Century*, Little, Brown, 2009

Reynolds, David, *In Command of History: Churchill Fighting and Writing the Second World War*, Penguin Books, 2005

Sheffield, Gary, *Forgotten Victory. The First World War: Myths and Realities* Headline, 2001

Sheffield, Gary (ed.), *Leadership and Command*, Brassey's, 1997 (essays by John Bourne and Michael Howard)

Sheffield, Gary, *Leadership in the Trenches: Officer–Man Relations, Morale and Discipline in the British Army in the Era of the First World War*, Macmillan, 2000

Sheffield, Gary, *The Somme*, Cassell paperback, 2004

Sheffield, Gary and Todman, Dan (eds.), *Command and Control on the Western Front: The British Army's Experience 1914–1918*, Spellmount, 2004

Sixsmith, E. K. G., *British Generalship in the Twentieth Century*, Arms and Armour Press, 1970

Smyth, John, *Leadership in War 1939–1945*, David and Charles, 1974

Stevenson, David, *1914–1918: The History of the First World War*, Allen Lane, 2004

Stevenson, David, *With Our Backs to the Wall: Victory and Defeat in 1918*, Allen Lane, 2011

Strachan, Hew (ed.), *The Oxford Illustrated History of the First World War* Oxford University Press, 1965 (essays by Paul G. Halpern, B. J. C. Mc-Kercher and Tim Travers)

Taylor, A. J. P., *English History 1914–1945*, Oxford University Press, 1992

Taylor, Frederick, *Dresden: Tuesday 13 February 1945*, Bloomsbury paperback, 2005

Terraine, John, *Haig: The Educated Soldier*, Hutchinson, 1963

Todman, Dan, *The Great War: Myth and Memory*, Hambledon, 2005

Tooze, Adam, *The Wages of Destruction: The Making and Breaking of the Nazi Economy*, Penguin Books, 2007

Travers, Tim, *How the War was Won: Command and Technology in the British Army on the Western Front 1917–1918*, Routledge, 1992

White, Peter, *With the Jocks: A Soldier's Struggle for Europe 1944–45*, Stroud: The History Press, 2009

Wilson, Trevor, *The Myriad Faces of War: Britain and the Great War 1914–1918*, Polity Press, 1986

Winter, Denis, *Death's Men: Soldiers of the Great War*, Allen Lane, 1978

Winter, J. M., *The Great War and the British People*, Macmillan, 1985

Journal articles

Bailey, J. A., 'The First World War and the Birth of the Modern Style of Warfare', Occasional Paper 22, The Staff College, Camberley, 1996

Bourne, John, 'British Divisional Commanders during the Great War', *Gunfire: A Journal of First World War History* 29, nd

Cox, Sebastian, 'A Loose Canon Who Should Have Been Fired: Sir Arthur Harris and the Bomber Offensive, September 1944–April 1945', unpublished paper, nd

Cox, Sebastian, 'Sir Arthur Harris and some Myths and Controversies of the Bomber Offensive', *Royal Air Force Historical Journal* 47, 2010

Egerton, George W., 'The Lloyd George Memoirs: A Study in the Politics of Memory', *Journal of Modern History* 60, 1988

Grigg, John, 'Nobility and War: The Unselfish Commitment?' [also described on the cover as 'Idealism and Two World Wars'], *Encounter*, March 1990

Hays Parks, W., 'Precision and Area Bombing: Who Did Which and When?', *Journal of Strategic Studies* 18(1), March 1995

Mortimer, Mark, 'The Snobbery of Chronology: In Defence of the Generals on the Western Front', *The Historian*, Spring 2009

Ramsden, John, 'Refocusing "The People's War": British War Films of the 1950s', *Journal of Contemporary History* 33(1), 1998

Senior, Mike, 'Learning Curves and Opportunity Curves on the Western Front', *Stand to!* 93, January 2002

INDEX

Advanced Air Striking Force 29, 147
Aldington, Richard 4
All Our Yesterdays newsreels 10
Allies, WWII strategy 145, 146–163
Amiens
  Battle of 64, 140–141
  Gestapo prison bombing 107
Anzio, combat conditions 80–81
appeasement 28, 170
area bombing 112–114
Armistice, WWI 95, 166, 167–168
Army–Air co-operation, failure of 147
Arnhem 160–161
  casualties 161
Arras, Second Battle of
  improvements in warfare 132–133
  tunnels 132–133
artillery, WWI, modernisation 55, 129,
  131, 132–133, 136–137
Asquith, Herbert Henry, German
  invasion of Belgium 27
Attlee, Clement 165
Australian Corps, WWI 139–140, 142

B-17 bombers 115
battlefield conditions
  WWI 4–5
    Western Front 4–5
  WWII 4
Belgium, threat from Germany 1914 27
Berlin, bombing of 105

Beyond the Fringe 11
Blackadder Goes Forth 21–22, 48–49,
  127
Blitzkrieg 70, 147
blood transfusion 71
Blunden, Edmund 4, 126–143
Bomber Command
  defence of British Isles 36
  strategic bombing of Germany
    100–124
  accuracy 106–107, 112–114
  arguments in favour of 102
  Berlin 105
  casualties 105, 115–116, 117, 123:
    friendly fire 108–109
  contribution to victory 123
  criticism of 102–103, 119–122
  Dam Busters raid 106–107
  Dresden 114–119
  Hamburg 105
  Lancaster bombers 104, 110, 115
  Mosquito fighter-bomber 106–107,
    110, 115
  oil targets 111–112, 114, 116
  Operation Overlord 106, 107–109
  P51 Mustang fighter-bomber
    109–110
  railways 112
  Ruhr 104–105, 112
  Sir Arthur Harris: bombing priorities
    110–115; successes 104–105

bombing
  Bomber Command 100–124
  Luftwaffe 101
Britain
  post-WWI
    industrial and financial crisis 169,
      175–176
    military position 168
    national prestige 170
    public appreciation of Army
      169–170
  WWI
    economic vulnerability 90
    friction with Allies 37
    peace negotiation with Germany 37
    propaganda against Germany
      38–39
  WWII, loss of power 7, 164, 173–174
British Army, WWII, learning process
    144–163
British Expeditionary Force
  WWI 31, 49–51
    combat conditions 62–63: boredom
      68; comradeship 68; rest and
      recreation 66–67; training and
      fatigues 67
    improvements in warfare 137
    problems of expansion 49–50
    unpreparedness at outset 127–130
  WWII 29, 55–56
  see also Field Force
Britten, Benjamin, *War Requiem* 23
Broodseinde, Battle of 135
Brooke, Rupert, *Peace* 62
Burma campaign 36

Cambrai, Battle of, improved artillery
    136–137
Canadian Corps, WWI 142
Casablanca Conference 1943 173
casualties
  WWI 3, 70–71, 72, 138–139
  WWII 6, 70–71, 72
    Arnhem 161
    Bomber Command 105: Dresden
      115–116, 117; friendly fire
      108–109
    medical advances 71
    Operation Overlord 158

cavalry, WWI 142
Chamberlain, Sir Neville
  appeasement of Hitler 28, 170
  Hitler's opinion of 28–29, 170
  hopes Hitler will withdraw 29, 32
  reluctance to bomb Germany 101
Chantilly, Allied Military Conference
    1915 34
Christmas Truce 1914 65
Churchill, Sir Winston
  aggressive strategy 172–173
  appeasement of Roosevelt and Stalin
    171–172
  as saviour of nation 60, 61
  as writer 9–10
  attitude to bombing campaign 101
  electoral defeat 1945 165
  First Lord of the Admiralty 26
  keeps France in WWII 32–33
  on persecution of Jews 13, 14–15
  optimistic strategy post-Dunkirk
    33–34
  plan to attack Soviet Union 1945
    174–175
  Poland 1945 174
  portrayal by Hitler 40
  Potsdam Conference 175
  Prime Minister 1940 171
  promotion of tank warfare 43
  reputation as leader 7, 9
  support for Gallipoli campaign 31
  support for strategic bombing of
    Germany 120
  The Second World War 3, 9, 162
  The Valiant Years 9
  The World Crisis, criticism of generals
    43–44
  WWII propaganda 5
  Yalta Conference 174
cinema
  interpretation of WWI 2
    Battle of Somme 4
  interpretation of WWII 3, 10–11
Clark, Alan, *The Donkeys* 18,
    126–141
comics, role in popularising WWII 10
command structure
  WWI 141
  WWII 146

communications
  North Africa campaign 152
  North-West Europe, WWII 146
  Operation Overlord 160
  Western Front, WWI 50–51, 138, 141
Communism, East and Central Europe
  176
comradeship, WWI 68
concentration camps 1, 3, 13
conscription
  WWI 31–32
  WWII 5
Coventry, bombing by *Luftwaffe* 101
creeping barrage 131, 132

Dad's Army 11
Dam Busters raid 106–107
Declaration of London 88–89
Desert Air Force 153
Dresden
  bombing of 114–119
    political reaction to 116–117
    post-war arguments about 117–119
Dunkirk
  Field Force 147, 148
  Royal Air Force 147

Eastern Front, WWII, defeat of German
  forces 3
Eden, Sir Anthony
  capture of Messines Ridge 134
  meeting with Karski 13–14
El Alamein, Battle of 153
evacuation, children 5

Field Force 28, 29, 55–56, 73–86, 145,
  146, 149–153
  Dunkirk 147, 148
films *see* cinema
First World War
  Armistice 166, 167–168
  attrition towards Germany 88–99
  Britain's failure to negotiate peace 37,
    40
  casualties 138–139
    comparison with WWII 70–71, 72
  cavalry 142
  combat conditions 4–5, 62–63, 64–71
    boredom 68

  comparison with WWII 68–71,
    86–87
  comradeship 68
  rest and recreation 66–67
  training and fatigues 67
  communications 50–51, 138, 141
  defence strategy 29–30, 31, 34–35, 37
  elite regiments 65, 66
  futility of 1
  German atrocities 38
  German reparations 166–167
  German war aims 38
  leadership 42–55
  media interpretation of 2, 63–64
  military achievements 6–7
  naval blockade 88–99
    restrictions on neutrals 91–92, 97
  negative stereotypical view of 1–3, 5,
    7, 8, 17–24, 126–127, 165
  post-war settlements 6–7, 95,
    165–169
  reasons for Britain's involvement 3–4,
    12
  siege conditions 50, 62–63
  state control of economy 32
  transformation of warfare 6–7, 64,
    125–143
    artillery 55, 129, 131, 132–133,
      136–137
    command structure 141
    Royal Flying Corps 55, 137–138,
      141
    tanks 55, 130–131, 136
    transport 50, 138
  Treaty of Versailles 95, 165–169
France
  invasion by Germany 1940 32–33,
    35–36
  'blessing' for Britain 35–36

Gallipoli campaign 31
generals
  cavalrymen 53–54
  WWI 42–55
    misconceptions about 51–55
  WWII 56–61
  see also leadership
Germany
  armaments production

WWI 94–95
WWII 124
atrocities, WWI 38
control of Mediterranean 33
defeat
WWI 139–141, 168–169
WWII 41
invasion of Low Countries and France
32–33, 35–36
invasion of Poland 29, 31
lack of hostility towards 1914 26
naval blockade by Royal Navy WWI
88–99
civilian death rate 93–94
civilian shortages 90–91, 92–94,
95–97
military shortages 94
professionalism
WWI 51
WWII 60, 145–146, 147, 149,
156–157
reparations, WWI 166–167
strategic interest, WWI 4
submarine warfare, WWI 97, 99
threat to Belgium, WWI 27
war aims, WWI 38
Gordon Highlanders, Normandy 82–83
Gort, Field Marshal Sir John, WWII
146
Graves, Robert 4
emphasis on horror of war 66,
126–143
Grayling, A. C., criticism of strategic
bombing 121–122
Grey, Sir Edward, response to German
invasion of Belgium 27
Guards regiments 65
gunnery see artillery

Haig, Sir Douglas
as national hero 169–170
attitude to new technology 55
attitude to Press 57–58
criticism of 42
Basil Liddell Hart 46–47
Lloyd George 44–45
Somme campaign 131–132
Hamburg, bombing of 105
Hamel, capture of 139–140

Hancock's Half Hour 11
Harris, Sir Arthur
Chief of Bomber Command 103–104
criticism of bombing priorities
110–115
oil targets 111–112, 116
successes in Germany 104–105
Hastings, Max, criticism of strategic
bombing 120–121
Hitler, Adolf
attack on Soviet Union 40
occupation of Prague 1939 28
opinion of Chamberlain 28–29, 170
opinion of Churchill 40
unsystematic strategy 33–34
Horrocks, Lieutenant General Sir Brian,
showmanship 71–72

idealism 15–16, 39
Irving, David, The Destruction of
Dresden 117
Italy campaign 36, 155–156
combat conditions 77–81

Jews, persecution by Nazis 12–15
Journey's End (R. C. Sherriff) 22

Karski, Jan, reports of persecution of
Jews 13–14
Katyn Forest, massacre of Polish officers
14
King's Own Scottish Borderers, 4th
Batallion, combat conditions
83–86
Kitchener, Field Marshal Lord, strategic
plan 30, 31, 62–63

Lancaster bombers 104, 110, 115
Larkin, Philip 62
leadership
WWI 42–55
age 54
cavalrymen 53–54
challenge of BEF expansion 49–50
communications 50–51
German professionalism 51, 60
innovation 54–55
misconceptions about: 'lives of
luxury' 51–53

leadership (*cont.*)
  WWII 56–61
    charismatic 58–59
    lack of suitable officers 59
    misconceptions about 53
League of Nations, President Woodrow
    Wilson 166
lend-lease agreement 171–172, 175
Lewis gun 131
Liberal government 1914, ignorance of
    warfare 26, 27, 29–30
Liddell Hart, Captain Basil H. 45–48
  criticism of Haig 46–47
  influence on media 48
  on the Royal Navy blockade 97–98
literature
  WWI 2
  WWII 11
  see also poetry; writing
Littlewood, Joan, *Oh! What
    a Lovely War* 18–20,
    126–127
Lloyd George, David
  criticism of Haig 44–45
  friction with military leaders 35
  'Khaki Election' 164
  Memoirs 44–45
  Treaty of Versailles 164
Locarno Treaty 1925 7
London, bombing by *Luftwaffe* 101
Loos, Battle of 50, 63, 128
low-level marking techniques 111
Lübeck, bombing of 104
Ludendorff, General Erich, Armistice 95,
    139, 140
Luftwaffe 73
  bombing of London and Coventry
    101
  dominance in 1940 147
  fearsome reputation 29
  lack of strength 33
  loss of morale 110
Lusitania 91

Machine Gun Corps, WWI 138
Maginot Line 145
Messines Ridge, capture of 134
Middle East campaign 36
militarism, 'Prussian' 39–40

Monte Cassino, combat conditions
    78–80
Montgomery, Field Marshal Bernard
  as all-conquering general 61
  Arnhem 160–161
  commander of Eighth Army 153–155
  Operation Overlord 159–160
  public relations 58–59, 71–72
Mosquito fighter-bomber 106–107, 110,
    115
Munich Agreement 1938 28
Mustang *see* P51 Mustang fighter-bomber

national solidarity, WWII 16–17
naval blockade
  WWI 88–99
  restrictions on neutrals 91–92, 97
Nazi persecution of Jews 12–15
Nazi–Soviet Non-Aggression Pact 16, 31
Normandy 1944
  combat conditions 81–83
  role of Bomber Command 106,
    107–109
North Africa campaign 36, 149–155
  British successes 150–151, 153–155
  British weaknesses 150, 151–153
  Desert Air Force 153
  Eighth Army 151, 153–155
    Field Marshal Montgomery
      153–155
  poor communications 152
  Royal Air Force 152–153
  see also Montgomery; Rommel
North-West Europe, combat conditions
    81–86
Nuremberg Trials 3, 13

OBOE electronic guidance system 104,
    105, 108, 111
Oh! What a Lovely War 18–20, 126–127
oil targets, Bomber Command 111–112,
    114, 116
Operation Battleaxe 151, 152
Operation Brevity 151
Operation Crusader 151, 153
Operation Overlord 157
  casualties 158
  communication failures 160
  Field Marshal Montgomery 159–160

manpower shortage 159
role of Bomber Command 106,
  107–109
tactical failures 160
USA 173
Ordnance Corps, WWI 138
Ottoman Empire, British attack on 31
Owen, Wilfred 22, 23

P51 Mustang fighter-bomber 109–110
Panzer Group Africa 151–152
Passchendaele see Ypres, Third Battle of
Patch, Harry 22–23
Pathfinder Force 104
Pearl Harbor, Japanese attack on 36–37
penicillin 71
phoney war 16, 29, 146
Plumer, Field Marshal Herbert
  capture of Messines Ridge 134
  Third Ypres campaign 135
  visits to trenches 52–53
poetry, WWI 2, 5, 22, 62, 126–143
Poland
  Churchill strives to secure
    independence 174
  German invasion of 29, 31
Polygon Wood, Battle of 135
Potsdam Conference 165, 175
propaganda
  WWI 38–39, 93, 96
  WWII 5–6, 162

railways, bombing of 112
rationing 5
Remarque, Erich Maria
  All Quiet on the Western Front 22
  emphasis on horror of war 66
Rommel, Field Marshal Erwin 60,
  151–152, 155
Roosevelt, President Franklin D.
  Churchill 171–172
  Karski 14
Royal Air Force
  defence of British Isles 36
  Dunkirk 147
  North Africa campaign 152–153
  see also Royal Flying Corps
Royal Artillery, WWI 138
Royal Engineers, WWI 138

Royal Flying Corps 55, 137–138, 141
  see also Royal Air Force
Royal Navy
  contraband control of Germany
    89–90
  defence of British Isles 36
Royal Sussex Regiment 65
Royal Welch Fusiliers 65
Ruhr, bombing of 104–105, 112
Russia
  offensive against Austria 1916 34
  see also Soviet Union

Sassoon, Siegfried 5
  criticism of leadership 43
  emphasis on horror of war 66,
    126–143
Scots Guards, 2nd Battalion, casualties
  72
Second World War
  attrition towards Germany 100–124
  Britain's decline as world power 7, 8,
    164, 173–174
  British Army learning process
    144–163
  casualties
    Arnhem 161
    comparison with WWI 70–71, 72,
      162
    medical advances 71
    Monte Cassino 80
    Operation Overlord 158
  civilian privations 5–6, 16
  combat conditions
    comparison with WWI 68–71,
      86–87
    Italy campaign 77–81, 155–156
    North-West Europe 81–86
    Western Desert 73–77, 150
  command structure 145, 146–163
  communications 146, 152, 160
  defeat of Germany 41
    disarming 168–169
  defence strategy 28–29, 30–31, 33–34
  lack of idealism 15–16
  leadership 53, 56–61
  manpower shortage 159, 164, 174
  as moral crusade 13
  national solidarity 16–17

Second World War (*cont.*)
  propaganda 5–6, 162
  reasons for Britain's involvement 4,
    12–13
  stereotypical view of 1–2, 3, 5–6, 165
    creation of myths 8–17, 161
  strategic bombing of Germany
    100–124
    see also Bomber Command
  transport 155–156
shell shortage, WWI 50
shellshock 69–70
Somme campaign 2, 34
  civilian reaction to 4, 63
  reasons for failure 129–130
  role of Haig 131–132
  strategic success? 132
Soviet Union
  Allies' good relations with 15, 16
  Churchill plans to attack 174–175
  defeat of *Wehrmacht* 164
  influence of Communism in Europe
    176
  invasion by Germany 36, 40
  Katyn Forest massacre 14
Speer, Albert
  Minister of Armaments and War
    Production 124
    on Hamburg bombing 105
    on Ruhr bombing 104–105, 124
Stokes mortars 131
submarine warfare, WWI 97, 99
sulpha-drugs 71
Sweden, effect of naval blockade, WWI
  92

Tank Corps, WWI 138
tank warfare
  WWI 55, 130–131
    Battle of Cambrai 55, 136
    promotion by Churchill 43
    Third Battle of Ypres 136
  WWII
    lack of preparedness 147–148
    Western Desert 74–77
Taylor, A. J. P.
  on the naval blockade legacy 98
  reinforcement of myths about WWI
    126–141

Teheran Conference 1943 173
television
  interpretation of WWI 2, 20–22,
    63–64
  interpretation of WWII 10
  parody and satire 11
Terraine, John, *Haig: The Educated
    Soldier* 20, 48
The Great War BBC television series
    20–21
The Monacled Mutineer 22
theatre, interpretation of WWI 2
transport
  WWI 50, 138
  WWII 155–156
Treaty of Brest-Litovsk 166
Treaty of Bucharest 166
Treaty of Versailles 95, 165–169
  disarming of Germany 168–169
  Lloyd George 164
  resentment against 166–167
trench warfare
  WWI 1, 63, 64–65
    relaxation of hostilities 65–66
  WWII 70, 73, 78, 81
Truman, President Harry S., terminates
    lend-lease 175
Turkey, Gallipoli operation 31

USA
  dominance in 1944 164, 173–174
  entry into WWI 91
  entry into WWII 36–37, 173
    Operation Overlord 173
  lend-lease agreement 171–172,
    175
USAAF, bombing accuracy 112–114

Verdun, Battle of 1916 34
veterans, WWI 22–23
Vimy Ridge, capture of 133

Wehrmacht
  decision-making 161
  North Africa campaign 150
  professionalism, WWII 60, 72, 73,
    145–146, 147, 156–157
Weimar Republic 166, 168
  downfall of 167–168

Western Desert, combat conditions
 73–77
Western Front
 Britain increases war effort 34–35
 casualties 70–71, 72, 138–139
 cavalry 142
 combat conditions 4–5, 62–63,
  64–71
 command structure 141
 communications 50–51, 138,
  141
 leadership 42–55
 siege conditions 50, 62–63
 transformation of warfare 125–143
 transport 138

Wilson, President Thomas Woodrow
 Fourteen Points 166
 League of Nations 166
writing
 WWI 18–20, 126–143
 WWII 11
 see also cinema; literature; poetry;
  theatre

Yalta Conference 1945 174
Ypres, Third Battle of 2, 63, 132,
 134–136
 Lloyd George's criticism of Haig
  44–45
 Plumer's Second Army 135

Why did historians wait until the 1970s before exploring a wide range of sources?